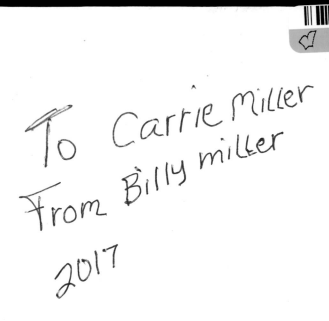

To Carrie Miller
From Billy miller
2017

Published by Straight Talk Books
P.O. Box 301, Milwaukee, WI 53201
800.661.3311 · timeofgrace.org

Cover image: GraphicStock

Printed in the United States of America
ISBN: 978-1-942107-44-6

TIME OF GRACE and IT ALL STARTS NOW are registered marks of Time of Grace Ministry.

set *free* by
GRACE

Daily Reminders
of God's Love

Introduction

At the restaurant where I worked in my student days, one of the waitresses sighed one day. "I wish I had faith," she said. "I really would like to believe in God." But if all she did was sigh now and then, nothing would ever change.

Where does faith come from? How can a small faith become a strong faith? God has the answer. **"Faith comes from hearing the message, and the message is heard through the word about Christ"** (Romans 10:17). It is contact with the Word of God that makes you more knowledgeable, more confident, more secure, more connected, more passionate, more Christ-like in your behaviors, and more armored against Satan's attacks. Only the Word of God can help you find the roots of your origin, find the purpose and meaning for your life, and find certainty for eternal life in heaven.

It is only the Word of God that assures you of God's unconditional love for you; the free and full forgiveness of your evil words, thoughts, and actions; and the incredible works of God in human history on your behalf. Only the Word of God can guide you in choosing how to please God with your life and find joy in service over self.

My hope is that these Grace Moments, which are a taste of the Word for each day, will encourage you as you serve God and that through them the Word will do its wondrous work in your heart of strengthening your faith in our wonderful Savior Jesus.

Pastor Mark Jeske

january

"Forgetting what is behind and straining toward what is ahead, I press on toward the goal to win the prize for which God has called me heavenward in Christ Jesus."

Philippians 3:13,14

Jesus' resolution

Linda Buxa

As far as resolutions go, I think Jesus had the strangest one. **"As the time approached for him to be taken up to heaven, Jesus *resolutely* set out for Jerusalem"** (Luke 9:51).

Now, I'm guessing your resolutions are all about how you are going to decrease your suffering and improve your life. Because January 1 is a clean slate, you woke up excited and hopeful that this year—*finally!*—you would get things under control.

From the moment Adam and Eve sinned, God knew his relationship with you was broken—and your life would be eternally out of control. There is no way you could exercise enough, be sorry enough, organize enough, or earn your own salvation enough to change your hopeless situation. So he gave Jesus the job. As he lived on earth, Jesus resolved that—even though he started his task seemingly weak in a manger—he would finish strong to the cross.

Our resolutions fizzle out because we allow ourselves to be distracted. Jesus stayed focused, resolving to increase his personal suffering so he could improve your life. The moment he said, "It is finished," he became the only one ever to keep a resolution perfectly. And in that moment, your life came back under control, because you were put back on God's side.

Now, not only is every year a clean slate; every morning is too. **"Because of the LORD's great love we are not consumed, for his compassions never fail. They are new every morning; great is your faithfulness"** (Lamentations 3:22,23). Happy New Year!

Hurt by the church

Jason Nelson

As I've made my rounds in life, I've run into some hurting people. None with festering wounds quite like those hurt by their church. The circumstances vary, but when they needed it most, the ministry of God's grace in its various forms was withheld from them by their church. They were disfellowshiped, shunned, made to humiliate themselves publicly, denied sacred rites, or given an irrelevant penance to perform. These are high hurdles for the weakest people to clear in order to satisfy the *true believers.*

A woman caught in adultery was almost killed by her church. The rules said that such a grievous sin was punishable by death and the fatal pummeling could be a group activity. That group taunted the bowed-low Jesus: "What do you say, rabbi, you want in on this?" Then Mercy stood up. With God's authority Jesus said, **"Let any one of you who is without sin be the first to throw a stone at her"** (John 8:7). No one hung around to take him up on the offer. Jesus said, **"Neither do I condemn you . . . go now and leave your life of sin"** (verse 11). She did and never stopped following him.

It is amazing that I have met most of these people in a church, not the church that hurt them but one that helped them heal because the love of Jesus predominates everything there. This is praiseworthy evidence that God's grace, in its various forms, will trump anyone's foolish mistakes, bind up a broken heart, heal all wounds, and redirect a wayward soul.

Superglue

Pastor Mark Jeske

There are various kinds of attraction forces that hold people groups together. One is ethnicity and language, which gives scared and lonely immigrants a better shot at survival. One is race—centuries of underdog status have made all black folks in America brothers and sisters to each other. Another is a common economic and social philosophy, which keeps political parties together year after year.

Christians hold together through several glues. One of the most powerful is Lord's Supper, which not only binds people more closely to their Savior Jesus, but it also has a horizontal dimension, bonding the people who experience the holy meal together. The Christians in Corinth badly needed this healing and power because their young congregation was so riven into factions: **"Because there is one loaf, we, who are many, are one body, for we all share the one loaf"** (1 Corinthians 10:17).

Cult leaders, concentration camp commandants, and the devil all use the same strategy to break people down— isolation from the group and steady indoctrination of lies. The Lord's Supper is a priceless gift from Christ to bond us to a band of fellow believers. No matter how lonely you may feel during the week, there is no mistaking the comfort and strength you can derive from the sacramental communal meal. You aren't crazy to believe all the wondrous and invisible things in the gospel.

You are not alone.

Stay positive

Pastor Mark Jeske

One of many indicators that the Bible really did come from God and is not man-made is that so many of the heroes are portrayed warts and all. Only a God-inspired letter to a famous congregation like the one in Corinth would have dared to expose so many of the group's sins and weaknesses.

The Christians in Corinth were riddled with cliques and factions, confused about the last times, careless in what they did with the Lord's Supper, and way too lax about the gross immorality in their midst.

And yet. And yet Paul looked for and found reasons to praise them and build them up. He had plenty of corrective criticism in his letters to them, but he also celebrated the Spirit's powerful and effective working in them. **"I always thank my God for you because of his grace given you in Christ Jesus. For in him you have been enriched in every way—with all kinds of speech and with all knowledge"** (1 Corinthians 1:4,5).

They weren't hopeless, and you aren't either. Paul knew that only the message of God's love and mercy can give people forgiveness from their burdens of guilt and failure, that only God's message of hope can move us forward even when we feel like quitting. The wonder isn't that we have failed sometimes but that we have overcome Satan's overwhelming attacks, still held onto our faith though surrounded by unbelievers, and are still exhibiting love and service to one another.

I thank God for you too.

Be deaf occasionally

Pastor Mark Jeske

The great composer Beethoven began to lose his hearing when he was only 30, and by the last decade of his life he was totally deaf. He never heard his own majestic Ninth Symphony. Can you imagine how devastating it must have been for a musician and composer not to be able to hear what his music sounded like?

It may surprise you to hear me recommend occasional deafness. I don't mean doing any physical damage to God's masterful inventions on either side of your head. I mean choosing not to hear certain things in your life, and if you did hear them, to act as if you hadn't. **"Do not pay attention to every word people say, or you may hear your servant cursing you"** (Ecclesiastes 7:21).

Bosses should let some muttered comments fly by and take no notice. Teachers should not feel that they have to scold every sinful student word. Nor should husbands and wives think that they have to fix, correct, or argue with everything that comes out of their spouse's mouth. People say things when they are tired, peevish, or argumentative that they probably don't mean. If you choose not to "hear" those words, they won't be trapped in the official record of your communications. You can keep arguments from starting, let a foolish temper cool down, and maybe even save a relationship.

Your employees, students, or spouse may think you are losing your hearing (or possibly your mental sharpness). Just smile.

Help is on the way

Pastor Mark Jeske

Epiphany is one of those "church words" whose meaning keeps slipping from your mind no matter how often you hear it. It comes from two Greek words meaning "shining through." It is a reference to how at select times the Father authorized Jesus in his humility to let his true glory "shine through" his earthly disguise.

Those glory moments were sights for sore Israelite eyes. Their nation had been battered, defeated, shrunk, impoverished, and incorporated into various empires. To gloomy Israelites, the prophet Zechariah's words gave hope while they waited for God to bring relief: **"[Christ, your King] will proclaim peace to the nations. His rule will extend from sea to sea and from the River to the ends of the earth. As for you, because of the blood of my covenant with you, I will free your prisoners from the waterless pit. Return to your fortress, you prisoners of hope; even now I announce that I will restore twice as much to you"** (Zechariah 9:10-12).

Like little Israel, we are still in the time of warfare. How encouraging it is for us to hear of Jesus' Epiphany miracles! It gives us hope that peace is coming; it gives us inspiration to see that he truly is the King of all the world; it gives us patience to bear with suffering and want now, knowing that in heaven God will double compensate us for everything we gave up for him here.

Let the Epiphany glory of God's Son shine on your face and make you smile today.

A foolish nostalgia

Pastor Mark Jeske

Every so often I'll get an e-mail that has been chain-forwarded featuring a slideshow of nostalgic pictures from life in the "good old days." There will be pics of freckle-faced kids in cuffed blue jeans riding in a red Radio Flyer coaster wagon, a family sitting around an enormous console radio in the living room, and gigantic heavy cars with flying tail fins at a drive-in movie. The fantasy is that life back then was safer, healthier, you know, *better*.

The past has always been a place of mental and emotional escape for people who are stressed out by the present and fearful of the future. Nostalgia, however, is usually a selective slideshow. Former times weren't always that hot. You won't see nostalgia slides of black folks being abused by Jim Crow laws, the millions of people suffering in Stalin's mass starvation, or Holocaust SS death camps.

Solomon was aware of the lure of nostalgia: **"Do not say, 'Why were the old days better than these?' For it is not wise to ask such questions"** (Ecclesiastes 7:10). It's one thing to study the past and appreciate it. It's another to use the study of history as a dreamy way to run away from the challenges, dilemmas, and work of today.

History is important because it is the record of God's working out of his magnificent plan of salvation. History also informs you about how to make decisions right now.

Generosity convection

Pastor Mark Jeske

Your cereal boxes probably have this disclaimer near the top: "Some settling of contents may have occurred during shipping." The company doesn't want you cranky because there seems to be two inches of air inside the box.

In an open-air market in the Middle East, long before shrink-wrap, glass jars, cans, or cardboard, a merchant would fill the measuring container before pouring it out to you. Sellers who wanted you to be sure that you were getting the full measure would shake the container to settle the grains, even tamping the surface down and refilling to make sure you got the full load.

Jesus spent a lot of time teaching his disciples about generosity convection, i.e., the more you give, the more you get: **"Forgive, and you will be forgiven. Give, and it will be given to you. A good measure, pressed down, shaken together and running over, will be poured into your lap. For with the measure you use, it will be measured to you"** (Luke 6:37,38).

It sounds so counterintuitive, doesn't it? If I give things away, by definition I will have less. The opposite is true! God went first with his gracious gospel, fronting us his love and forgiveness. It is imperative that believers do the same, being generous with both their words of mercy and with their financial gifts.

Jesus said it, not I—God has his hand on the resources faucet of your life, and he watches your generosity as he decides how far to open it.

Remember who you are at work

Linda Buxa

"Whatever you do, work at it with all your heart, as working for the Lord, not for human masters, since you know that you will receive an inheritance from the Lord as a reward. It is the Lord Christ you are serving" (Colossians 3:23,24).

Do you have multiple personalities? You know, one for work and one for church.

Whether you're a welder, waitress, nurse, teacher, businessperson, or soldier, God thinks there is no difference between the worship you offer in church and the worship you offer at work. (Well, except that you happen to be getting paid at your job.)

In God's view, you are his child all the time, not only when you are in his house. As his child, you are a living sacrifice and everything you do is a spiritual act of worship. You worship him when you distinguish yourself by your work ethic and commitment to the company. You worship when you serve your coworkers by praying for them. Worship is looking for people who aren't in the family of believers yet and praying for ways to reach them with the gospel.

By the way, remembering who you are at work isn't always easy. It means making tough choices, reporting theft, not blaming your mistakes on someone else, and working faithfully when everyone else is texting their friends. It means your coworkers might actually be offended by you because of your worship.

Remember: Great is your reward in heaven.

No limits to his power over matter

Pastor Mark Jeske

"A man's got to know his limitations"—wisdom from Harry Callahan (a.k.a. Clint Eastwood) in *Magnum Force*. Clint's right—we are all limited: limited vision, limited brainpower, limited physical capacity, limited lifespan. The God we worship, however, has no such limitations. The entire physical universe was created by him and every day still must submit to his word and will. Absolutely every molecule in every place is under his supervision and direction.

Look what he did in Egypt to Egypt. When the arrogant and hard-hearted pharaoh refused to release his Israelite slaves, God sent his man Moses for a little demo of what unlimited divine power looked like: **"He raised his staff in the presence of Pharaoh and his officials and struck the water of the Nile, and all the water was changed into blood. The fish in the Nile died, and the river smelled so bad that the Egyptians could not drink its water"** (Exodus 7:20,21).

Is your jaw dropping? The Nile is over four thousand miles long, with billions upon billions of gallons of water sliding downhill in its banks. God turned physics into biology by making something inorganic organic.

It is nothing for God to stop the earth's rotation, feed five thousand people with five loaves and two fish, or turn water into wine. He has the unlimited power to do everything for you that he said he'd do, and he uses that power to bring benefit to your life.

Put me in chains

Jason Nelson

Why do subordinates of all kinds harbor resentment toward those over them? There were no ranks in Eden. There was God walking with two people made in the image of God, working together in perfect harmony. What happened? Well, God had a short list of tough consequences for breaking that world. **"You'll get your food the hard way, planting and tilling and harvesting, sweating in the fields from dawn to dusk"** (Genesis 3:18,19 MSG). So we sing the working person blues because we have to slave away under people we don't admire. **"Angry people without God pile grievance upon grievance, always blaming others for their troubles"** (Job 36:13 MSG).

We work in broken organizations where those in the cubicles think the person in the corner office is pretty clueless. It's been so long that the *boss man* has been the adversary that it's hard to imagine it any other way. But there are model companies where collaboration, shared decision-making, and better-than-living wages raise everyone's morale and grow the bottom line. Those serving there sing a different tune. **"There's nothing better to do than go ahead and have a good time and get the most we can out of life. That's it—eat, drink, and make the most of your job. It's God's gift"** (Ecclesiastes 3:13 MSG). So let's start a worker's revolt. Put this on your desktop: *I am here to serve. Put me in chains.*

Captive thoughts

Linda Buxa

Just the other day my son said, "Sometimes I wish I could just say everything I am thinking!"

I get that, don't you? I mean, I would love to just let those thoughts fly! Ah, what sweet relief to say what is *really* on our minds!

Of course, I am not talking about the nice, sweet, thoughtful things. I am thinking about saying the mean things. The thoughts that I let stew, simmer, and boil. The ones that make my eyes glare and my chest tighten. The ones that would probably leave a trail of pain and tears.

Thankfully, the Holy Spirit—who lives inside of me and gets all the credit for this—reminds me of the truth: **"We demolish arguments and every pretension that sets itself up against the knowledge of God, and we take captive every thought to make it obedient to Christ"** (2 Corinthians 10:5).

Our thoughts are like evil minions frolicking around, spreading toxic thoughts, and enjoying the anxiety they work in us. Those thoughts set themselves up against the knowledge of God that calls for speaking the truth in love, which calls for patience, words that heal. The apostle Paul suggests that we throw those anti-kingdom thoughts in jail, no longer giving them permission to wreak havoc.

A drawback of our current society is that moral relativism and personal freedom have become such a rallying cry that we have forgotten personal responsibility—even in our own minds. Just because we *can* give full rein to our thoughts, doesn't mean we *should*.

Think before you drink

Pastor Mark Jeske

The big breweries still advertise heavily on television, guaranteeing that if you buy and consume their products, you will have much more fun and romance in your life. But aware of alcohol's destructive power and nervous about lawsuits, the companies make sure the ads end with this: "Drink responsibly."

Holy Communion is a big deal. It is the holiest thing that people can do this side of heaven. It is a direct encounter with the very body and blood of the Son of God, and God says that he views disrespect shown to those holy things as disrespect to Christ himself. Ignorance is no excuse. Think before you drink. **"People ought to examine themselves before they eat of the bread and drink of the cup"** (1 Corinthians 11:28).

So what does it mean to examine yourself? Four things: 1) Recognize that evil lives inside your heart and that you have sinned against God in thought, word, and deed. Admit it without excuses or blaming. Know that you need a Savior to keep you from condemnation. 2) Rejoice that your Savior Jesus has suffered, died, and risen again to purchase your freedom. 3) Realize that he gives you his body and blood to guarantee your forgiveness. 4) Reaffirm your desire to live a newer and holier life from today on.

Holy Communion is holy food for your soul, to sustain you in your daily warfare against Satan and to comfort your heart with the gospel. Enjoy the Supper!

No limits to his power over animals

Pastor Mark Jeske

Over the centuries people have fantasized about having power over animals to get them to help us. They domesticate and train horses and dogs one by one to be our companions and pull loads for us. But only God can utter a command to an entire genus or species and expect complete and immediate obedience.

The flies in Egypt didn't have to go to obedience school to be trained one at a time when God called for them. He spoke once, and trillions of them poured in immediately from all over the Mediterranean world, swarming over Egypt and the Egyptians: **"'I will make a distinction between my people and your people. This sign will occur tomorrow.' And the Lord did this. Dense swarms of flies poured into Pharaoh's palace and into the houses of his officials; throughout Egypt the land was ruined by the flies"** (Exodus 8:23,24).

Power that unlimited calls for our worship. It also demands our respect. The flies knew their Creator and responded to his will immediately. Their behavior gave glory to God and demonstrated how universal and unlimited are his power and authority. Pharaoh on the other hand was unimpressed and refused to submit. You might say he was dumber than a fly. His land and its people suffered terribly because of him.

The animals where I live know God's voice too.

Lord, help me keep my house in order

Jason Nelson

I got a warning from the laundry police. "Put your dirty clothes in the hamper and not in a pile next to the hamper." I'm sorry. It was a momentary lapse in judgment. I promise it will never happen again. Please don't send me to husband jail.

Actually, my wife and I are on the same page when it comes to the importance of a tidy house, and we share household duties well. We know our home is our launching pad for being civilized, organized, and effective people everywhere else. **"By wisdom a house is built, and through understanding it is established"** (Proverbs 24:3). It all starts on the home front.

It may seem archaic to voice this concern in the 21st century. But families living in squalor and neighborhoods with trash laying everywhere are still problems. I don't want to be impolite, but people's hygiene and housekeeping are windows into their state of mind. When addiction, depression, or socioeconomic backwardness disorganize people's thinking and siphon away their ambition, it shows in telltale ways. Any social worker can report that helping people recover from behavioral health breakdowns and live productively necessitates monitoring their progress with these very basic tasks.

"Cleanliness is next to godliness" is not a Bible passage. But cleanliness is a Christian virtue and the outward evidence of a well-ordered inner life. With such a life God is very pleased.

Watch your mouth

Pastor Mark Jeske

The gem industry would like you to think that diamonds are forever. You know what else never dies? Stuff you put on the Internet. Somehow the tech nerds who invented computer servers developed such automatic and redundant backup programming and capacity that everything that ever entered the 'Net will live forever. Somewhere in a server farm in Lapland is an astonishing record of your words and life, the good and the bad.

Watch your mouth! Think before you click! **"Do not revile the king even in your thoughts, or curse the rich in your bedroom, because a bird of the sky may carry your words, and a bird on the wing may report what you say"** (Ecclesiastes 10:20). "Friends" who love drama and excitement will pass on your remarks about other people to those very people. People of dubious judgment will forward your e-mails and tweets. Your cell phone texts, tweets, and GPS locations are indefinitely available to smart people. The proliferation of public digital cameras and computerized video recording also means that you are a movie star every day whether you realize it or not.

Here's a self-check for what you speak and send today: Is it true? Is it kind? Is it helpful? Would I be ashamed if this got out? You know, it is good also to be mindful, even apart from your massive cyber audience, that our Lord hears all we say and sees all we do.

The sanctity of life and hope

Jason Nelson

The Roman orator Cicero (106–43 B.C.) is credited with saying, "Where there is life there is hope." He made that astute observation decades before a young Jewish woman felt the Son of God kicking inside of her, giving mankind the hope of eternal life. Much later, another Jewish girl turned the phrase to sustain herself through the daily torment of the Holocaust. Her observation was equally profound: "Where there's hope, there's life. It fills us with fresh courage and makes us strong again" (Anne Frank, 1929–1945, *The Diary of a Young Girl*). Hope and life are inseparable companions, and they deserve equal protection.

Solomon said, **"Anyone who is among the living has hope"** (Ecclesiastes 9:4). We feel hopeful because we're alive. We enjoy life because we have hope. Anytime a human life is cut short, there is a second great tragedy. Some hope also dies. Real human potential goes unfulfilled. Something important will be left undone.

We have been among the living from our first moments inside our mothers. God's holy angels and many wonderful people worked very hard to keep it that way. Because they did, we have fulfilling lives in Jesus Christ. And there is hope for others through us as we live for him. We owe a great debt. Let us pay it forward as guardians of life and hope.

No limits to his power over the weather

Pastor Mark Jeske

"Everybody talks about the weather but nobody seems to do anything about it." That amusing line is generally attributed to Mark Twain, and what has given the sentiment legs for more than a century now is that we have all wished we could influence what was happening in the atmosphere, at least on certain occasions.

Mothers of brides with outdoor receptions wish they could control heat and humidity. Farmers would love to be able to control the sunshine and rainfall that their crops need. If they were in charge of the weather, there would never be a killing frost again. Airlines would never lose a dime again to flights canceled due to storms in flight paths.

There is Someone in heaven who always gets the weather he wants: **"Then the Lord said to Moses, 'Stretch out your hand toward the sky so that hail will fall all over Egypt—on people and animals and on everything growing in the fields of Egypt.' When Moses stretched out his staff toward the sky, the Lord sent thunder and hail, and lightning flashed down to the ground"** (Exodus 9:22,23).

Perhaps the Egyptian farmers, huddling in their little huts and watching the destruction, cursed their bad luck. The amazed Israelite slaves were treated to a display of unlimited power over the weather that made them glad to be believers. They knew who had made hail happen.

Stay in sync

Linda Buxa

Years ago I participated in a sound effects show at Disney World. While watching a black-and-white movie, we used props to re-create sounds: thunder, doors creaking, glass breaking. I was horrible at it. The movie, which was supposed to be a Disney "horror" movie, quickly became a comedy. The sound of knocking came after the door was open. You heard the glass break three seconds after it hit the floor. The click of footsteps kept going after the man stopped walking.

It's easy to get out of sync in life too, reacting at the wrong time and the wrong way to what's going on around us. That's why the apostle Paul reminds us, **"Since we live by the Spirit, let us keep in step with the Spirit"** (Galatians 5:25).

Your temper doesn't sync up with the call to live in peace. Avoiding conflict because it's easier, even when you really need to lovingly confront someone, isn't actually love. More stuff doesn't lead to contentment. And inner peace won't come when you drink because you're miserable, eat when you're lonely, and flirt on social media because you don't feel beautiful.

Want to get back in sync? The Holy Spirit is ready and can't wait to show his work through your life: **"But the fruit of the Spirit is love, joy, peace, forbearance, kindness, goodness, faithfulness, gentleness and self-control"** (Galatians 5:22,23).

Jesus, plain and simple

Jason Nelson

I really think we need to strip it down. I don't think we should dumb it down, but I think we need to strip it down. Most Christians know that for decades now, churches in America have been declining in membership. There is no denominational exception. And most Christians are aware that the number of non-Christian people in the world is increasing. In an attempt to address these problems, different brands of Christianity have recommitted themselves to do better what they believe distinguishes them from everyone else and will attract people to them. And there's a lot of "inside baseball" discussion about what it means to be *a truly authentic* (you can fill in the blank here). The force of persuasion and resources has been directed at a lot of external things that are likely to trend away.

So I think we need to strip it down because we may have no choice. Like the acoustic version of a well-orchestrated song, we can grab people's attention with the compelling beauty and simplicity of God's essential message to us.

May I ask that if by God's providence and grace a lost soul stumbles upon your gathering—amid the cherished bells, smells, sights, sounds, traditions, and rituals—no one leaves without hearing this message, plain and simple? **"God so loved the world that he gave his one and only Son, that whoever believes in him shall not perish but have eternal life"** (John 3:16).

Serve and you will be served

Pastor Mark Jeske

"What have you done for me lately" is not just a Janet Jackson music video. It is a life and business philosophy that says that you turn on the charm and effort only when the other person goes first. That isn't particularly good business, and it is terrible Christianity.

The gospel of God's grace teaches us that he went first, bearing great gifts, risking rejection, hoping for a faith and life response. God did that not only to change your status with him from prisoner to friend but to inspire you to treat other people that way. King Solomon's wise and older royal advisors recommended a humble strategy to the late king's young son, crown prince Rehoboam: **"If today you will be a servant to these people and serve them and give them a favorable answer, they will always be your servants"** (1 Kings 12:7). Brilliant advice.

Unfortunately Rehoboam sought out advice also from spoiled and immature younger advisors who advised a hard-edge approach. He adopted their strategy, and a bitter civil war resulted that permanently split the country.

"Serve people and they will serve you" is a beautiful and concise summary of how you and I can put the gospel into action in our lives. It carries God's promise that you will not impoverish yourself by being generous, by taking the risk of going first. As you meet other people's needs, God will see to it that yours will be met too.

New clothes

Pastor Mark Jeske

Hans Christian Anderson's tale about a vain emperor's invisible clothes continues to delight one generation of children (and adults) after another. Though the emperor could not see his royal robes, he imagined that he looked regal and elegant as ever. He was, in fact, naked.

Through your faith in Christ you have been named a member of God's royal family, cleared of all charges against you in God's court, and given new clothes to wear. Satan, however, cannot bear to see you happy and secure, and like the loud child piping up in Anderson's tale, mocks you as a fraud. As he did to Christ in the desert, the devil claims to be lord of the earth, that all mankind are his slaves, and that Christ's work is a failure. "You're naked losers!" he hisses.

But you aren't. Though you can't see your new clothes, they are there. Their existence is guaranteed by God's own promise and sealed through your baptism: **"In Christ Jesus you are all children of God through faith, for all of you who were baptized into Christ have clothed yourselves with Christ"** (Galatians 3:26,27). That means that when God looks at you he doesn't see the flaws, failures, and fears—he sees only the golden holiness of his Son. Your new clothes are God's gift to you. Though free to you, they are priceless, for they were bought at the cost of the blood of the Savior.

Wear them with pride.

Victory in the courts

Linda Buxa

"**Instead, they were longing for a better country—a heavenly one. Therefore God is not ashamed to be called their God, for he has prepared a city for them**" (Hebrews 11:16).

Every time the Supreme Court rules on a hot social topic, my Facebook feed is filled with opinions from both sides. Television reports show the chaos created when throngs of supporters and protestors converge. People either celebrate or decry the direction the nation is headed. In the middle of every ruling, it seems we are looking to make this world into a place that we like. But when we start looking to that group of judges to give us hope, we're looking in the wrong place.

Look at the people around you, fighting so vehemently for their earthly causes, and see them as Jesus did, people who have a very specific number of days to hear what Jesus has done for them. People who need to know that no matter what they think about this country, there is a better country—a heavenly one.

Then talk to them, both the ones with similar political leanings and the ones who are on the opposite end of the spectrum. Listen to them. Love them. Tell them of the God who didn't come to create an earthly kingdom but who came to make sure that God the Judge will rule in their favor when it comes to the heavenly country.

No limits to his power over death

Pastor Mark Jeske

Play characters like Dr. Faust traded his soul to avoid it. And in the novel *The Picture of Dorian Gray*, Dorian Gray tried to cheat it by having his mortality trapped in a painting. We are all afraid of death, the dark stalker, who is after us all. Because of the curse of death hovering over us, it will get us all.

Human mortality is absolutely no problem for our Savior Jesus. The One who created us in the first place can re-create us in the twinkling of an eye. His mission for coming to earth two millennia ago was to reconnect lost people with their aching Father, to undo the death sentence, and to open up a second life after the first death.

A synagogue president named Jairus had a sixth-grade daughter whom he dearly loved. Her untimely death devastated him. Jesus arrived at Jairus' home and encountered funeral bedlam: **"Meanwhile, all the people were wailing and mourning for her. 'Stop wailing,' Jesus said. 'She is not dead but asleep.' They laughed at him, knowing that she was dead. But he took her by the hand and said, 'My child, get up!' Her spirit returned, and at once she stood up"** (Luke 8:52-55).

Only God could call death a nap. Only God could do something about Jairus' daughter. Only God can give you life after death.

Soon, soon you will personally witness the Son of God's unlimited power over death as he forces graves all over the world to yield the bodies in them.

Don't give up on me

Pastor Mark Jeske

King Manasseh of Judah was the worst. He did everything in his power to destroy the worship of the Lord and reinstitute the worship of Baal and Asherah that his father, good king Hezekiah, had gotten rid of. He practiced sorcery and witchcraft and even performed child sacrifices. He was a lost cause, right?

"The Lord brought against them the army commanders of the king of Assyria, who took Manasseh prisoner, put a hook in his nose, bound him with bronze shackles and took him to Babylon. In his distress he sought the favor of the Lord his God and humbled himself greatly before the God of his ancestors" (2 Chronicles 33:11,12). The Lord heard his repentant prayers and allowed him to return to Jerusalem and even take up the kingship again. Manasseh then devoted his energy to undoing all the spiritual damage he had done, getting rid of the Baals and reinstituting the worship of the God of Abraham.

You and I cannot see into people's minds and hearts; nor can we predict their future with 100 percent accuracy. We don't know who might one day repent and who will not. We will let God sort that out. Our job is simply to speak the solemn warnings of God's law and the sweet promises of his gospel—not just to nice people, but to bad boys and girls too.

There are going to be some very surprising people in heaven with Jesus.

How much is enough?

Pastor Mark Jeske

It's fairly easy for me to criticize other people for being materialistic. I can see conspicuous consumption in others; I am not quite so sharp in seeing it in myself. Even though I don't have a Porsche, golf club membership, or second home, I am just as at risk in being seduced by the addictive allure of MoneyMoneyMoney as any wealthy person.

Money is an amazing tool. It concentrates power and makes it portable. It allows you to accumulate things that you want and get other people to do what you want. To some degree those are good things. But it is a small step from working hard to accumulate wealth to falling in love with the power it brings you.

How do you know when you have enough? **"Whoever loves money never has enough; whoever loves wealth is never satisfied with their income"** (Ecclesiastes 5:10). You know you're in trouble when money is at the core of what makes you feel safe and secure, when money is at the core of whether or not you feel that your life is a success, when money is at the core of your personal happiness. God made us to be connected in love to other people. Even more, God made us to find our greatest fulfillment, satisfaction, and happiness in loving and serving him first.

Do you believe that?

I know your deeds

Pastor Mark Jeske

"Do you love me?" Tevye the milkman asks his wife, Golde, in *Fiddler on the Roof.* "I'm your wife," she says. "I know. . . . But do you love me?" Golde can't give him an answer, "Do I love him?"

Does it surprise you to know that God is intensely interested to know if his love for you and me is requited or unrequited? What difference has the gospel made in your life? Did you know that through your baptism he adopted you into his family? Have you heard his call to your personal ministry and service? Are you proud to be his child? eager to be his royal priest? dedicated to organizing your life around obedience to his commands and adopting his philosophy of life?

Or not? In God's eyes, lukewarm might as well be rejection. He told an indifferent congregation in Laodicea, **"I know your deeds, that you are neither hot nor cold. I wish you were one or the other!"** (Revelation 3:15). Believers drifting along and not caring much is Satan's doing. Wake up! Indifference is one small step away from unbelief, from sliding back into idolatry, selfishness, and eternal condemnation.

Reclaim your first love. Clear your head, take stock of your true treasures, and make the changes you need to make sure that God knows he is your #1. Put Jesus back on the throne in your heart, tune up your ears to listen for his voice, and rededicate yourself today.

I mean it! Right now!

Time to sharpen yourself

Linda Buxa

In Stephen Covey's *The 7 Habits of Highly Effective People*, he tells the story of a woodcutter. On the first day of work, the man brought down 18 trees. The next day he tried harder, but could only do 15 trees. The third day's results were worse: 10 trees.

The woodcutter apologized to his boss, explaining he couldn't understand what was going wrong.

"'When was the last time you sharpened your axe?' the boss asked.

'Sharpen? I had no time to sharpen my axe. I have been very busy trying to cut trees . . .'"

Is something off in your life and you just can't understand what's going wrong? Maybe it's time to think about how you're spending your time—and with whom you're spending that time. Wise King Solomon knew this when he wrote, **"As iron sharpens iron, so one person sharpens another"** (Proverbs 27:17).

When you invest in Christian friendships, you surround yourself with people who will encourage you and support you. If you choose well, they will also challenge you and hold you accountable. Then you have the energy and the strength to go out to a world full of both hurting hearts hungry for Jesus and hostile hearts wanting to see you fail. You will be far more effective—with less effort— if you make sure you are sharp. If you keep working and working without regrouping with your Christian friends, you will quickly get dull.

Which people keep you strong? Text them this Proverbs passage and thank them for keeping you sharp! Better yet, pick up the phone and tell them.

Spur one another on

Jason Nelson

A regular reader of these devotion books asked me who my literary influences are. I was flattered anyone thought I had literary influences. Without giving it much thought, I rattled off in no particular order C.S. Lewis, the apostle John, Erma Bombeck, and Garrison Keillor. And then I smirked, "And if I can turn a phrase it's because I spent most of my life listening to country music. *"She loves the singer; she just couldn't live the song."*

The hope we profess has also rubbed off on us from others. And through us that hope will rub off on someone else. That's why we get together and work together as Christians. So, **"Let us consider how we may spur one another on toward love and good deeds"** (Hebrews 10:24). May the circle of positive influences be unbroken.

When I hear Pastor Jeske share one of his excellent messages, I want to try to write something really decent to follow his good example. When I read the meaningful devotions of my writing buddies, I want to make sure I don't drop the ball. I need to see it to try it myself. The excellence modeled by others in the Christian community is the gentle kick in the flank that keeps me moving in the right direction. Their best effort spurs me on. And then if one of you dear readers expresses appreciation, that just makes me want to try even harder.

Mercy, not sacrifice

Pastor Mark Jeske

Counterfeiting is not dead. The digital age we live in has made faking currency easier, and so governments have to resort to special tricks in paper and ink to foil counterfeiters. You know, you can fake a relationship with God too, at least to casual observers. It's not particularly hard to perform religious rituals, but they are meaningless and worthless before God if your heart isn't in it.

God's prophet Hosea was his spokesman to Israelites who thought religious performance was an acceptable substitute for real faith and love in action: **"What can I do with you, Ephraim? What can I do with you, Judah? Your love is like the morning mist, like the early dew that disappears. For I desire mercy, not sacrifice, and acknowledgement of God rather than burnt offerings"** (Hosea 6:4,6).

Real faith comes from a painful awareness of the human evil that lives within you. It comes from hearing the gospel of God's merciful atoning sacrifice in your place and on your behalf and believing in his precious forgiveness. Real faith expresses itself not only in the performance of religious ceremonies, which may bring real value, but also in daily works of service and kindness to people around you.

Attending worship services, placing religious art around your house, and contributing money to religious organizations and their ministries are all good, as long as they flow from real faith in Christ and are validated by the way you treat other people.

No limits to his power over Satan

Pastor Mark Jeske

"Resistance is futile. You will be assimilated." With that monotone threat, the alien Borg collective announced the imminent defeat of the starship *Enterprise* and her crew. Captain Picard needed all of his resources to save the ship and its people.

I know where the *Star Trek* scriptwriters got their material for this story. They lifted it from Satan's ongoing marketing campaigns. Satan wants you to stop struggling, stop trying to live a moral life, stop believing that there's anything worth living for, stop denying yourself, and just surrender to your appetites and desires. "Resistance is futile," he whispers. "Everybody lives like this now. The earth is mine. God is gone, but I am here. It is your destiny to be part of my kingdom."

What a thrill to know that that depressing message is a lie. Jesus' acceptance of our guilt, humble suffering, horrible crucifixion, sad burial, and triumphant resurrection have won a permanent victory. Satan's power is broken. Jesus won.

On one of their training tours his disciples got a little taste of this victory: **"The seventy-two returned with joy and said, 'Lord, even the demons submit to us in your name.' He replied, 'I saw Satan fall like lightning from heaven. I have given you authority to trample on snakes and scorpions and to overcome all the power of the enemy; nothing will harm you'"** (Luke 10:17-19).

Seriously. You are safe in Jesus' arms. Soon you'll see. Soon.

february

"Let us love one another, for love comes from God.
Everyone who loves has been born of God and knows God."

1 John 4:7

Marriage is hard: We're prideful

Pastor Mark Jeske

Have you ever seen the sappy Ryan O'Neal/Ali MacGraw movie romance entitled *Love Story*? MacGraw played a character who was dying, and at her bedside O'Neal, choking and tearful, said he was sorry. MacGraw then unloaded a line that has done a lot of damage to relationships and marriages everywhere: "Love means never having to say you're sorry."

Apologizing is hard work. Apologizing *and* changing your behaviors is even harder, and what makes it so hard is pride. Dating and marriage always to some degree involve each person's struggling for control. When your behaviors are driven by pride, you want to win every argument, always be right, see difficulties as your partner's fault, bring up your partner's admitted failures of the past, and explain away or deny your own sins and weaknesses.

You need other people's input and critique to know how you sound, how you look, how your actions affect other people. In humility realize that you aren't quite as brilliant and infallible as you think you are: **"Do not think of yourself more highly than you ought, but rather think of yourself with sober judgment, in accordance with the faith God has distributed to each of you"** (Romans 12:3).

When your spouse has an issue with something you've said or done, listen twice and think three times before you say anything. It may just be that the best thing you can say is, "I'm sorry."

Marriage is hard: We're selfish

Pastor Mark Jeske

Ever hear one of your friends say, "I have to take care of me for a change." "It's my time now." "I need to be looking out for number one." Unfortunately the people who say these things don't mean Jesus Christ. They mean themselves.

Sinners like you and me do not need to go to grad school or subscribe to webinars on how to be selfish. We are born with software already installed and functioning. Our parents (hopefully!) slowly trained us to overcome that selfish streak and learn to share our toys, wait in line, take turns, and listen to the views and stories of others. It is embarrassing how fast those old behaviors come back under stress, and it hurts marriages.

Husbands and wives can drive each other crazy because they don't notice things that are really important to each other. Both what they do and what they neglect can really hurt. Being self-absorbed comes naturally. Focusing energy and thought on other people's well-being is learned behavior. It is Christ-behavior: **"No one should seek their own good, but the good of others"** (1 Corinthians 10:24).

It is a major triumph of the cross when you think first, "What does he or she need?" instead of, "Here's what I want." It is part of the magic of the Christian way of life that when you put others first, your needs always get taken care of too. Always.

Marriage is hard: We're different

Pastor Mark Jeske

One of you is a neat freak, and the other doesn't worry much about a few socks on the floor here and there. One of you is a saver; one is a spender. One is always on time; the other is much more relaxed about the clock. One of you loves noise and energy and parties, and the other loves quiet time at home. One of you is creative and passionate, which is nice, but also prone to leave a trail of debris behind, which drives the other crazy.

Just as Felix and Oscar argued and battled all the time in *The Odd Couple*, husbands and wives are vulnerable to Satan's plotting to drive the tip of a crowbar into their differences and use them as a fulcrum to pry them apart. God made us different not to drive each other crazy but to enrich our lives and give us a bigger and wider and more interesting perspective on life. **"We have different gifts, according to the grace given to each of us"** (Romans 12:6).

Manage your differences! Celebrate your differences! Do *not* allow Satan to manipulate you into arguing over them. How boring your marriage would be if you and your spouse had identical views and habits. Any fool can complain about what you don't like about another person. It takes a Christian to celebrate the treasure you have in your spouse.

Funny . . . the more you do that, the more your spouse will appreciate you (and your quirks).

Marriage is hard: We're stubborn

Pastor Mark Jeske

Apologizing is hard work. You know what else is hard? Forgiving an apologizing spouse.

Why? Why should that be hard? Well, for one, it's easy to suspect that the apology isn't sincere ("I'm sorry." "You are *not!*"). For another, when this isn't the first argument on a certain misbehavior, the wounded party sees a trend and fears it will continue indefinitely. Am I enabling more of this bad behavior? For another, staying angry gives you emotional leverage. For another, staying wounded gives you the moral high ground in future negotiations. Your injury is an asset—why would you give away this form of capital?

Holding onto anger, however, poisons your soul. It marinates your spirit in toxins that will affect everything else in your life and especially in this most important of all your human relationships. Holding anger blinds you to your spouse's gifts and values for your life and keeps you from seeing his or her efforts to make things better.

There's a better way. **"Bear with each other and forgive one another if any of you has a grievance against someone. Forgive as the Lord forgave you"** (Colossians 3:13). What breaks you out of these anger ruts is the sweet remembrance of the massive debt of ours that our Lord Jesus forgave. If we show a bitter and unforgiving spirit to our spouse, we are daring God to do the same to us.

Let it go.

Rise, respect, and revere

Pastor Mark Jeske

The culture of the United States is notorious for its obsession with youth, health, beauty, and strength. That's how we measure the worth of others; that's how we believe that people measure ours. We fear the aging process and grieve over each new wrinkle and gray hair. We collect aging jokes, laughing nervously because we're so afraid of becoming old, disabled and forgetful, helpless and incontinent.

There's a better way to live. Since we know we are immortal, we don't have to see the aging process as stealing all our reasons for living. Each day we live is a step closer to heaven. We can accept ourselves as we are, and even more important, we can give value and worth to the seniors who are ahead of us in age. **"Rise in the presence of the aged, show respect for the elderly and revere your God. I am the Lord"** (Leviticus 19:32).

Did you know that this is a spiritual issue? The attitude you show the elderly shows what you think of God. We owe much of our lives to the older generation. Their hard work, sacrifice, values, patience, suffering, and determination bequeathed us our government, churches, community organizations, and schools.

Listen to their stories. Value their opinions and philosophy. Appreciate their work. Make them feel important. In so doing, you will be revering your God.

Arrogant, overfed, and unconcerned

Linda Buxa

Sodom and Gomorrah live on in infamy. After all, when the Creator of the universe destroys your city with burning sulfur because your people are wicked, you must be *really* wicked. So wicked that, even thousands of years later, sins are still named after you.

Because I am prone to comparison, I used to become incredibly self-righteous when I read this story. Then one day a friend pointed out Ezekiel 16:49,50, where God tells Jerusalem, **"Now this was the sin of your sister Sodom: She and her daughters were arrogant, overfed and unconcerned; they did not help the poor and needy. They were haughty and did detestable things before me. Therefore I did away with them as you have seen."**

Oh. That's not why I thought they were destroyed. Those cities were burned to the ground because they were arrogant, overfed, unconcerned, and didn't help the needy—in addition to the other sins that I thought were the main reason.

If I am truly prone to comparison (and it's not working in my favor at this point), I realize I am far more like Sodom and Gomorrah than I originally thought. Arrogant? Check. Overfed? Check. Unconcerned? Check.

Ezekiel's words sound a warning that my personal comfort, status, and agenda are not a priority. In God's world, **"Anyone who wants to be first must be the very last, and the servant of all"** (Mark 9:35).

God's motif

Jason Nelson

The origin of our word *motive* can be traced to an old French word: *motif*. It conveys the idea of *causing movement*; an underlying stirring that pushes itself outward. Great works of music have motifs you can hear. Decorators hold their designs together with motifs you can see. God always operates with a motif you can believe in.

What moves God? The list of things that stir his heart is long, but one motif always comes through. **"We know and rely on the love God has for us. God is love"** (1 John 4:16). Love is God's essence and the motivation for everything he does. Love caused him to create people to express it to and not abandon them when they became unlovable. He led wandering Israelites with his big loving glory so they would go where he would keep his promise to save the world by sending his Son as the Jewish Messiah. He upset the apple cart many times in history so your ancestors would have to pick up the pieces and migrate in the direction of his love for you. When the noise of a conflicted world muffles God's motif, you can hear it in the peace of God that surpasses understanding. When the fog of trouble—lots of trouble—obscures God's motif, it streaks through so we can see solutions to our problems. There is no question about what moves God.

The question is, Does what moves God move you?

What do you mean "grace"?

Pastor Mark Jeske

The Bible has some powerful and important words that have their own unique divine meanings within the biblical narrative that are different from everyday English usages: *covenant* and *faith* and *testament*, for instance. Another is *grace*. In secular talk, *grace* means fluidity of movement, poetry in motion. It means skill in manners and social behaviors, knowing the right thing to say or do in a social situation.

The core meaning of *grace* in the Bible, however, is an attitude of kindness, mercy, and love toward us that God has chosen, not because of what we have done for him but because of his decision to show kindness, mercy, and love to us. Our salvation originated in the mind and heart of God. Jesus' forgiveness and the promise of heaven are gifts, not deferred compensation. None of this was our idea, our choice, or our accomplishment. He is not rewarding us. He is in fact loving the loveless, saving the hopeless, and enlightening the clueless.

Jesus revealed the meaning of God's grace to his stunned disciples: **"He is kind to the ungrateful and wicked. Be merciful, just as your Father is merciful"** (Luke 6:35,36). Even the very faith we need to believe the message is a gift of God's grace. What can we do but worship and praise our marvelous God!

And show that same mercy to the fools and sinners around us.

I'm single and I love my life

Pastor Mark Jeske

Parents really love it when their 20-something kids start settling down with a steady boyfriend or girlfriend, and they really get excited when there is engagement news. Pre-grandparents get all giggly when they envision holding a baby in their arms again.

Those feelings are understandable and natural. But parents (and grandparents) need to be careful about marriage pressure. It's okay to want to set up your granddaughter with your friend's handsome grandson. But accept and respect the fact that singleness is a great way to serve the Lord as well as marriage and production of children. Singleness as a life platform can enable absolutely remarkable service to the Lord. St. Paul recommended it heartily: **"I would like you to be free from concern. An unmarried man is concerned about the Lord's affairs—how he can please the Lord. But a married man is concerned about the affairs of this world—how he can please his wife—and his interests are divided"** (1 Corinthians 7:32-34).

Independence is a sweet joy of singleness. When you don't have a spouse and dependents, you can change your mind and change your life on short notice. You can take greater risks if nobody else needs your income stream. You can live small and accept greater hardships if you are not dragging somebody else along.

For many centuries Christian missions and Christian schools have been blessed by single people. Are you single? Let me hear you say, "I love my life."

Straight talk

Linda Buxa

We want straight talk. We want doctors to tell us the real problem so we know the right course of treatment. We want politicians to tell us what they really believe, not what they think will get them elected.

This doesn't seem to carry over into our personal lives. We want everyone to agree with us all the time because then we can feel good about ourselves. How do you react when your friend reminds you it is not a wise idea to commit to someone who does not share your faith? Maybe they ask if you have been meeting with other Christians regularly—in church or at Bible study. What if they share that—faith issues aside—people who live together before they get married have a higher divorce rate? Sometimes they stop you in the middle of a story and say, "That's gossip. I really don't want to hear it."

Proverbs reminds us that even though straight talk might hurt, **"wounds from a friend can be trusted, but an enemy multiplies kisses"** (27:6).

Honestly, I prefer "kisses," but those are not in my best interest. Without people holding me accountable, I'll do what is comfortable and makes me feel good. That's where our trusted Christian family comes in. Out of love they absolutely care about our eternal well-being and are courageous enough to tell the truth. If you don't have somebody like that in your life, find somebody. And listen up.

The Bible's words are God's words

Pastor Mark Jeske

It is common practice for Christians to quote the authors of the various books of the Bible as though they were just like all other authors, i.e., responsible for generating their own content. While Scripture does indeed use each writer's own linguistic style and life situation, God in fact inspired and controlled all content. The Bible is not a collection of man's words about God; it is a collection of God's words about God.

The apostle Peter could be very humble about certain things. He was acutely aware of the shame and hurt that his early boasting and later denials of Christ on Good Friday brought about. But he was absolutely fearless about the source of the material in his two letters, and in all of Scripture for that matter: **"Above all, you must understand that no prophecy of Scripture came about by the prophet's own interpretation. For prophecy never had its origin in the will of man, but men spoke from God as they were carried along by the Holy Spirit"** (2 Peter 1:20,21).

Powerful concept: if people don't like something in the Bible, they can't just blow it off as the private opinion of a nice but misguided fellow. They are now messing with God. Peter's strong words relieve you of an impossible task—trying to figure out which if any of the Bible's words might be true and from God.

Yo—they're all true.

Your time of grace

Pastor Mark Jeske

When the wicked witch wanted to terrify Dorothy into giving up the ruby slippers, she took an hourglass and turned it upside down. "That's how much longer you've got to be alive, and it isn't long, my pretty!" Dorothy watched in horror as the grains of red sand rushed into the lower glass.

All of us have an invisible hourglass, marking off the minutes until there are no more. Our lifetime is slipping away. Does that thought terrify you? Solomon wants to tell you something about the importance of having God at the center of all your thoughts, about the meaning of your life, your relationship with him, and immortality: **"Remember him—before the silver cord is severed, or the golden bowl is broken; before the pitcher is shattered at the spring, or the wheel is broken at the well, and the dust returns to the ground it came from, and the spirit returns to God who gave it"** (Ecclesiastes 12:6,7).

Your days on this earth are your time of grace—your opportunity to be reconnected with your Creator, your time to hear the gospel message of your Savior Jesus, your time to believe it and live it through the power of his Spirit. Jesus tells you that whoever believes in him will never die. Remember him!

Everything you lose on earth will be replaced in heaven. Don't be afraid. Live every day God gives you with zest and appreciation for his blessings. When the last grain of sand has dropped, your new Adventure begins.

Love is a war

Diana Kerr

The day before Valentine's Day you're probably expecting a classic lovey Bible passage for the devotion, such as "Love is patient, love is kind . . ."

How about this instead? Love is a *war*. "It sure is," you might be thinking. "You should have heard the fight I had with my spouse last night."

I don't mean you're at war *against* your spouse, though. No, you're at war *alongside* your spouse. Because *Satan* is the enemy.

Paul reminds us of this truth in Ephesians 6:12: **"For our struggle is not against flesh and blood, but against the rulers, against the authorities, against the powers of this dark world and against the spiritual forces of evil in the heavenly realms."**

Adopt this mind-set shift and suddenly your battle changes. With this perspective, you're able to view the petty arguments with your spouse for what they truly are—an attack by the devil. Are you going to allow him to damage your faith and your marriage without putting up a fight? I hope not.

Thankfully, Paul goes on in verses 13 to 17 to give you advice for battle: **"Put on the full armor of God,"** have **"the belt of truth buckled around your waist,"** **"take up the shield of faith,"** and **"take the helmet of salvation and the sword of the Spirit, which is the word of God."**

See the battles in your marriage for what they truly are, and make sure you're equipped to fight and overcome them *together*.

Love for all

Diana Kerr

Did you pass out Valentine's treats in school when you were young? Remember how you gave a card to *every* classmate no matter what? Every kid received Valentine's love without discrimination.

Now we're grown up, and love doesn't work that way. We show love only to the people we like and to the ones who will reciprocate that love. The writer of Hebrews suggests a different approach to challenge and encourage us: **"Keep on loving one another as brothers and sisters. Do not forget to show hospitality to strangers. . . . Continue to remember those in prison . . . and those who are mistreated"** (Hebrews 13:1-3).

How do your actions stack up against those verses? Do you treat a stranger at the grocery store with less respect than you treat your best friend? Do you shy away from the new guy at your church who just got out of jail for drunk driving? Do you watch the woman with a disability who lives in your neighborhood walk blocks and blocks to buy her groceries without ever offering her a ride? Do you join in the gossip about the single mom at your child's school? There's not one of us who hasn't failed in this area of Christian living.

This Valentine's Day, pause and consider how you might show love to everyone. If you need a role model or some good ideas, look no further than your Savior as the ultimate example.

The raw power of no

Jason Nelson

God is very accommodating, and I appreciate him for that. I can't think of too many prayers he hasn't answered to my liking or longings in me that he has left unfulfilled. Maybe that's why I struggle when he says no and means it. I have mixed feelings about him when he will not honor my requests; when there are no ifs, ands, or buts about it. *No, this threat won't end. No, your child won't recover. No, this cup of suffering can't be avoided. No. No. No.* No from the Almighty is a shattering demonstration of raw power. All we can do is sit in stunned silence and revere his absolute certainty.

Ezekiel and other prophets had the unenviable task of saying no to God's people on his behalf. They told them, **"I will not look on them with pity or spare them. Although they shout in my ears, I will not listen to them"** (Ezekiel 8:18). Sometimes no is the only answer that accomplishes God's purposes. It's something we need to hear to remember who he is and completely submit to his will.

I don't take no for an answer well. I'll grit my teeth and try one more plea from another angle. "Perhaps, Lord, you didn't hear me right." "Maybe you don't get what's at stake here." But when he still says no, all that I have left to say is a thoroughly humble, "Your will be done."

Stamina

Pastor Mark Jeske

The story of King Joash of Judah is the mirror image of Manasseh's. He had an outstanding beginning to his reign and enjoyed great favor from the Lord. He listened to the wise counsel of elderly Jehoiada the priest, carrying out a major renovation and rebuilding of the temple in Jerusalem.

Then came the crisis: **"After the death of Jehoiada, the officials of Judah came and paid homage to the king, and he listened to them. They abandoned the temple of the LORD, the God of their ancestors, and worshiped Asherah poles and idols"** (2 Chronicles 24:17,18).

What a sad, sad story. It shows us that Satan can get his hooks into people even if they have been active believers for many years. People *can* lose their faith. Like Joash, we are strongly influenced by the people we choose to have around us. Other strong believers can lift us up. Bad company corrupts even good people.

Learn from Joash. Your faith needs not only an initial flame but stamina for the long haul. Don't get careless and let down your guard. Let God's Word speak to you daily. Choose your friends carefully. Have a pastor whom you can trust and who will tell you the truth about yourself. Feast on the Lord's Supper to build your faith. Make weekly worship and Christian fellowship a life priority.

Build your spiritual stamina so that you can finish well.

Just too small

Jason Nelson

In 1977 I had tea in the seaside cottage of an extraordinary woman named Svetlana Peters. I was there to recruit her five-year-old daughter to be a student in my very new, very small school in southern California. We discussed the blessings of Christian education, Olga's future, and not a word of her family's infamous past. I left optimistic that I would have the privilege of teaching Joseph Stalin's granddaughter about Jesus. The next day I got the call I was waiting for. Svetlana said, "Mr. Nelson, I think you have a very nice school and that you would be a good teacher for Olga—but I am not going to send her, because your school is just too small." Thud.

I thought of the verdict about another small place. **"But you, Bethlehem Ephrathah, though you are small among the clans of Judah, out of you will come for me one who will be ruler over Israel, whose origins are from of old, from ancient times"** (Micah 5:2). I wanted to call Svetlana back and plead with her to reconsider because salvation often starts small. A new life starts small. But I didn't. Shortly afterward, they moved on.

Svetlana craved anonymity. There's nowhere to hide in a small place. She traveled far and wide so that her notoriety wouldn't eclipse her privacy. In 2011 Svetlana died unnoticed in a nursing home in a little town in Wisconsin very near where I live. Sometimes the whole world is just too small.

It's all about me

Pastor Mark Jeske

Jewish scholars have a tradition that Solomon wrote the Song of Songs as a young man, Proverbs in the middle years, and Ecclesiastes as an old man. Makes sense to me. The voice coming from Ecclesiastes sounds like one who has been wealthy and accomplished, who has known pleasures in abundance, but who lost spiritual focus.

The book of 1 Kings shows that Solomon's loyalty to the Lord waned in his later years, and the following words express the futility of a worldview that is not organized around God: **"I denied myself nothing my eyes desired; I refused my heart no pleasure. My heart took delight in all my labor, and this was the reward for all my toil. Yet when I surveyed all that my hands had done and what I had toiled to achieve, everything was meaningless, a chasing after the wind; nothing was gained under the sun"** (Ecclesiastes 2:10,11).

The key words here are "under the sun," a refrain that echoes through Ecclesiastes. When God is not the center of things, when he is not honored as Creator and Redeemer, when one's labors are only for personal fulfillment, there is no satisfaction. Pointless. Meaningless. God programmed us to find our greatest joy in worshiping him and serving one another. Not ourselves.

Solomon's staggering wealth, immense power, palaces, armies, fortresses, and pampered lifestyle left him sad and empty at the end. Do you still think that more money will buy you more happiness?

Why did you let me get my hopes up?

Linda Buxa

We don't know her name; the Bible only calls her the Shunammite. This wealthy woman loved God and provided for his prophet Elisha. Deep down she desperately wanted to be a mother, but that hadn't happened yet. So when Elisha told her she would have a baby in a year, **"'No, my lord!' she objected. 'Please, man of God, don't mislead your servant!'"** (2 Kings 4:16).

He didn't mislead her. His prophecy came true and her son was born. Not many years later, the son complained about a pain in his head—and died on his mother's lap. She went to find the prophet, **"'Did I ask you for a son, my lord?' she said. 'Didn't I tell you, "Don't raise my hopes"?'"** (verse 28).

(I promise this story has a happy ending. Read 2 King 4:8-37.) Though it seems unusual, we can relate. We all have a deepest desire. We wait, pray, hope . . . and God just doesn't seem to be hearing us. Maybe we are too afraid to ask . . . because what if God says no? What if God takes away our good things and the pain makes us wish we had never been blessed in the first place?

I promise, thanks to Jesus, that your ultimate story has a happy ending. Meanwhile in this world, as you are waiting, praying, questioning, grieving, God is working. Maybe he'll show you how. Maybe he won't. So you and I simply pray for the faith to say, **"The Lord gave and the Lord has taken away; may the name of the Lord be praised"** (Job 1:21).

Watch and pray

Pastor Mark Jeske

There are times for casual conversation; times for napping; times for fooling around, mindless tasks, and passive entertainment. And then there is the time for spiritual rearmament because you are at war.

Jesus' disciples were not listening to Jesus' repeated warnings and exhortations about the time of spiritual testing that was about to come upon them. All the forces of hell were gathering on the eve of Good Friday, and Jesus spent hours carefully teaching them what lay ahead. Then came the time for prayer. Jesus took them to his special quiet place, an olive grove with an oil press, but they did not perceive the urgency. **"Then he returned to his disciples and found them sleeping. 'Simon,' he said to Peter, 'are you asleep? Couldn't you keep watch for one hour? Watch and pray so that you will not fall into temptation. The spirit is willing, but the flesh is weak'"** (Mark 14:37,38).

The same devil who made monkeys of the 12 disciples is coming after you too. Acknowledge your accountability to God. Review his high standards. Confess your failures. Hear with gratitude the stories of the Savior's saving work. Marvel at the cost. Love him for his great love for you.

After the shock and sadness and awe of Good Friday, you will be ready for the triumphant ecstasy of Easter.

Open a window

Jason Nelson

I don't think *infiltrational* is a word. My computer put a red line under it suggesting it isn't, but I tricked it into accepting it by adding it to my dictionary. I know *confrontational* is a word, and it's our tendency when we meet people whose ideas don't sync with the Christian worldview. We are tempted in good conscience to argue the point. As they say, "to defend the faith." But any kind of defensiveness is counterproductive communication. People stop listening because they don't like our tone. Door closed. They feel put down because they have gaping holes in their knowledge of the Bible. Those gaps are our opportunity to slip in there like fresh air through an open window.

There's a lot of stale thinking in a room full of people. Dead air lingers around people dead in their sins. It gets recirculated when people exchange very common and very cynical ideas. That's just suffocating. We have a different outlook because the resurrected Jesus breathed on all of his disciples and empowered them: **"If you forgive anyone's sins, their sins are forgiven"** (John 20:23). We are forgiven and deputy *forgivers.* Our thinking is freshened up with all Scripture, which is **"God-breathed and useful for teaching"** (2 Timothy 3:16). We can open a window on any discussion when we listen with respect, make sure we understand why people think what they do, and graciously offer insights that reflect the Bible's teachings.

Self-deception

Pastor Mark Jeske

Are you even remotely as good as I am at self-deception? I scare myself sometimes. I can talk myself into anything. I can cover my tracks, forget inconvenient facts, pretend that my motivations are pure, fabricate justifications for sketchy deeds, dodge probing questions, spar with Bible passages, dance around self-criticism, and blame others—all the while pretending to be righteous.

I would imagine that you are pretty good at self-justification too. My wife told me once, two days after an argument, "I am so sorry. I was wrong, but at the time I just felt so right!" Join the club: **"All a man's ways seem innocent to him, but motives are weighed by the Lord"** (Proverbs 16:2). We fool ourselves all the time. We can't fool God.

How can you tell when you've drugged yourself with self-deception? Listen to your family. They are way more onto your scams than you realize. When they tell you things about yourself, clamp down on your tongue and don't argue with them. Listen humbly and reflect. They may be God's voice.

Listen to the Word of God and keep comparing it to your life and ways. Psalm 119 says the Word is a lamp for your feet and light for your path. Hebrews chapter 4 says it is sharper than a sword, penetrating even to the dividing of soul and spirit, joints and marrow, and judges the thoughts and attitudes of the heart.

That's good news for us self-deceivers.

An examined life

Jason Nelson

Socrates said, "The unexamined life is not worth living." Like other philosophers in the single-digit centuries, he asked a big question: What gives life meaning? He answered with ideas that became basic material for the philosophical building blocks of Western civilization. Such as, because we are people and not animals, vegetables, or rocks, we can take a long, hard look at ourselves. We can live an examined life.

The examined life is the cornerstone of the Christian life. Embracing our Savior requires making ourselves aware of what he saved us from. We have to be brutally honest with ourselves about ourselves. Only then can we see how we defeat ourselves and fail to measure up to everything that is holy. It takes self-imposed discipline to review all of our choices and repent of the sins we commit every single day. It takes determination to follow our Lord because we love him for redeeming us from a very inadequate life and giving us a life worth living.

Use that special capacity that God gave people. **"Examine yourselves to see whether you are in the faith; test yourselves. Do you not realize that Christ Jesus is in you—unless, of course, you fail the test? And I trust that you will discover that we have not failed the test"** (2 Corinthians 13:5,6).

Spirit of the living God, enable each of us to examine ourselves daily and realize that through Jesus Christ we have lives worth living. Amen.

Balance sheet

Pastor Mark Jeske

One of the most stressful but important times in a company's business year is audit time. Trained analysts descend on the offices and compare the company's published financials with actual bank and investment statements and issue an opinion of the company's stated financial health.

St. Paul occasionally performed a self-audit, not of finances or personal possessions, but of spiritual wealth. **"But whatever were gains to me I now consider loss for the sake of Christ. What is more, I consider everything a loss because of the surpassing worth of knowing Christ Jesus my Lord, for whose sake I have lost all things. I consider them garbage, that I may gain Christ and be found in him"** (Philippians 3:7-9).

Everything tangible in our lives will be left behind when we die and ultimately burned up on the Last Day. Rank, special awards and titles, and an elegant house will soon pass away. What matters is one's personal relationship with Jesus, for that will last into eternity. You could be penniless, but your heavenly balance sheet would show that you are a spiritual millionaire.

The British poet and pastor Isaac Watts took personal inventory of his life and identified the triumphant cross of Christ as his greatest treasure:

When I survey the wondrous cross
On which the Prince of glory died,
My richest gain I count but loss
And pour contempt on all my pride.

February 25

Encouraging coworkers

Linda Buxa

Coworkers can drive you nuts, can't they?

After a day dealing with the guy who takes all the credit, the boss who belittles you, and the woman who never stops complaining, working from home sounds better and better.

So what the apostle Paul suggests that you do can be pretty hard—especially at work, especially with the difficult ones. **"Be wise in the way you act toward outsiders; make the most of every opportunity. Let your conversation be always full of grace, seasoned with salt, so that you may know how to answer everyone"** (Colossians 4:5,6).

As a believer in Jesus, your job isn't only a place to earn money; it is your personal mission field. God has placed you in one specific setting for four, eight, or ten hours a day—and he has another job for you to do. He wants you to make the most of every opportunity to shine Jesus' light into your coworkers' lives.

You walk with them as their family members face illness; you share the hope that you have even in stress; you talk about the way God has provided for you. You purposefully encourage others by thanking them for their hard work or writing a note when they are struggling. You choose your words wisely. You are prepared to **"give an answer to everyone who asks you to give the reason for the hope that you have"** (1 Peter 3:15).

Because when they see how differently you live and work, they will ask. Be ready.

The color of Lent

Linda Buxa

Please don't tell anyone, but Lent is not my favorite time of year. I think it's because somewhere along the line I started believing that the purpose of Lent was to make me feel guilty. I thought that Lent's whole job was to point its accusing fingers at me and shout that I am a terrible, horrible, no good, very bad person.

Maybe you have that impression too.

Actually, Lent has a different job. It isn't to dredge up guilt for sins that have already been forgiven. Lent is all about Jesus. That's why the color of Lent is purple. Purple is not the color of our sin (those are scarlet). Purple shows that our royal and majestic King came to us righteous and victorious, yet lowly and riding on a donkey.

Lent shows that our King has taken our past sins, put them on himself, died for them and with them on the cross, and buried them. When he came alive again, he shared that victory with us and made us children of God.

"Now if we are children, then we are heirs—heirs of God and co-heirs with Christ, if indeed we share in his sufferings in order that we may also share in his glory" (Romans 8:17).

So by all means, observe Lent with humility, because you used to be a slave to sin. But celebrate it with awe because the King of glory has made you glorious.

And we shall wear purple.

Damn you

Pastor Mark Jeske

There isn't much real understanding of the meaning of the word *curse* today. People love to use "cuss words" to add intensity and flavor to their conversations, but cuss words just let you pretend that you're an adult and demonstrate that you're upset. They don't really mean that they expect God the Great Judge to impose the punishment of hellfire on the people they're cussing.

But that's what *damn* means—that the verdict of guilty has been imposed by the legal authority and that the punishment is physical and eternal death in hell. That curse hung over you and me because of our sins; that curse was placed by the Father on the Son, who bore it for us. But because Christ placed himself between us and the Father's righteous wrath, we are spared: **"Christ redeemed us from the curse of the law by becoming a curse for us, for it written: 'Cursed is everyone who is hung on a pole'"** (Galatians 3:13).

Some of the Christian Scotch-Irish mountain folk who lived in the Blue Ridge wrote a poem about Christ's magnificent sacrifice, and they coupled it with a haunting Appalachian tune:

What wondrous love is this, O my soul, O my soul!
What wondrous love is this, O my soul!
What wondrous love is this that caused the Lord of bliss
To bear the dreadful curse for my soul, for my soul,
To bear the dreadful curse for my soul!

By his wounds: Condemned!

Pastor Mark Jeske

If you ever serve on jury duty, you might learn more about our judicial system than you care to know. The courtroom world of endless waiting, obscure arguing, behind-the-scenes plea bargains, and delays can diminish your confidence in our system.

But nothing you see in our courts could compare with the dreadful miscarriages of justice we read in Scripture about our Lord Jesus. He actually had four judicial hearings in the middle of the night as Maundy Thursday turned into Good Friday. He was arraigned before the retired high priest Annas; tried and "convicted" by the high council of the Jewish people and its chairman, Caiaphas; sent for a hearing to the Roman governor of Galilee, "King" Herod; and finally sentenced again to death by crucifixion by the governor of Judea, Pontius Pilate.

The kangaroo courts were bad enough. You know what's really scary about the trials of Jesus? God took those unjust guilty verdicts *and endorsed them*! Seriously! He let those unworthy judges speak for him as they cried out, "He is worthy of death!" Isaiah revealed that God wasn't just watching Jesus' trial; he was joining in the condemnation: **"The Lord has laid on him the iniquity of us all"** (Isaiah 53:6).

That's pretty good news for you, you know. Because you and Jesus switched places, he gets your guilty verdict and you get his not guilty verdict.

march

"The Word became flesh and made his dwelling among us.
We have seen his glory, the glory of the one and only Son,
who came from the Father, full of grace and truth."

John 1:14

It begins

Pastor Mark Jeske

When God wanted to show *intentionality*, i.e., that the things which were happening did not come about by accident but by divine plan and power, he often chose the number 40.

In Scripture, when something took 40 days or 40 years, it wasn't a coincidence: God was up to something. Likewise when Christians long ago decided to set aside a time of preparation before Easter, it seemed like the perfect choice to use God's special number and set aside that many days for a season of repentance and prayer. Only the weekdays are counted in the solemn 40; Sundays are still thought of as feast days. We call the season *Lent.*

Repentance is always a good mind-set and posture for Christians, but never more so than in the run-up to the commemoration of the awe-full day of the crucifixion of Christ. His savage torment and death made the payment for our sins and moral failures. It is appropriate for us to reflect on our own unworthiness, so that the beauty of his free gift of forgiveness will shine more gloriously.

Abraham's humility before God is our Lenten model: **"I am nothing but dust and ashes"** (Genesis 18:27). Whether you wear Lenten ashes metaphorically or actually apply them to your forehead, the spirit of Ash Wednesday is one of sober reflection of the terrible cost of human rebellion against God.

Only Jesus can lift you from the dust and ashes of your own making.

Rediscover reading . . . your Bible

Linda Buxa

In honor of Theodor Seuss Geisel's birthday, mayors are reading in classrooms and teachers are tying their lesson plans to Dr. Seuss books—all to celebrate Read Across America Day. They want students to rediscover a love of reading.

What if Christians seized this day to celebrate Read the Bible Across America Day? If we rediscovered a love of God's message with the same excitement and energy as kiddos who read silly rhyming words?

But we have grown-up excuses, don't we? Maybe the Bible seems as confusing as the tongue twisters in *Fox in Socks*. Maybe your schedule seems as chaotic as *The Cat in the Hat*, and you can't find a moment to rest. Maybe God didn't answer your prayers the way you wanted so he seems more like the Grinch who stole Christmas than a heavenly Father who loves you.

When you take time to read the book by the Author of Life, you'll see how much he offers. In Matthew 11:28 he invites you to come when you're tired, to climb on his lap, to *Hop on Pop*, because he gives your weary soul rest. He tells you *Oh, the Places You'll Go!* because you can do all things through Jesus who gives you strength (Philippians 4:13). You'll see he has never broken a promise, so you can trust that "he meant what he said and he said what he meant. Your God is faithful one hundred percent!" (altered from *Horton Hears a Who!*).

Happy reading!

Run away!

Pastor Mark Jeske

Okay, I'll admit it. One of my guilty pleasures is watching *Monty Python and the Holy Grail*. It's a mad funny send up of the legend of King Arthur and his knights of the Round Table. Arthur is bedeviled by the multitude of fools around him who won't cooperate in his quest for the Grail, and what's worse, his knights are idiots and cowards. Every time they encounter an enemy they wail, "Run away!" and they all flee.

Which is exactly what Jesus' disciples did when he was arrested in the Garden of Gethsemane. Though earlier that evening they had all protested loudly that they would never leave Jesus, at the first sign of trouble they bolted: **"Then everyone deserted him and fled"** (Mark 14:50). Peter came partway back, as far as the high priest's courtyard, and only John actually witnessed the crucifixion.

Lest we too smugly scorn the 11, however, we might ponder how often we have concealed or evaded our Christian identity, ashamed or embarrassed at being thought stodgy or prudish or out of it. Through the transporting magic of the gospels, we can witness the crucifixion for ourselves, trembling at our sins, trembling at the horror, but trembling also with relief that the sacrifice was made for us once for all. Long ago some Christian slaves made up this lament:

> *Were you there when they crucified my Lord?*
> *Were you there when they crucified my Lord?*
> *Oh, sometimes it causes me to tremble, tremble, tremble.*
> *Were you there when they crucified my Lord?*

Disruptive Jesus

Jason Nelson

Entrepreneurs change the world with disruptive innovations. The Internet is now the standard for accessing information and has put encyclopedia salesmen out of business. Elon Musk is hoping his Tesla Motors and SolarCity make dinosaurs out of fossil fuels. Amazon.com has brick and mortar retailers scrambling to stay viable. Drone strikes have disrupted warfare. An innovation is disruptive when it captures the marketplace because there's nothing better.

Jesus disrupted religion. Before he came along the relationship between God and man was based on following tedious rules under the supervision of imperfect clerics. People were used to it that way and there was no incentive to change it. But Jesus was different. **"Such a high priest truly meets our need—one who is holy, blameless, pure, set apart from sinners, exalted above the heavens. Unlike the other high priests, he does not need to offer sacrifices day after day, first for his own sins, and then for the sins of the people. He sacrificed for their sins once for all when he offered himself"** (Hebrews 7:26,27).

What a novel idea! One sacrifice by a new kind of mediator that is good forever. It is an idea that is still catching on because old habits die hard and getting saved the Jesus way is counterintuitive for many. That's what makes it disruptive. **"Therefore he is able to save completely those who come to God through him, because he always lives to intercede for them"** (Hebrews 7:25).

The unlearning curve

Jason Nelson

One of the great inefficiencies of life is spending time and energy unlearning things we spent time and energy learning. It's frustrating because we would have been better off without those monkeys on our backs to begin with. That's why folks often say, "If I knew then, what I know now." If I knew then that dumping information on students through a lecture was ineffective instruction, I would have been a better teacher sooner. If I knew then that a pedantic writing style was boring, I might have been published sooner. It's an irritating irony that the first step in learning anything new is unlearning the old.

I should have known that there's an unlearning curve in being a Christian. **"You were taught to change the way you were living. The person you used to be will ruin you through desires that deceive you. However, you were taught to have a new attitude. You were also taught to become a new person created to be like God, with a life that truly has God's approval and is holy"** (Ephesians 4:22-24 GW). Let's face it. We have to unlearn some nasty habits in order to live our faith.

That's true of every other aspect of our individual and collective lives. Change for the better begins when we first ask, "What do we need to unlearn here?" If I knew then how transforming this question can be, I would have asked it much sooner.

By his wounds: Scourged!

Pastor Mark Jeske

Every story needs a villain in order for the hero to shine. It sure isn't hard to find villains in the Lenten stories of Jesus' suffering—clueless and faithless disciples, hard-hearted Pharisees, Sadducees protecting their privileged positions, cruel and inhuman soldiers, and a cynical imperial governor. To this list could be added our names, for it was our sins that made Jesus' terrible ordeal necessary.

You can add God's name to the list as well. What!? God caused Jesus' suffering? Yes. Behind the lash of the scourge was the hand of God, who was pouring out the judgment, wrath, and punishment for the sins of the entire world upon the Son. Isaiah's prophetic insights allow us to see what was really happening in Jerusalem on Good Friday: **"Yet it was the Lord's will to crush him and cause him to suffer, and though the Lord makes his life an offering for sin, he will see his offspring and prolong his days"** (Isaiah 53:10).

As you are compelled to visualize the leather lashes cracking down on Jesus' bare back, first raising red welts, then drawing blood, and finally tearing the flesh apart, realize all over again how bad sin is—your sin. This is what hell is like, and Jesus offered to experience it so that you wouldn't have to. If God actually followed through and did this to his Son, he will certainly do what he says he will do to unbelievers on the Last Day.

The price was paid. Jesus got to see his offspring (you and me) and live again.

Time to go Home

Linda Buxa

Jack, my family's black Lab, loves walks. What really gets him excited, however, is going home. The minute we turn into our driveway, he grabs the leash and pulls us.

He doesn't care that we have a 420-foot driveway—uphill. He is asking us to do the equivalent of a hill sprint, leaving us breathless and worn out, but he doesn't care because he's going home. He loves home!

This is exactly what the writer of Hebrews meant when he wrote, **"Let us consider how we may spur one another on toward love and good deeds, not giving up meeting together, as some are in the habit of doing, but encouraging one another—and all the more as you see the Day approaching"** (Hebrews 10:24,25).

It's great to be walking in this world together, but when we know the Day is coming when God is going to create our new Home, we get even more excited. We grab the leash and pull each other up. Jumping around (figuratively, maybe not literally) saying, "We're going Home! Look! I can see it!"

Who cares if the last bit of our earthly walk is uphill? What does it matter if it's a sprint and it's hard and we're tired? We're almost Home. Look around—especially for the people who seem worn down—grab 'em by the hand and give them a tug. Encourage them. Because we are almost Home. Let's go!

Taking up a fatal cross

Jason Nelson

Polycarp (A.D. 69–155) may have been taught directly by John. He was an apostolic father who learned the faith from someone who learned the faith from Jesus. His Christianity wasn't safe like mine is. It wasn't practiced in the friendly confines of a nice church by reciting familiar liturgies. His trust in Christ's sacrifice was fresh and intense, and every day he faced the likelihood he would have to make his own sacrifice. When he refused to burn incense to the emperor, he was burned at the stake. He was heard to say, "I bless you father for judging me worthy of this hour, so that in the company of martyrs I may share the cup of Christ" (Martyrdom).

We are horrified that Christians around the world are being forced to share the cup of Christ. They authenticate their trust in Jesus' sacrifice by dying for him. They probably made a promise early in life that they would be willing to give up everything rather than deny their faith. I did too. The difference being, they knew it could mean a lot more than reluctantly rolling out of bed early on a Sunday morning.

It makes me wonder how committed to Christ I really am. Discipleship becomes real when the threats against following Jesus are serious. I know I've had it very easy. I hope a brutal captor would hear me say, **"For to me, to live is Christ and to die is gain"** (Philippians 1:21).

A word of grace

Pastor Mark Jeske

The prophet Isaiah had been allowed to peer seven centuries into the future. There he saw in metaphorical pictures the great drama of salvation played out before him. There was the great Suffering Servant of the Lord, represented as a sheep, helpless and about to be slaughtered.

And silent. Jesus had very little to say at the three "judicial" hearings that condemned him and nothing at all to the guards and soldiers who abused him. They beat him, pounded a crown of thorns into his head, and flogged him. He bore it meekly. Even the brutal crucifixion did not wring curses, threats, and hate from his lips. But the four gospels record that he did speak seven times in those six horrible hours.

His first utterance was a word of grace. **"When they came to the place called the Skull, they crucified him there, along with the criminals—one on his right, the other on his left. Jesus said, 'Father, forgive them, for they do not know what they are doing'"** (Luke 23:33,34). In those few words, Jesus summarized the entire purpose of his mission to earth—he came to bring the forgiveness of sins to people who are lost and clueless.

The cross of Christ did not cut short his saving work. *It was his saving work.* There the price of our forgiveness was paid in full. There you will find the forgiveness that you need for a happy life, a peaceful death, and a jubilant resurrection.

A word of hope

Pastor Mark Jeske

Eager suitors sometimes despair that they will ever be thought worthy of the hand of the beautiful woman they are pursuing. Mid-level managers wonder if they will ever be thought worthy of executive rank. Bonehead sinners like you and me wonder if we will ever make it to heaven.

We do believe in Jesus, but we still keep sinning. How depressing! What if he stops loving us? What if he finally gets sick of us? What if we are disqualified? When doubts and fears like these creep into your mind, let your eyes look at the evil criminal who was being crucified next to Jesus. In shame and urgency he cried out to the Man in the middle, **"'Jesus, remember me when you come into your kingdom.' Jesus answered him, 'Truly I tell you, today you will be with me in paradise'"** (Luke 23:42,43).

What magnificent comfort! What an incredible display of the gospel! What priceless hope! This man had done nothing to earn his way into God's favor. All he had was his sorrow and his confidence that Jesus had come to bring him the rescue he needed. Jesus' mercy was greater than his evil. A lifetime of crime was washed away in the moment of his repentance and faith.

He was now Jesus' friend. That very day the angels would come to bear his soul home to paradise.

A word of compassion

Pastor Mark Jeske

When I'm in pain, I have no patience or compassion for anybody else but me. If I bang my thumb with a hammer and my wife asks me if I'm all right, I bark back, "No! Of course I'm not all right."

All the more extraordinary that while he was in his death agony, Jesus was thinking about his mother. Left unsaid in the biblical narrative is where his stepdad Joseph was (maybe dead) and where Mary's other sons were (perhaps not believers at this time). But Mary was there and, as had been prophesied 33 years earlier, a sword was piercing her own soul.

Jesus cared deeply for her and wanted to make some important arrangements: **"Near the cross of Jesus stood his mother, his mother's sister, Mary the wife of Clopas, and Mary Magdalene. When Jesus saw his mother there, and the disciple whom he loved standing nearby, he said to her, 'Woman, here is your son,' and to the disciple, 'Here is your mother'"** (John 19:25-27).

John, the "disciple whom Jesus loved," was the only one to come back to witness the crucifixion. It was to him that Jesus entrusted the care of his mother, a charge that John would certainly execute faithfully. In an era without a government safety net, John would be her source of support.

A true servant till the end, our Savior was thinking about the needs of others.

A word of desolation

Pastor Mark Jeske

The fourth word Jesus spoke from the cross was the worst. It revealed how utterly alone Jesus was in his death struggle with Satan.

This battle was fought not with swords or spears, light sabers or lightning bolts, energy blasts or physical strength. The battleground was in the mind of Christ himself, where he fought Satan's temptations alone and physically exhausted. He had been abandoned by his disciples (save one), condemned by the religious leaders of his own people, and condemned by the Roman government that was supposed to dispense justice.

All Satan had to do was get him to sin once. Just once. Satan was whispering constantly that the foolish mortals on earth were vermin not worth dying for, that there were far easier ways to do this. Just one little act of rebellion against his Father. And now the Father had abandoned him! **"From noon until three in the afternoon darkness came over all the land. About three in the afternoon Jesus cried out in a loud voice, 'Eli, Eli, lema sabachthani?' (which means 'My God, my God, why have you forsaken me?')"** (Matthew 27:45,46). Why? Jesus knew why. Because he alone had agreed to pay the price for human sin. What he was really crying out was his shock at how awful it was to have God turn his back on you and withdraw all love, mercy, hope, and support.

At that moment Jesus was experiencing hell. For you.

A word of fulfillment

Pastor Mark Jeske

Jesus once told his disciples and the Pharisees a parable about a beggar named Lazarus who went to heaven and a rich man who ended up in hell. So severe are the torments of hell that not even one drop of water would be given to relieve the agony.

Perhaps Jesus knew already then that he would be describing his torments on the cross. Though offered something to drink Good Friday morning, he refused. He was determined to experience the full measure of physical torment that was needed to pay in full the sinful debts of mankind. But he knew also that Psalm 69 had prophesied that the Suffering Servant would be given vinegar to drink.

And so as death drew near, Jesus asked for the drink— not to diminish his suffering, but to fulfill the Scripture: **"Later, knowing that everything had now been finished, and so that Scripture would be fulfilled, Jesus said, 'I am thirsty.' A jar of wine vinegar was there, so they soaked a sponge in it, put the sponge on a stalk of the hyssop plant, and lifted it to Jesus' lips"** (John 19:28,29).

Even on the cross Jesus was taking great care to show that the portrait of the coming Savior, painted over the course of many centuries throughout the Old Testament, was accurate in every detail. He came not to discard the Old Testament but to fulfill it and complete it. In his dying moments the Son of God demonstrated that God keeps his promises.

A word of victory

Pastor Mark Jeske

Have you ever noticed how time crawls when you're sick or undergoing major stress? What seemed like an hour you found out later was only five minutes. Can you imagine how long Jesus' six hours on the cross must have seemed to him? Every minute was an hour and every hour a day. Worse even than the physical torment was the tension over whether or not Satan would make him crack. His obedience to the Father had to be perfect, compensating for all of our disobedience. Even one little sin and all would be lost. No anger, no bitterness, no vengeance fantasies, no hate.

But he didn't crack. Our Champion stayed strong until the end. With intense relief Jesus knew that his death was now maybe just seconds away. With intense relief he uttered a confident statement of fact that sent the devil howling. **"When he had received the drink, Jesus said, 'It is finished'"** (John 19:30). His suffering is finished. Satan is finished. Our condemnation is finished. Death is finished. The grave is finished. Hell is finished.

When Satan tempts you to despair, rebuke him with the reminder that he lost. He is a spent force. He is not the king of hell; he in fact will be its most notorious prisoner. Forever. Jesus' victory is your victory. It is now locked in the past, and for all his tricks Satan cannot undo it.

You are safe.

A word of trust

Pastor Mark Jeske

Ever see children play the "falling game"? One kid stands about two feet behind the other. The one in front intentionally leans backward and falls, trusting that the one behind will catch her. That momentary buzz of terror is what makes the game fun—you're pretty sure the other person will catch you, but there is still that little jolt of fear and panic that makes your adrenal glands fire.

Jesus had come to the final moment of decision— would he use his almighty power to burst from the cross, self-heal his battered body, and unleash divine fury on his enemies? It is to our everlasting benefit and relief that he surrendered not only to physical torment but to our last enemy, to the dark pit of death. **"Darkness came over the whole land until three in the afternoon, for the sun stopped shining. And the curtain of the temple was torn in two. Jesus called out with a loud voice, 'Father, into your hands I commit my spirit.' When he had said this, he breathed his last"** (Luke 23:44-46).

He trusted his Father to catch him as he let go, trusting that the holy plan was a good one, trusting that his work had been sufficient, trusting that the Father's promises of resurrection would come true.

Jesus' word of trust can be yours also. Whether you say it or just think it on your deathbed, the Father will catch you. He will keep all his resurrection promises to you too.

3:16 on 3/16

Pastor Mark Jeske

There's a reason why Christians like to hold up signs at sporting events that read, "John 3:16." Those 25 words express the mystery and beauty of the gospel of Christ more clearly and tenderly than almost any other Scripture passage you could think of. It helps people remember what Jesus is all about and gives them a simple but powerful vocabulary for sharing their faith.

To a learned but simultaneously ignorant Pharisee named Nicodemus, Jesus once gave an insightful explanation of his divine mission on earth: **"God so loved the world that he gave his one and only Son, that whoever believes in him shall not perish but have eternal life"** (John 3:16). Jesus' words elegantly express two important but seemingly contradictory truths. First, God's love is *universal*. It is for everybody, literally the whole world. But it is also *restrictive*—only those who believe the gospel will have eternal life. This is the grace/faith tandem; both are true.

What you need to know is that the proclamation of God's unlimited and universal grace is what creates the very faith in people's minds and hearts that they need. Only believers in Jesus can enjoy a guilt-free and hope-filled life; only believers in Jesus will enjoy an eternity in heaven.

You, yes you, are an important part of God's communication network. Do you know someone who needs to hear 3:16 on 3/16?

Be one of his

Jason Nelson

The Irish are really on to something. For at least one day every year, everyone wants to be one of them. The Norwegians missed that boat. But the Irish own our alter egos. With enchanting customs and good merchandising, things Irish are everywhere on St. Patrick's Day. I'm not aware of any resentment from the true Irish that a bunch of imposters are crashing their party. They say, "Be one of us."

That's in keeping with the work of St. Patrick. He wondered himself, "How is it that in Ireland, where they never had any knowledge of God but, always, until now, cherished idols and unclean things, they are lately become a people of the Lord, and are called children of God?" (*The Confession of St. Patrick*).

It's because Patrick showed them God is everywhere on the Emerald Isle. He used familiar tokens to teach the Celts who God is and relentlessly urged them to become his children. He styled a cross to suit their tastes. That's a winning approach for all missionaries. It imitates Paul in Athens: **"What therefore you worship as unknown, this I proclaim to you"** (Acts 17:23 ESV). It's a gracious invitation. No matter who you are, be one of his.

Happy St. Patrick's Day! Feel free to be one of them. But with all due respect, I don't think beer should ever be green.

By his wounds: Crowned!

Pastor Mark Jeske

If you visit the Tower of London, you may wish to see the dazzling display of the royal crown jewels. Included in the treasury is Queen Elizabeth's consort crown, platinum and purple velvet, encrusted with a dazzling array of gems including the 105-carat Koh-i-Noor diamond. Its value is beyond estimating.

King Jesus was given a crown to wear as well, but there was no velvet, platinum, or jewels. The "obeisance" he received from the Roman soldiers was mockery and jest. The "scepter" he was given was a reed, and his "crown" was a strip of thorns twisted into a circlet. As a gesture of total contempt, they beat it into his dear head, intensifying the humiliation and agony. The idea that he claimed to be the King of the Jews brought only resentment—they wanted no further claims on their accountability.

Isaiah had said it would be like this: **"He was despised and rejected by mankind, a man of suffering, and familiar with pain"** (Isaiah 53:3). It is the paradox of the gospel that Jesus' path to glory lay through humiliation, that his path to delight lay through pain, that his path to victory lay through suffering, and that the way in which he could crush Satan involved letting himself be crushed first.

It is the paradox of the gospel that it is through the wounds of Christ that you and I are healed.

By his wounds: Crucified!

Pastor Mark Jeske

Of the many paradoxes of Good Friday, one of the strangest is the way in which Jesus' death transformed something totally ugly into something stunningly beautiful. Crucifixion was a punishment reserved for the worst of the enemies of the state. It was cheap—prisoners could be nailed to any tree and left to hang there till dead. It was public—the passersby could come by and gawk, suitably discouraged from committing such crimes. And it was excruciating—beheading was instantaneous, but a crucifixion victim could linger in agony for days.

The Romans' worst punishment was God's choice for the punishing of his Son, whom he now considered to be the worst sinner of all time. The prophet Isaiah, seven centuries before Christ, was allowed to look into the future to see the strange way in which salvation for the human race would be won. **"He was pierced for our transgressions, he was crushed for our iniquities"** (Isaiah 53:5). There is no longer any condemnation or punishment for those who believe in Christ. His precious body was pierced by dreadful nails; his precious wounds bring you healing.

The death of Jesus has transformed an instrument of torture into a symbol of inspiration for our churches. The cross has become our logo, our "mark." We use it for artistic decoration, place it atop our steeples, and hang it above our altars. It is now such a beautiful symbol that Christians use it as jewelry.

Wear your cross with pride.

Surprise! Hatred is a form of murder

Pastor Mark Jeske

You probably know people who make up their own version of Christianity based in part on things they've heard, part on their own logical conclusions, and part on wishful thinking. Quoting the "Good Book," they say things like, "God helps those who help themselves," unaware that those words don't come from the Bible.

Jesus spent a lot of time in his Sermon on the Mount correcting various aspects of the "folk religion" of his day. For instance, he saw that people's understanding of God's law was very superficial. God's holy requirements run not only to deeds but also to words and even thoughts: **"You have heard that it was said to the people long ago, 'You shall not murder, and anyone who murders will be subject to judgment.' But I tell you that anyone who is angry with a brother or sister will be subject to judgment"** (Matthew 5:21,22). Surprise!

Hating and hurting someone in your mind are not only sins needing the forgiveness and healing of Jesus, but they do real damage to the hater. They are acids that burn in your stomach and corrode your soul. Anger is a prison. It can keep you trapped in negativity and make it hard for you to sustain healthy relationships with other people and with God too. Is there any hate in your heart right now? Wash it out with the daily grace that comes to you from Christ.

Choosing to love sinners is the work of Christ and the angels.

Sibling rivalry

Diana Kerr

The Bible tells some intense stories of sibling rivalry. Cain and Abel, Jacob and Esau, Joseph and his brothers . . . their drama is worthy of the *Jerry Springer Show*!

Most of us have experienced sibling rivalry, but probably to a lesser degree. I doubt that you murdered a sibling, stole his birthright, or sold him into slavery. So what does God teach us through these stories?

Do you notice a common theme? Jealousy and hurt. **"When** [Joseph's] **brothers saw that their father loved him more than any of them, they hated him and could not speak a kind word to him"** (Genesis 37:4). Joseph's brothers' hateful thoughts turned into hateful actions when he told them about his vision of them bowing down to him.

Maybe you can relate to the brothers' pain. All of us have felt slighted or less important than our siblings at one time, and it hurts.

When you're the Joseph in a situation with your siblings, show them some love and be careful what you say. It's natural to want to share the wonderful ways God is blessing you, but be careful how you do it. You might need to be gentle with the news of your pregnancy to your sister who just miscarried or your excitement about your lavish trip to Europe with your brother who's struggling to make ends meet.

Sticks and stones may break someone's bones, but words can break hearts and relationships.

Free friends

Pastor Daron Lindemann

Would you believe it if I told you that someone needs you to be a friend to them? God wants you to know and believe that you can be that friend.

Never fake, always faithful, Jesus loves you with a sincere love. Who needs your love to be more sincere?

Jesus rebukes evil, chases temptation from bullying you, and provides you opportunities to do what is right. What group of friends needs your help to avoid evil and pursue good?

Jesus prayed for his enemies: "Father, forgive them." Who is an enemy you can pray for and forgive?

Jesus welcomed strangers and shared his greatest gifts with them. Who is estranged from the church or homeless, needing your hospitality?

Jesus wept with Mary and Martha and celebrated with his disciples. Who needs your companionship in a time of grief or a time of joy?

So, as a friend of the resurrected Jesus, empowered with his love, be a better friend. **"A friend loves at all times"** (Proverbs 17:17).

Befriend others like Jesus has befriended you.

The Meal is the price of your salvation

Pastor Mark Jeske

What is actually happening when people receive Lord's Supper?

You can't see much. It may only look like some reverent people getting a morsel of bread and a sip of wine. But what is really going on is a personal encounter with the risen Christ, their Savior from sin. Through the mystery and miracle of the sacrament, they are *receiving* the body of Christ; through faith they then *become* part of the body of Christ, i.e., the great union of all believers past, present, and future.

That personal encounter was instituted by Christ, guaranteed by Christ, and explained by Christ: **"Take and eat; this is my body. . . . Drink from it, all of you. This is my blood of the covenant, which is poured out for many for the forgiveness of sins"** (Matthew 26:26-28). The Meal guarantees people's forgiveness before God *because the Meal is the very price of their salvation.* The body you receive was nailed to the cross for you. The blood you receive came out of his body for you.

The message behind Lord's Supper is the same message brought by the spoken gospel of Christ: you are loved, you are forgiven, you are empowered to live a new life. What the Supper does is make that message personal. You cannot possibly mistake whom God means with that love, forgiveness, and power because the Meal is in your mouth.

It's personal.

Forgiveness for the "worthy"

Linda Buxa

Professional golfer Tiger Woods was serially unfaithful to his wife. Still, he draws crowds. Adrian Peterson beat his son. Fans hate what he did yet root for him to help his team win. Michael Vick found work again after time in jail for dog fighting.

One commenter, referring to sports stars' relationships with their fans, caught my attention with his insight: "In our society forgiveness is not for those who truly repent, it's reserved for those who still have something to offer."

He was right. We are outraged by sports stars, celebrities, and elected officials whose behavior seems outrageous. But we forgive, mainly because they offer victories, entertainment, the promise of better living conditions. Still, *forgiveness* isn't the right word. We overlook, rationalize, minimize, judge—and make the person earn our forgiveness.

We have it wrong though. Our great God doesn't forgive that way. **"But God demonstrates his own love for us in this: While we were still sinners, Christ died for us"** (Romans 5:8). He forgives because he knows we have nothing to offer, because he wants to, because he loves us.

Jesus' performance—not ours—is the only thing that brings us back into a real relationship with our Father. This is the only relationship that gives us peace.

We've been given the privilege of passing along that forgiveness to the people in our lives. Not because they've earned it or have something to offer, but out of gratefulness to Jesus.

Death is dead wrong

Linda Buxa

"When Jesus had cried out again in a loud voice, he gave up his spirit. At that moment . . . the bodies of many holy people who had died were raised to life. They came out of the tombs after Jesus' resurrection and went into the holy city and appeared to many people" (Matthew 27:50-53).

For hours, Jesus suffered the horrible wrath of his Father and battled death. Then, at the moment of his choosing, he died. Death thought it had won, but death was wrong.

When Jesus died, holy people came back to life.

The day Jesus took our punishment is filled with so many incomprehensible, overwhelming details, that this portion of the story easily gets overlooked. When the temple curtain was torn, an earthquake rocked the area, and dead people came back to life. They came out of their tombs, waited three days until Jesus came out of his, and then went around the city, putting the full power of his resurrection on display.

Jesus' victory over death is just as real for you too. When Jesus died on the cross, he took your punishment. When Jesus died, your sinful self died. When Jesus died, you were set free. *When Jesus died, you came back to life.*

Death still pretends it is winning, but death is still wrong. You are alive. Now you get to appear to many people. You get to put the full power of his resurrection on display.

Today is a good day to do that.

Eternity in my heart

Pastor Mark Jeske

Blaise Pascal was a 17th-century French mathematician, physicist, and Christian philosopher. He said once, "There is a God-shaped vacuum in the heart of every man which cannot be filled by any created thing, but only by God, the Creator, made known through Jesus."

Pascal was right. There is no meaning in the universe if you deny the Creator, no love in the universe if you deny Christ the Savior, and no wisdom in the universe if you deny the Spirit. King Solomon, speaking as "the Preacher" (i.e., "Ecclesiastes") wrote brilliant lines on the emptiness of life without God: **"I have seen the burden God has laid on men. He has made everything beautiful in its time. He has also set eternity in the hearts of men; yet they cannot fathom what God has done from beginning to end"** (Ecclesiastes 3:10,11).

Even unbelievers believe in the afterlife and want to go to heaven, because that yearning to be reunited with the divine has been put in their hearts whether they realize it or not. Alas, they cannot fathom what God has done and with reckless abandon design their own roads to heaven, every last one of which is a dead end.

Don't live your life with a vacuum inside you. Let the Word of Christ fill your soul and spirit so that you may enjoy your eternity.

Let other people praise you

Pastor Mark Jeske

"Don't blow your own horn," my mother used to tell me. "Let other people figure out on their own how brilliant you are." Great advice! She was right, of course.

We are all somewhat insecure, and some of us are seriously insecure. We all want to be noticed, admired, and loved, and when those things aren't happening fast enough, we figure we have to use an accelerant, like more charcoal lighter on damp briquettes. The trouble is, people don't like braggarts, and our efforts at self-promotion easily backfire.

It is enough that God notices our hard work, sincerity, and sacrifice. If we truly believe that he takes care of his people, we can be patient about being recognized and wait for God's time. If we know that we are pleasing him with our lives, we won't be so needy about having to manipulate others into noticing us. Then—when people think that their words of approval were their own idea, they will be much more sincere and real: **"Let someone else praise you, and not your own mouth; an outsider, and not your own lips"** (Proverbs 27:2).

Much better than praising yourself is to look for things to praise in other people. Try it for three months. You will start to acquire more friends, who for some mysterious reason find that they enjoy being around you.

What makes you write a check?

Jason Nelson

"Freely you have received; freely give" (Matthew 10:8). Let's assume everyone's resources are limited. Mine are. So what makes you get out your checkbook and give money you could use to someone else? It takes money to live. And it takes money to share the Bread of Life and some daily bread with others. Just about anyone will take a check. But writing one is a targeted expression of faith.

I regularly attend church where I regularly hear about the love of Jesus in a very relevant way. And I regularly leave feeling inspired to get through the drudgeries of life, so I regularly write them a check.

And then I scatter some checks. When I've seen people suffer because of natural disasters, I've called the number on the screen and cut them a check. To honor the memory of someone who meant a lot to me, I've written checks to ministries that meant a lot to them. Some Christian organizations doing very good work have gotten checks. A television preacher delivering the timeless truths of God's Word has gotten a check. And I'm on the lookout for anyone who can win souls for Jesus by teaching the gospel in a way that can't miss. I think I would like to write them a check.

Whenever I am moved to express appreciation for everything God has done for me, I write a check because everyone's resources are limited.

Thinking the worst

Linda Buxa

Every year there are government elections of one sort or another, and they always leave me a little worn out.

Between the ads, the debates, the news reports, we are geared to start looking for and thinking of the worst in every candidate. I completely understand that to be informed voters, we need to be, well, informed. But after a while, I get weary of all the mean-spiritedness.

It seems like it carries over into how we treat not only the people running for local and national office but also how we treat the people around us. We think the worst of their intentions, their politics, their personal decisions—without any hint of love, mercy, or kindness.

We need to stop. The Holy Spirit wants to develop qualities in us—the Bible calls them fruit—and he does it by first renewing and transforming our minds. With the Holy Spirit's prompting, we remember that we have been given the mind of Christ. His mind will change the way we think and change the way we think about the people around us. We stop seeing them as adversaries but, rather, as people he created, people he loves, people he wants to see in heaven. So instead of listening to the negative today, **"brothers and sisters, whatever is true, whatever is noble, whatever is right, whatever is pure, whatever is lovely, whatever is admirable—if anything is excellent or praiseworthy—think about such things"** (Philippians 4:8).

When no one's watching

Jason Nelson

The body language of people ready to do something wrong is a dead giveaway. They look left. They look right. They maybe even look up to see if anyone will notice. And then they cheat or steal because no one is watching. Sadly, we all have those motions in our muscle memory. We have violated the commandments of God, the trust of our employers, and our own ethics when we think no one is watching.

It would be an abuse of God's place in our lives to try to keep people honest by reminding them that "God is always watching, so behave yourselves." It is *because* of his place in our lives that we keep ourselves honest when no one is watching. Jesus taught this enduring truth: **"Whoever can be trusted with very little can also be trusted with much, and whoever is dishonest with very little will also be dishonest with much"** (Luke 16:10).

A contributor to the decline of America's economic might is workers filling their lunch boxes with company stuff when no one is watching and taking it out the door. Employee theft costs our economy billions of dollars annually, and we all pay for it. Jesus taught that the shrewdest thing we can do in the workplace is return more than we were given because trustworthy people are the exception. Every boss is looking for ethical workers who add value to the enterprise when no one is watching.

Follow your heart

Linda Buxa

High school and college seniors are on their senior slide already. (If they aren't, they'll be there soon.) In just a few weeks, they will be sitting in their caps and gowns listening to valedictorians and celebrity speakers telling them to do what they love, follow their hearts, and make a difference in the world.

Let's face it, those speeches offer nothing more than a syrupy, shallow view of life. You see, when I hear that I should follow my heart, I think, "No way." Deep down I know what a dope I really am. I know that left to my own devices, **"out of the heart come evil thoughts—murder, adultery, sexual immorality, theft, false testimony, slander"** (Matthew 15:19). In my most honest moments, following my heart means that I am selfish. The only difference that makes in the world is a negative one—one that ignores people as I look for my own comfort.

Thankfully, Philippians 2:3,4 offers real wisdom with an honest, deep view of life that reminds me to follow God's heart: **"Do nothing out of selfish ambition or vain conceit. Rather, in humility value others above yourselves, not looking to your own interests but each of you to the interests of the others."**

Want to make a real difference in the world? Serve God by loving the people he placed in your life. Do the good works he prepared in advance for you to do. Be willing to sacrifice time, money, and energy to look out for others.

april

"Humble yourselves, therefore,
under God's mighty hand, that he may lift
you up in due time."

1 Peter 5:6

April 1

A done deal

Pastor Mark Jeske

The New York press corps loved Yogi Berra because he delighted them with the most quirky and delicious quotes. Commenting on the possibility of ninth inning comebacks he said once, "It ain't over until it's over." Funny, but people derive a certain sense of hope from thinking that it's never over, that there will be endless chances for do-overs and many different ways to arrange a successful transition in the next life. Sorry. Ain't gonna happen.

Scripture teaches two crisp and important truths. One, people have their time of grace and then will immediately face judgment—no endless cycles of reincarnation where you can circle back and have another go at achieving a good enough life. **"Just as people are destined to die once, and after that to face judgment, so Christ was sacrificed once to take away the sins of many, and he will appear a second time, not to bear sin, but to bring salvation to those who are waiting for him"** (Hebrews 9:27,28).

Did you note the sweet second point? The work needed to bring everlasting life to you and all believers is not ongoing, a work in progress, or iffy in any way. It's a done deal. He was sacrificed on the cross *once and for all*. Lift up your face and your eyes to heaven. Look for him! Watch for him! Wait patiently for him!

He's almost here—come soon, Lord Jesus!

God designed it that way

Pastor Mark Jeske

The single life is great. The freedom and independence you enjoy open up many possibilities for travel, sudden employment changes, risk taking, use of your time, and lifestyle. Still, marriage offers some powerful advantages over the single life. God designed it that way.

Solomon's concise poetic verses in Ecclesiastes summarize four powerful blessings of married life: **"Two are better than one, because they have a good return for their labor."** In this country, by retirement age each married person's net worth on average is double that of a single person. **"If either of them falls down, one can help the other up."** Marriage is the ultimate buddy system—life is full of hard knocks, and your spouse will always be there for you. **"If two lie down together, they will keep warm."** A double marital promise—not only does marriage provide the only God-pleasing way to express your sexuality, there is a great emotional warmth and security that only married people can enjoy. **"Though one may be overpowered, two can defend themselves"** (Ecclesiastes 4:9-12). A husband-wife team has twice the skills and twice the brainpower of a lone individual.

You theoretically only get to do this once. So when you're in the dating game, don't just settle for people who are fun to be with. Have an eye on what kind of long-term partner he or she would be.

And whether or not he or she is a Christian.

Someone to fight for you

Linda Buxa

Thomas Edison was dyslexic and struggled in school. He liked to see things for himself and ask questions. He couldn't just sit and memorize; he suffered under the teachers' rigid ways—and whippings. His mother became so angry with the school that she chose to educate him at home.

Years later, Edison said, "I remember I used to never be able to get along at school. I was always at the foot of the class. I used to feel that the teachers did not sympathize with me, and that my father thought I was stupid." But then he said, "My mother was the making of me. She was so true, so sure of me; and I felt I had something to live for, someone I must not disappoint."

You feel the shame he felt because you've felt it too, both as a child and an adult. You can, without hesitation, name the insults you suffered at the hands of grade school friends. The sting from a failed relationship lingers. You're embarrassed because you were fired. You know the humiliation of being jailed.

In Jeremiah 1:19, God promised the Israelites, **"They will fight against you but will not overcome you, for I am with you and will rescue you."** The promise is for you too. You are more than a conqueror because the Lord God is your defender.

Your God is the Maker of you. He is so true, so sure of you that you have something—someone—to live for. Now. Forever.

Forgiveness begins at home

Pastor Mark Jeske

Home is where children are discipled most and best. Home is where they learn to obey those who have authority over them, learn to listen, to share, and to serve. They learn manners and politeness. But home is also a place where adults can work on their Christian life skills.

I have a theory that it is harder to live like a Christian in your home than out in the "world." We can put up with unfair and disagreeable people for short bursts of time. But there's nowhere to run at home. If you can't learn to manage conflict at home, if you find yourself going to bed angry or resentful, there can be no healing. It is endlessly surprising to me how many Christian homes are hotbeds of pain and conflict.

Home is where you can fuel up on the power of the gospel to know and experience your forgiveness from God. Home is where you can practice letting mercy flow not only *to* you but *through* you. **"Bear with each other and forgive one another if any of you has a grievance against someone. Forgive as the Lord forgave you"** (Colossians 3:13). Letting go of anger and cutting others some slack is not optional for believers. It is a fruit of faith that God absolutely demands to see.

Let's practice. Repeat after me: "I was wrong about that." "Nice job." "I don't get why you said those things. Help me understand." "I forgive you."

Average Joes

Pastor Daron Lindemann

"Careful now, Joseph, be gentle with him. His journey is just beginning."

"Careful now, Joseph, be gentle with him. His journey is just about done."

"Watch out for splinters from the manger."

"Watch out for splinters from the cross."

"Here, Joseph, I'll hold his head . . . there . . . now use those cloths and wrap him tightly. That's it."

The caring hands of one Joseph, taking the role of Dad, tended to Jesus at his birth. He was a hard-working craftsman, loyal and helpful, and tempted to leave Mary when he discovered she was pregnant. Years later the caring hands of another Joseph, Joseph of Arimathea, tended to Jesus at his death. He was a rich man, a church man, on the council, and expected to conform to his male peers like men do.

Neither of these men, of their own doing, would be described as great. One of them was poor. The other hid his faith behind religious rituals. Yet both stepped up when it was time to serve the kingdom of God.

You don't have to be great to make a difference. You just have to be near Jesus. Touched by his birth. Moved by his death. **"From now on all generations will call me blessed, for the Mighty One has done great things for me—holy is his name"** (Luke 1:48,49).

Where do you need to step up? Don't be afraid. Stay close to Jesus. Because of him, average Joes get involved in great things.

Think ahead

Pastor Mark Jeske

One of the hardest and yet most important skills for parents to teach their children is the ability to think ahead, to delay gratification, to save money, to think before speaking, to do the hard jobs first, to put work before pleasure. In a small mind, there is no tomorrow. There is only now. Now. NOW!

Jesus had some very important words for his disciples and for us, words that urge us to lift up our eyes from the ground and look ahead, because sometimes *our* minds are small too: **"Where your treasure is, there your heart will be also"** (Matthew 6:21). Materialism is a common disease—we chase what we can see, what brings us comfort, what brings us pleasures, what brings us recognition. If your chief treasures are earthly, your heart will be earthbound too, and you will be totally unprepared to be forced to let go of everything on your deathbed.

Jesus invites his disciples to make their money and property decisions with a long-term view—how will my asset management look from a heavenly perspective? What kind of life am I trying to build? What will I be proud of as I sit in my nursing home? What would I be ashamed to show Jesus about my life decisions?

Here's what will bring the most satisfaction: people first. A generous hand. A grateful heart. And a mind completely convinced that the Lord in heaven will more than compensate us for every sacrifice on earth.

He laughs

Pastor Mark Jeske

What makes something funny? Let's admit it—a lot of our humor is based on the misfortune of others, on ridicule, on someone else's embarrassment or pain. When Jerry hits Tom in the face with a frying pan, when someone slips on a banana peel, people laugh.

Does God have a sense of humor? You would probably think not. The Bible presents his thoughts and words with such intensity, such earnestness, such solemnity, that you just can't imagine Father, Son, or Holy Spirit ever cracking a joke. Still, he laughs. Just as the absurdity of life seems funny now and then, God looks at human pretension and pride and puffery and sometimes just loses it. In Psalm 2 the Father looks down at the high and mighty of earth and their proud defiance of him. Their puny plans look silly to him: **"The One enthroned in heaven laughs; the Lord scoffs at them"** (Psalm 2:4).

Read 1 Samuel chapter 5. When the Philistines had seized the holy ark of the covenant and placed it in the temple of their god Dagon, God could have brought any manner of catastrophe upon them—burning sulfur from heaven, lightning bolts, plagues, the angel of death. Do you know what he did? He struck them with what were probably severe hemorrhoids. They begged the Israelites to take their ark back.

Tell me that God doesn't have a sense of humor.

I'm a participant in Holy Week

Pastor Mark Jeske

It's a common thing for people to identify with the protagonist in a movie or story. The adventure and emotions pull us in, and we can't help rooting for the hero. Internet and video game technology today can make the stories even more intense because they are interactive, i.e., you can participate virtually in the *Halo* or *Assassin's Creed* narrative and feel like you're there.

The gospels' account of Holy Week, especially the three-day stretch of Good Friday/Holy Saturday/Easter Sunday, is not only a fascinating and compelling story to read. Your baptism actually plunges you personally right into the story. What happened to Christ is shared by you. Seriously! **"Don't you know that all of us who were baptized into Christ Jesus were baptized into his death? We were therefore buried with him through baptism into death in order that, just as Christ was raised from the dead through the glory of the Father, we too may live a new life"** (Romans 6:3,4).

It's not the splash of water that transports you there. The water just personalizes and identifies the participant by actually touching his or her skin. The real power is the Word of God that works in and through the water. That Word puts you on the cross so that your sin is condemned and punished there. That Word puts you in the tomb with Christ, and it raises you up with him, forgiven, refreshed, and empowered to lead a new life.

You aren't just a spectator. You're there.

Hosannas that last

Diana Kerr

I have to admit something—I think I was a little
stuck-up in my childhood Christianity. I remember
reading stories of disobedience in the Bible and thinking,
"I would *never* do that." I'd watch the *Ten Commandments*
movie starring Charlton Heston with complete disgrace
during the scene when the Israelites create the golden calf
they then begin to worship. "Could they be any dumber?"
I'd think.

Hearing the story of Palm Sunday each year was no
exception. I couldn't grasp how the people of Jerusalem
could gather around praising Jesus as King one day, only
to delight in his torturous murder later that week. Do you
know what I mean? Do you find yourself shaking your head
in disapproval at the people whose mouths shouted both
"Hosanna!" and "Crucify!" in nearly the same breath?

As my faith matures and God deals out healthy doses
of the humility I deserve, I now read about Palm Sunday
and my heart pains me with truth. I am just as guilty of
turning my back on my Savior. When I'm in church, I sing
"Hosanna!" When I read my Bible, I revel in the majesty
of the King of kings; but when I leave church or close my
Bible, my "Hosanna!" doesn't always continue.

Let's confess our insincere praise and pray instead for
a life of ceaseless hosannas. **"Hosanna to the Son of
David! Blessed is he who comes in the name of the Lord!
Hosanna in the highest heaven!"** (Matthew 21:9).

Palm Monday is a big day too!

Linda Buxa

Palm Sunday was a pretty big day. A spontaneous parade, shouting, palm branches, praising. You wouldn't blame Jesus if he wanted to rest after all the excitement. Instead, Matthew tells us that Jesus woke up on Monday and headed straight for the temple because he had work to do.

"Jesus entered the temple courts and drove out all who were buying and selling there. He overturned the tables of the money changers and the benches of those selling doves. . . . The blind and the lame came to him at the temple, and he healed them. But when the chief priests and the teachers of the law saw the wonderful things he did and the children shouting in the temple courts, 'Hosanna to the Son of David,' they were indignant. 'Do you hear what these children are saying?' they asked him. 'Yes,' replied Jesus, 'have you never read, "From the lips of children and infants you, Lord, have called forth your praise"?'" (Matthew 21:12-16).

Jesus has that same work ahead of him each day in your life:

Driving out distractions. What in your life gets in the way of actual worship or distracts you from your true purpose? Overturn it.

Healing you. You have hurts and scars and failures that he came to handle for you. He provides comfort now until you are perfectly healed in heaven.

Listening to praise. As God's child, you were created to praise him. He loves to hear it. Don't let anyone shush you!

Happy: Accept your lot

Pastor Mark Jeske

Americans have a special love affair with happiness. How many other nations have a chartering document that asserts their God-given right to life, liberty, and the pursuit of it?

The freedom to chase happiness, however, does not mean that you'll get it. Happiness is not something that you can pursue and then acquire externally. It doesn't come with more money, more possessions, more power, more friends, or more fame. Happiness is a choice you make about how you look at your world. Happy believers rejoice in their relationship with God through Christ; rejoice in the people God has given them in their lives; rejoice at the promises he's made of provision, protection, and guidance; and feel blessed by whatever material possessions he has chosen to give.

Let the sunlight of King Solomon's wisdom shine in your mind: **"When God gives someone wealth and possessions, and the ability to enjoy them, to accept their lot and be happy in their toil—this is a gift of God. They seldom reflect on the days of their life, because God keeps them occupied with gladness of heart"** (Ecclesiastes 5:19,20).

If you catch yourself saying things like, "I'll be happy when . . ." you're already off track. That day may never come, or when it does you'll be caught up in chasing something else. You can decide to be happy *today*. Happy are those who accept their lot.

Let me hear you say, "I love my life!"

Happy: Sing a song

Pastor Mark Jeske

The digital music explosion has been a huge blessing for Christians—never before have we had access to so many kinds of sacred music for our home audio systems, smart devices, and cars. And yet there is a risk—I fear that the more music we have to *listen* to, the less able we become of making our own.

God gave us throats, lungs, lips, and gospel good news for the purpose of personal musical worship. **"Is anyone happy? Let them sing songs of praise"** (James 5:19). Martin Luther said, "Music is one of the fairest and most glorious gifts of God, to which Satan is a bitter enemy; for it removes from the heart the weight of sorrow and the fascination of evil thoughts. . . . If the devil suggests cares or sad thoughts, then defend yourself with a will and say: 'Get out, devil. I must now sing and play to my Lord Christ.' Take some good fellows and sing the devil down until you learn to despise him. . . . Next to the Word of God, music deserves the highest praise."

You don't have to be a trained musician to make a joyful noise to God, although each person's voice and ear can be trained for improvement. When people hear joyful singing coming from you, it will encourage them, heal your own heart, and gladden God's to receive your worship in this personal and emotional way.

Sing! Sing! Sing!

Happy: Enjoy being single

Pastor Mark Jeske

Every time congregations advertise an event, they are tempted to use the descriptor *family* with it—you know, "family" Bible hour, "family" potluck dinner, "family" workday. They intend that descriptor to be inclusive, warm and fuzzy, and kid-friendly. Single people have told me, however, that "family" as a tag might as well say, "No singles wanted." Aargh!

Pastors know that many marriages in their congregations are struggling and so will speak on marriage a lot. I did a three-part series on marriage that had the unintentional consequence of a single woman in disgust refusing to attend services for that series. "Singles not wanted," she concluded.

Single life is *great*! I gave up mine only with a profound sense of loss and appreciation for its independence. St. Paul, while recommending marriage for all because his world was so full of immorality, also said this about widows: **"If her husband dies, she is free to marry anyone she wishes, but he must belong to the Lord. In my judgment, she is happier if she stays as she is"** (1 Corinthians 7:39,40). Seriously!

This side of heaven, nobody gets everything. Our lives are a mix of pleasure and self-denial, having it now and waiting, struggle and peace. Remarriage for widows and widowers might turn out wonderfully, but take it from St. Paul—you might be happier solo.

Christians, help get the message out that the single life is great!

Happy: Appreciate good leadership

Pastor Mark Jeske

The country of Yemen today is not known in the West for much beyond its poverty, khat chewing, and terrible civil wars. But back in biblical times, when it was known as Sheba, it was renowned for its oases in the desert and for its wealth.

Sheba's queen came to visit King Solomon in Israel to see if his reputation for wisdom could possibly be true. Her trip summary tells us a few things about what makes for a good life. Speaking to Solomon she said: **"How happy your people must be! How happy your officials, who continually stand before you and hear your wisdom! Praise be to the Lord your God, who has delighted in you and placed you on the throne of Israel"** (1 Kings 10:8,9).

The queen offers keen insight into human interaction. How miserable it is when you are trapped in an organization, a business, or a country that is poorly led. Good leadership makes everyone's life better. Good leaders attract talent, inspire confidence and optimism, recognize and promote talent, and help the group imagine the future. Good leaders understand the times and help prepare people to respond to changing situations. Good leaders are calm and resilient, resourceful and curious, flexible, and know how to delegate. How fascinating that the queen didn't comment on how happy Solomon must be, but rather on how happy the palace staff must be!

Do you appreciate good leadership in your life?

Happy: Find joy in your children

Pastor Mark Jeske

I love children. Mine are big now, and I find special joy in talking about parenting with young moms and dads and playing with their kids. Only seldom can I resist the temptation to offer guidance in how to think about their lives.

I look at pictures of my own kids when they were small and deep pangs of guilt and regret wash over me. How did I not realize how magic those days were! Why did I not spend more time with them? If only I could bring those days back!

There is no experience on this earth like that of raising children. If it is that big for a male like me, I can barely imagine what it must be like for a woman to bring forth a new life from her own body. The patriarch Jacob (sadly) had two wives and two, ahem, concubines. His wife Leah was not so good-looking, and so she yearned for vindication and love through providing children for Jacob, even when they came through a concubine, her maidservant: **"Leah's servant Zilpah bore Jacob a second son. Then Leah said, 'How happy I am! The women will call me happy.' So she named him Asher"** (Genesis 30:12,13).

The Hebrew word *Asher* means "happy" or "blessed." I tell you what—why not pretend to call your child or grandchild Asher today, even if only in your heart, to show your intense gratitude to God for letting you be part of his process of bringing new life into the world.

Three are better than two

Pastor Mark Jeske

One of the persistent myths that hobbles people's mental architecture of how marriage is supposed to work is the notion that good marriages are "made in heaven." True enough—the blueprints were designed by God himself. But marriage comes in kit form—you have to build it yourselves. Good marriages are divinely designed in heaven, but they are *built on earth* by the daily choices, words, and attitudes of ordinary human beings like you and me.

Marriage is possible without God in it. But it's way better when the two people who are twining their lives together make a conscious decision to twine God in too. **"A cord of three strands is not quickly broken"** (Ecclesiastes 4:12). Why are three better than two?

All the things a married person needs to give to a spouse must first come from God: patience to let a spouse develop, daily forgiveness for daily irritations and misunderstandings, unconditional love, steady kindness, a generous spirit, a willingness to take the other's words and actions in the nicest possible way, willingness to sacrifice personal preferences and comfort for the good of the team, the heart of a servant, finding greater satisfaction in benefiting another before yourself.

When God is your third strand; when your home is a place of prayer, Bible reading, singing, and giving of thanks; when you set aside a day for worship and build God into your financial budget, you are on your way to a happy life.

Overwhelmed?

Linda Buxa

It seems we are all overwhelmed. For some, the weight of loneliness, debt, grief, anxiety, change, poor health drags them down. For others, it is busyness. The schedules of work and kids and hobbies leave them gasping for breath.

When I feel that weight, my prayers quickly become pleas of "God, please make my life easier." Maybe yours do too. That's when we hear him tell us, **"In this world you will have trouble. But take heart! I have overcome the world"** (John 16:33).

That truth doesn't necessarily make our schedules less busy or take away the struggles, but it puts them in perspective. We take our eyes off our current struggles and place them on the One who overcame. We take heart that because our Brother said, "It is finished," Satan can no longer eternally overwhelm us. We look to the Creator, in awe that the One who placed every single star in the sky still knows our names and cares about our hurts. We see that the Father who anxiously runs to a prodigal child loves it when we come back home too. We are overwhelmed that the One whose voice strips the forests bare still whispers to us: "Be still." We stop thinking we are in this by ourselves and hear the Savior say, "Surely I am with you always."

Overwhelmed by the world? Not anymore.

Overwhelmed by the One who overcame? Absolutely!

Teach your girls about inner beauty

Pastor Mark Jeske

Men are dimly aware of the pressure on women to be beautiful. Women know it—they feel it every day. They know they are being evaluated every time they step out of their houses on their clothes, their hair, their makeup, their jewelry. Parents of girls need to be dialed in to the terrible peer pressures they face in their schools and on their streets.

That stress is so severe that it drives young women to anorexia, bulimia, and pills. It is a sacred duty of dads and moms to show their girls unconditional love, steady support, daily refuge, and daily affirmation that they are smart, precious, and pretty.

St. Peter has wonderful and encouraging words about what constitutes true beauty: **"Your beauty should come not from outward adornment, such elaborate hairstyles and the wearing of gold jewelry or fine clothes. Rather, it should be that of your inner self, the unfading beauty of a gentle and quiet spirit, which is of great worth in God's sight"** (1 Peter 3:3,4).

A girl who knows that she has great worth to her God and to her mother and father will be able to bear the abuse and rejection she will encounter in a world often cold and cruel. A girl who knows deep down inside that she has value and purpose will be able to deflect Satan's negative messages and fulfill her God-given purpose.

You go, girl!

Teach your boys about self-control

Pastor Mark Jeske

My wife and I had some rather high-minded ideas about keeping our boys away from violent play when they were little. We solemnly decided that we wouldn't buy toy guns for them. Ha! They just fastened two Lego blocks together at right angles to make guns of their own. When we took those away, they just used their fingers to shoot each other. We gave up. Boys want to live in a world of conflict in their play. Boys are by nature aggressive. They want to fight and compete and win.

Maybe it's the testosterone. Just as young women are at risk either of depression over their body image or fascinated by projecting their newfound sexual power, our boys are at risk because of their impulses toward sex and violence. Our culture glorifies men who seize both. Our Christian faith teaches us that real men show true strength by *restraint* of their passions: **"Encourage the young men to be self-controlled. In everything set them an example by doing what is good"** (Titus 2:6,7).

Boys long for heroes to look up to and to imitate. If a boy doesn't find a hero in his dad, he may choose a really bad one. Men, teach your boys about self-control. Demonstrate self-control (and look happy doing it). Help them use their strength and aggression to do great things for the Lord and to aspire to lead and protect their own families.

Quiet charity

Pastor Mark Jeske

It's not too hard to spot charity phonies—you know, people who do something for the community and then leverage every media outlet they and their staff can think of to trumpet that news as far and wide as possible. How much better it is to be generous and help people and let that be the end of it!

I have some friends who love to tell me what they contribute to and how they've been recognized. I wish they wouldn't do that. The only recognition they need is a receipt from the charity for IRS purposes and the approval of their generous Father in heaven who gave them the money in the first place.

Jesus taught his disciples that using generosity to stoke hunger for fame is cheap and unworthy of citizens of God's kingdom: **"Be careful not to practice your righteousness in front of others to be seen by them. If you do, you will have no reward from your Father in heaven"** (Matthew 6:1). If the recipients of your gifts want to use your name to encourage generosity by others, that's one thing. It's another entirely to use the neediness of others to make yourself look big.

Some congregations in the past used to publish the contribution records of all their members. It gives me the shivers even to think about that. Shaming won't help the low givers to be more generous, and flattering the big givers publicly won't help them carry out Jesus' instructions.

Shhh.

Tread lightly

Jason Nelson

I've been to a lot of churches in my life. I've always
been curious that there is so little discussion of the
environment in the Christian community. I've heard
some talk of subduing the earth and replenishing it with
people. I've heard sermons on the stewardship of time,
talent, and treasures but not much on good ol' *terra firma*.
We seem to shy away from that discussion. But if any
group should be at the forefront of concern for the
environment, it would be those who bow before the God
who made it.

> "O Lᴏʀᴅ, our Lord, how majestic is your name
> in all the earth!
> When I consider your heavens,
> the work of your fingers, the moon and the stars,
> which you have set in place,
> what is man that you are mindful of him?
> You made him ruler over the works of your hands;
> you put everything under his feet" (Psalm 8:1,3,4,6).

When the Bible wants us to appreciate the
transcendence of God, it glorifies him with the wonders of
the natural world. When the Bible wants people to
remember their dependence on God, it contrasts their
puniness with the expanse of everything he made. And
when the Bible wants human beings to be conscientious
with their dominion over God's creation, it puts the two
together so that we remember to tread lightly.

The earth is God's

Pastor Daron Lindemann

Some say that the first Earth Day, which was celebrated on April 22, 1970, marked the beginning of the modern environmental movement. A movement eager to say, "The earth is god!" As creatures of the earth who trust our Creator, however, we believe differently.

God miraculously created the earth out of nothing. He can do that because he is God and the earth is not. The earth serves him. The earth is not our mother, but dependent on her Creator like we are—more like a daughter. Without his constant care she would crumble.

Sadly, the earth is still wasting away, and not just because of poor choices by her inhabitants. No matter how much we recycle, we live on an infected planet cursed by God after humanity's sin.

Our Savior God, however, is fighting off the earth's curse and holding it together for a purpose. **"For the creation was subjected to frustration, not by its own choice, but by the will of the one who subjected it, in hope that the creation itself will be liberated from its bondage to decay and brought into the freedom and glory of the children of God"** (Romans 8:20,21).

The earth trembled when she held her Creator on a tree she grew, and she drank up his blood in the parched dust below the cross. And she will tremble again when she heaves our bodies from their graves on the Last Day before we are delivered forever to heaven and she is destroyed. Having served her Master well.

Sharpen the axe

Linda Buxa

"Give me six hours to chop down a tree and I will spend the first four sharpening the axe"—Abraham Lincoln

President Lincoln had it right. The time you spend preparing for your work makes the work so much easier.

Jesus gave us work to do too. Be salt and light in the world. Feed the hungry. Care for widows and orphans. Go and make disciples. Forgive as the Lord forgave you. Love your enemies. Serve one another. Know that you are blessed when you are persecuted.

That huge task means we need to make sure we spend enough time preparing for the task. Hebrews 10:24,25 tells us how: **"And let us consider how we may spur one another on toward love and good deeds, not giving up meeting together, as some are in the habit of doing, but encouraging one another—and all the more as you see the Day approaching."**

It is so much easier to do the work Jesus has for us when we first meet together and encourage each other. That is what keeps us sharp and gives us the motivation to seek out those who don't know Jesus—both the ones who are hurting and the ones who are hostile. Trying to do this by yourself will only wear you down and make you dull.

Has one of your fellow Christians missed out on their Christian axe sharpening? Give them a call and invite them to come back.

Surprise! Lust is a form of adultery

Pastor Mark Jeske

People like to assume that God's ways work pretty much the same as our ways on earth. People furthermore like to assume that his governance is a lot like ours. Since our country has freedom of belief and freedom of speech, isn't it reasonable to suppose that these two principles are operative in God's courtroom as well? Actually, no.

Listen to Jesus: **"You have heard that it was said, 'You shall not commit adultery.' But I tell you that anyone who looks at a woman lustfully has already committed adultery with her in his heart"** (Matthew 5:27,28). Jesus' statement probably drew two responses. First, "Yeah, right. I can think what I want in my own mind." The second, "What if he's right—dear God, I am in serious trouble."

Yes, he was right, and yes, we are all in serious trouble with the Sixth Commandment. No excuses, no stalling, no blaming allowed. The fact is, the inward and outward holiness demanded by that holy command is beyond anyone's ability to keep. We are all in desperate need of forgiveness, and we are in desperate need of the strength of the Holy Spirit to lead a life that respects the sexual boundaries set by our Maker. God set those boundaries not to torment us or remove what little fun we can have in this hard life. God built the excitement and fun into sexuality to enliven marriage and strengthen it as the basic building block of all society.

Eyes on your wives, guys.

Faith is never alone

Pastor Daron Lindemann

Faith alone saves. But for believers in Jesus, faith is never alone.

"Suppose a brother or a sister is without clothes and daily food. If one of you says to them, 'Go in peace; keep warm and well fed,' but does nothing about their physical needs, what good is it? In the same way, faith by itself, if it is not accompanied by action, is dead" (James 2:15-17).

Holding firm to the Bible's teachings can become a wicked trap if we stop there and think that God loves us only because we have the truth. True truth is accompanied by love.

Do you know what an *erg* is? It is the term of measurement for a unit of mechanical work. For example, it takes a certain number of ergs for you to walk to the kitchen. The Bible calls us to exercise our faith into acts of love and uses the Greek word *erg*.

Love is work. You are redeemed, not by God's good thoughts but by the loving work of Jesus Christ.

Love is work. A marriage relationship grows with work; it doesn't just happen and it isn't easy. Parenting is work (and having parents is work). Friendship is work. Going to church is work, and volunteering is work. School is work, and a career is work. Caring for people is work. Sometimes it's hard work! That's what faith does. It loves.

Christianity is nothing less than holding to the truth, but it is also so much more.

I'm a work in progress

Pastor Mark Jeske

The Bible's message has a lot of paradoxes and seeming contradictions. There. I've said it. It kind of helps to be able to hold two seemingly conflicting ideas in your head at the same time without going crazy. How can Christ be fully human and fully divine at the same time? How can God be three and one at the same time? *Hmm . . .*

One of those paradoxes that once may have confused you is the contrast between justification (complete) and sanctification (incomplete). Are you a sinner or a saint (i.e., holy)? The answer is yes. It's yes because in Christ you are declared to be as holy and sinless as Christ himself. But you are also a work in progress, a sinner who sometimes backslides, sometimes balks, sometimes doesn't understand, sometimes pushes back on God.

St. Paul did not hesitate to hold himself forth as an example of how to live the Christian life, but he also confessed his terrible failings and called himself the chief of sinners. But here's the deal—he didn't let his sins and guilt of the past become a dead weight on his shoulders: **"Not that I have already obtained all this, or have already arrived at my goal, but I press on to take hold of that for which Christ Jesus took hold of me"** (Philippians 3:12).

Knowing that we are loved, forgiven, and immortal, we can keep moving forward. God knows that we are works in progress. Glory awaits. Soon. Soon.

Pray for your leaders

Linda Buxa

Whenever there's a presidential campaign, based on the candidates' promises, it seems as if we are all hoping for an earthly savior, one who keeps us safe and makes our lives comfortable. Candidates want us to pretend we have amnesia, forgetting that scandals are often uncovered, exposing some at the top of the political food chain who have misused their power or acted out of selfish motives.

Why are we surprised? Thanks to sinful selfishness, every nation on earth has examples of corruption. King Herod killed baby boys two years and younger so he could retain power. King David had a top soldier killed to try to cover up his adultery. King Solomon, who had his share of adultery issues, knew how governments worked. **"If you see the poor oppressed in a district, and justice and rights denied, do not be surprised at such things; for one official is eyed by a higher one, and over them both are others higher still. The increase from the land is taken by all; the king himself profits from the fields"** (Ecclesiastes 5:8,9).

Let's listen to the One with eternal authority who establishes those with temporary authority: **"I urge, then, first of all, that petitions, prayers, intercession and thanksgiving be made for all people—for kings and all those in authority, that we may live peaceful and quiet lives in all godliness and holiness"** (1 Timothy 2:1,2).

Pray for your leaders.

The rooster crows

Linda Buxa

"Peter declared, 'Even if all fall away, I will not.' 'Truly I tell you,' Jesus answered, 'today—yes, tonight—before the rooster crows twice you yourself will disown me three times.' But Peter insisted emphatically, 'Even if I have to die with you, I will never disown you.' And all the others said the same" (Mark 14:29-31).

We all want to be Peter, don't we? In our hearts we want to believe with such fierce conviction that we would emphatically argue with Jesus. But we all know that Peter's example of conviction was quickly followed by a loss of courage. I know that my example of conviction can quickly fade through fear, indifference, and callousness. I bet you have your own examples too.

But the rooster always crows.

For Peter it took a literal rooster to wake him up. For me and you, it may take our consciences wrestling to the top or a dear friend who lovingly reminds us that we are off the rails.

Maybe you are the one who sounds the call, with gentleness and respect, to the people around you. There are many who don't know the ultimate sounding will be on judgment day, when it's too late to rush out like Peter to cry and repent.

As a footnote . . . Peter lived the rest of his life with conviction, and the moment did come when he was crucified—because he would not disown Jesus.

April 29

God's "perhaps"

Pastor Daron Lindemann

The blue ribbon in my front yard says that I appreciate police officers. The picture on my mantle of a police officer says even more. My son is a police officer.

I know. It's dangerous. But he is willing to take that risk for a greater reward: peace and safety in a wicked world. *Perhaps* at a personal cost to him. But I sure hope not.

I feel like the vineyard owner who **"sent a servant to the tenants so they would give him some of the fruit of the vineyard. But the tenants beat him and sent him away empty-handed"** (Luke 20:10). He sent more servants but the tenants beat and abused them too. Then the owner did the unthinkable: **"I will send my son, whom I love; *perhaps* they will respect him"** (Luke 20:13).

Perhaps?! He sees the vicious, abusive behavior and yet holds out only an iffy *perhaps*? Doesn't he understand the risk?

In this parable Jesus is teaching us that God's mercy goes beyond our norms of reality. God responds to our sins that hurt others, our abuse of his good gifts, and our repeat offenses of bad sinful habits by increasing doses of his patient love. Even if it costs him his own Son.

Let the "perhaps" of God be not a risky failure but a hope of God fulfilled in you because you will respect his Son. God didn't make a mistake when he sent his Son, Jesus, for you.

It's meant to be permanent

Pastor Mark Jeske

When two partners form a business venture, they are in it only so long as they realize a profit and get along with each other. If either one loses interest in the partnership, he or she may leave or buy the other out. There is no expectation that the partnership must last until death of the principals.

It's not hard to understand why people would enter marriage with the same attitude—who wants to make that kind of scary permanent commitment? It makes sense on a personal level to keep a back door or two open in case the relationship is no fun anymore.

That was certainly the view of marriage that the Pharisees at Jesus' time held. **"'Why then,' they asked, 'did Moses *command* that a man give his wife a certificate of divorce and send her away?' Jesus replied, 'Moses *permitted* you to divorce your wives because your hearts were hard. But it was not this way from the beginning'"** (Matthew 19:7,8). God sadly realizes that breakups are going to happen, but that was not his beautiful creative intent on the sixth day of creation, and it should not be seen as a spiritually acceptable option when two people get married.

Bottom line: husbands and wives need to change their behaviors, adapting to each other, serving each other, forgiving each other, and growing in the grace of self-control so that their inborn sinfulness won't destroy the relationship.

Marriage really is supposed to be till death us do part.

may

"See! The winter is past; the rains are over and gone.
Flowers appear on the earth; the season of singing has come,
the cooing of doves is heard in our land."

Song of Songs 2:11,12

Speak up for moms and their children

Linda Buxa

Mother's Day is coming up soon. Ads constantly remind us that the women in our lives would love flowers, chocolate, breakfast in bed, and jewelry. The abundance of pink cards praises the women who nurture, protect, and raise the next generation.

Still, I can't stop thinking that while individually we value mothers, we undervalue the children—some are willing to dispose of them before they are even born. But Psalm 139:13,14 tells us that mothers and children are inextricably linked: **"You created my inmost being; you knit me together in my mother's womb. I praise you because I am fearfully and wonderfully made; your works are wonderful, I know that full well."**

I can't change the entire culture, but I can influence the one around me. As Mother Teresa said: "Never worry about numbers. Help one person at a time and always start with the person nearest you." If you have some spare change, support pro-life groups, those who have resources to spread the message that each life is valuable. If you have time, volunteer at a crisis pregnancy center. If you have baby items, donate them to a women's shelter.

Finally, I know women who have had abortions. Sometimes Mother's Day isn't happy for them. They either have suffered or are still suffering, carrying guilt and sadness. When you plead the case for the unborn, remember to also love the already born. Adding to their burden doesn't help. Their guilty consciences won't pay for that sin. Jesus is the only one who can; he's the one who already did.

Dandelions and moms

Pastor Daron Lindemann

Dandelions and moms. They need no pampering to show their bright faces to a world busily speeding by them. **" . . . A happy mother of children. Praise the Lord"** (Psalm 113:9).

God uses mother dandelions to propagate new life in baby dandelions as he blows the floating seeds each to its new place. God opens or closes the wombs of women to bless them with no children, some children, or many children according to his perfect wisdom and love. **"As you do not know the path of the wind, or how the body is formed in a mother's womb, so you cannot understand the work of God, the Maker of all things"** (Ecclesiastes 11:5).

Dandelions tap their roots deep into the ground, pulling up nutrients to replenish the top soil. Mothers dig deep into their faith, hope, and love to nurture their children. **"She is clothed with strength and dignity; she can laugh at the days to come. She speaks with wisdom, and faithful instruction is on her tongue"** (Proverbs 31:25,26).

Their outward appearance changes—dandelions over a period of days, mothers over a period of years. But their roots remain; a mother's roots deeply imbedded in the promises of God that love and bless her, her children, and all people through Jesus. **"Charm is deceptive, and beauty is fleeting; but a woman who fears the Lord is to be praised"** (Proverbs 31:30).

Thank you, Lord, for dandelions and moms. Tough and tender, they color our world.

Thank you, teachers!

Linda Buxa

Online banking sites have a host of personal questions to verify who you are: mother's maiden name, high school mascot, first pet. They pick the tidbits of your life that you'll never forget. It's not surprising that "favorite teacher" always makes the list, because we all have that one teacher who immediately comes to mind. The one who encouraged you, challenged you, loved you, and disciplined you.

Whether in public school, private school, or home school, it's always good to take the time to say thank you to the ones who choose to spend their time, energy, money, and lives on teaching the next generation.

For the teachers who see their career choice as a way to not only teach the three Rs but to also show the Father's love, today is a great day to say, **"We always thank God for all of you and continually mention you in our prayers. We remember before our God and Father your work produced by faith, your labor prompted by love, and your endurance inspired by hope in our Lord Jesus Christ"** (1 Thessalonians 1:2,3).

For those educators who don't know Jesus yet, there is no better way to show your appreciation for them than to introduce them to the Teacher. Through your love, grace, and words, share with them the good news that **"the fear of the LORD is the beginning of wisdom, and knowledge of the Holy One is understanding"** (Proverbs 9:10).

Thank you, teachers! We appreciate all you do!

We made it

Jason Nelson

Don't you wonder what was running through Jesus' mind as he hiked up the Mount of Olives for the last time, his happy little band chattering along in anticipation of something? What did he recall with each step—a cow stall, carpenter shop, storms, healings, beatings, crucifixion, a first deep breath, the stench of hell? Who could blame him if he got to the top, looked heavenward, and whispered to himself, "I made it."

This little hill meant a lot to Jesus. He taught there and prayed there. He wept over Jerusalem there. He would return to God as God from there. We don't meditate on the ascension the same way we cherish the chain of events 40 days prior. But what Jesus finished on the cross he delivered to us in his ascension. His work was complete. We have redemption through his blood, the power of the Holy Spirit, the charge to be his witnesses, and the promise that he will return for us.

Jesus prepared his disciples for this mountaintop experience in the upper room: **"I am going there to prepare a place for you. And if I go and prepare a place for you, I will come back and take you to be with me that you also may be where I am"** (John 14:2,3).

We are going where Jesus is. Because he made it, we will too.

Worth the effort

Diana Kerr

Take a second and think about your prayer life.

How's it going? Do you find plenty of time for daily prayer, or do you sometimes rush through a busy day and barely spend a quality moment with God?

Our lives are full of endless tasks, meetings, and activities, most of which make it on our calendars or to-do lists.

Do you schedule one-on-one meetings with *God?*

I know, it feels weird to plan out something as beautiful and spiritual as prayer. Prayer should just happen naturally, right?

But if it *doesn't* happen naturally, or if you *don't* intentionally make time for focused prayer, what's at stake? Many of us can attest to the fact that the strength of our prayer life often directly correlates with our emotional strength as we navigate the daily challenges of life.

Our Lord lived here on earth way before smartphones and e-mails, but he still knew what it was like to feel the pressure of others' demands. And yet, he knew what he had to do to make sure that even *he* got his "God time" in each day. **"Crowds of people came to hear him and to be healed of their sicknesses. But Jesus often withdrew to lonely places and prayed"** (Luke 5:15,16).

Even with a lot going on, Jesus intentionally fit in alone time with his Father. If the benefits of prayer were worth the effort for Jesus, they are certainly worth our effort as well.

Dumb laws

Linda Buxa

Reading about states' dumb laws is an entertaining way to waste time on the Internet.

In Denver, Colorado, it's illegal to lend your vacuum to your next-door neighbor. (For the record, my neighbors are always welcome to vacuum my house.)

You may not run out of gas in Youngstown, Ohio. (Smart, but do you really need a law for that?)

Tennessee residents may not import, possess, or cause to be imported any type of live skunk, or to sell, barter, or exchange. (Who would want to?!)

In Walnut, California, you need a permit from the sheriff to wear a mask or disguise on a public street. (There has to be an exception for trick-or-treating, don't you think?)

Finally, the state code in Alabama only gives you five minutes to vote. (Hope you made up your mind before you went in there!)

Dumb laws made by humans were usually precipitated because of dumb actions by humans. God's law was given to humans, not because he calls us dumb, but because God is love. He knows that when we follow his laws his way, our lives are so much more at peace with him. Like King David, we say, **"Great peace have those who love your law, and nothing can make them stumble. I wait for your salvation, Lord, and I follow your commands. I obey your statutes, for I love them greatly. I obey your precepts and your statutes, for all my ways are known to you"** (Psalm 119:165-168).

Lord, I love your law!

Conspicuous consumption

Pastor Mark Jeske

It's a hard thing to suffer financial reversals, long stretches of unemployment, bad investments, rip-offs by family members, and debts from huge medical bills. It's hard to be cheerful in your faith when you feel as though you're in a deep pit in life. But did you know that the opposite scenario also brings great risk to your faith?

Accumulating financial resources can rot out your soul. Jesus knew that from the sad experience of studying the behaviors of the wealthy. He and his Father love to spoil their children with prosperity, but it takes a strong spirit to keep your head clear and not become selfish and materialistic as your net worth rises significantly. The prophet Amos had severe words for the upper class of the people of his day who not only lived the high life but used their power to squeeze even more from those at the bottom: **"Hear this word, you cows of Bashan on Mount Samaria, you women who oppress the poor and crush the needy and say to your husbands, 'Bring us some drinks!' . . . You will be cast out"** (Amos 4:1,3).

The remedy? As you take stock of your investments, give all the glory to the generosity of your heavenly Father. Scripture tells us that it is he who gave you the ability to produce wealth. Second, let his gifts flow through you generously.

You have been blessed to be a blessing to other people.

There is always a victim

Jason Nelson

It is a diabolical ruse to suggest private behavior is benign as long as no one else gets hurt. That allows people to rationalize doing destructive things in the privacy of their own homes or on their own computers. Society has played along by muting restraining statutes in deference to libertarian permissiveness. So people will smoke a little weed at home because no one else will get hurt. Or they will download dirty pictures for private viewing because no one else will get hurt. But someone always gets hurt. Sin always has a victim.

The National Institute of Health warns that pot smoking can stunt brain development and contribute to debilitating disorders like schizophrenia. We can see the correlation. Addiction to porn sabotages marriages and warps healthy sexual relations between husband and wife. We can see the correlation. Dabbling in any of these things is a dangerous experiment in self-indulgence and self-deception. Sin always has a victim. In most cases sin has several victims. The sinner suffers, and the people who love the sinner suffer even more.

And God suffers. God is a victim of our sins. **"He was wounded for our rebellious acts. He was crushed for our sins"** (Isaiah 53:5 GW). Christ is the long-suffering victim every time we undermine our well-being and pollute our moral standing. He is also an essential part of the long road back because **"he was punished so that we could have peace, and we received healing from his wounds."**

God's first law

Pastor Mark Jeske

Every so often there will be some hoo-ha over whether or not the Ten Commandments should be displayed in a public space, like city hall or a courthouse. While I believe it would be good for passersby to read and learn from the commandments, they are not binding in district or appellate court.

God's laws are binding, however, in *his* court. The list of ten commands in Exodus chapter 20 and Deuteronomy chapter 5 are a convenient summary of God's timeless will for mankind (although some of the phraseology is intended only for the temporary civil and ceremonial laws binding on Israel until the coming of Christ).

The most important of all the commandments of God is the first: **"I am the LORD your God, who brought you out of Egypt, out of the land of slavery. You shall have no other gods before me"** (Exodus 20:2,3). God's chosen personal adjective for himself is *jealous*—he absolutely will tolerate no competition for our worship, love, and obedience. Truly the story of humanity's fall from grace and our continued miserable struggles is the story of people loving and chasing other things. Whatever you love, trust, or follow more than God must go—idols seduce and corrupt and destroy those who love them.

Our Lord Jesus shows us the opposite of idolatry: **"Love the Lord your God with all your heart and with all your soul and with all your mind"** (Matthew 22:37).

God's second law

Pastor Mark Jeske

High on Mt. Sinai God gave Moses instructions for an entire way of life for the brand-new Israelite nation, recently freed from Egyptian slavery. In that mass of "covenant" material were his will for their society, their worship life, and timeless principles of their moral behavior toward him and each other. As a memory aid, God himself chiseled a summary of his divine instruction onto two tablets of stone for Moses to carry with him and to accompany the Israelites on the rest of their journey to Canaan.

Alas, the Hebrew Scriptures did not number them explicitly, and among Christians there are two main schools of thought on which commandment is which number. We'll call this one God's second law: **"You shall not misuse the name of the Lord your God, for the Lord will not hold anyone guiltless who misuses his name"** (Exodus 20:7).

Adulteration of God's holy message (or "name"), either by addition or subtraction, is strenuously forbidden and carries severe penalties. So does flippant or profane usage of God's precious proper names. Use them carefully and for the purposes for which he lovingly revealed them to you. Instead of hearing a lot of "dammits" and "swear to Gods" coming from your mouth, may your friends rather hear God's name in prayers, praises, and thanksgiving: **"Call on me in the day of trouble; I will deliver you, and you will honor me"** (Psalm 50:15).

God's third law

Pastor Mark Jeske

God's third law has a double meaning. **"Remember the Sabbath day by keeping it holy"** (Exodus 20:8) has both a temporary and permanent application. It was a temporary restriction of the Old Covenant, binding only until the time of Christ, that Saturdays were to be considered "no work" days. The Hebrew word *Shabbath* actually means "rest." Israelites were to remember God's creation week and rest as he rested on the seventh day.

The New Testament removed the "day" restrictions. Christians may hold their public worship services on the day of their choice. Most worshiping communities chose Sunday, the day on which the Father created light, the day on which Christ rose from the dead, the day on which the Holy Spirit came with power on Pentecost.

The Third Commandment's application for us today might simply be summarized, "Remember Sabbath," i.e., remember and appreciate the sweet joy, peace, and rest we enjoy because of the gospel message of the forgiveness of our sins. Remembering Sabbath means prizing the Word of God; reading and hearing it joyfully, regularly, and eagerly; celebrating your membership in God's family; and raising up words and songs of worship.

Here's how to remember Sabbath: **"Let the message of Christ dwell among you richly as you teach and admonish one another with all wisdom through psalms, hymns, and songs from the Spirit, singing to God with gratitude in your hearts"** (Colossians 3:16).

In Christ Jesus you will find your Sabbath, your rest.

God's fourth law

Pastor Mark Jeske

The first three of God's laws show people how to treat God; the rest of the Ten show us how God wants us to treat one another. Isn't it interesting that the first relationship for our instruction is that of a child toward his or her parents? **"Honor your father and your mother, as the Lord your God has commanded you, so that you may live long and that it may go well with you in the land that the Lord your God is giving you"** (Deuteronomy 5:16).

After figuring out how to keep their baby alive, the next most important thing parents can do is teach their children obedience and respect, the younger the better. Children will never take the concept of God seriously if they haven't learned about parental authority. Children will also never develop into employable young people if they haven't learned how to follow the instructions of others, feel accountable to other people's standards, keep their own egos in check, and accept responsibility for their own mistakes.

So important is this law that God attached two sweet promises to parent obeyers: your quality of life will improve and the quantity of your life will increase.

He attaches divine curses to people who choose to be authority defiers: **"Whoever rebels against the authority is rebelling against what God has instituted, and those who do so will bring judgment on themselves"** (Romans 13:2).

Parents, you should only have to give orders once.

God's fifth law

Pastor Mark Jeske

There's a reason why detective and cop shows, books, and movies are so endlessly popular. The never-fail plot line is murder, as we all have a nervous fascination with other people dying violently. Perhaps it's related to our own fear of death. You know, human life is fragile. It doesn't take all that much to take a life.

God knew that. He intentionally made human beings smaller and more physically vulnerable than many species in the animal kingdom. For protection he surrounded us not with a hard exoskeleton but with his Word and warning: **"You shall not murder"** (Exodus 20:13). Every society in human history, everywhere on the earth's surface, has known the deadly peril of toleration of murder and has outlawed it.

Murder not only cheats people out of years and even decades of the joys of life on earth. It may also cut short someone's opportunity to come to know and believe in the Lord Jesus and be saved (i.e., one's time of grace). You and I can respect and keep this commandment by doing what we can to help people live their earthly lives to the fullest.

The Lord Jesus not only kept this commandment perfectly for us as our divine substitute, refusing to do any bodily harm to those who were doing bodily harm to him, but he also taught his followers: **"Love your enemies and pray for those who persecute you, that you may be children of your Father in heaven"** (Matthew 5:44,45).

God's sixth law

Pastor Mark Jeske

When God invented the human race, he simultaneously invented the two genders, the mad wonder of sexuality, and human reproduction. His very last creative act during creation week was to invent marriage, the invisible bond that creates "one flesh" till death us do part. He was so excited about that gift to his first man and woman that he performed their wedding immediately upon creation of Eve.

God invented human sexuality for the delight of married couples and to bring about childbirth. Out of love for people and their marriages, he put his shield around married couples and forbade sexual behavior outside of marriage: **"You shall not commit adultery"** (Exodus 20:14). That prohibition includes two unmarried people, and even more important, sex with a person who is married to someone else.

Especially now in a fallen world, marriage from God's point of view is more important than ever for the stability and happiness of all human society. If men and women were sexually faithful only to their spouses, STDs would disappear. Every child would have a mommy and daddy to tuck her into bed each night. Without cheating and affairs, the divorce rate would plunge.

Governmental laws restricting sexual behavior are being dismantled one by one. God's sixth law has not been repealed: **"Marriage should be honored by all, and the marriage bed kept pure, for God will judge the adulterer and the sexually immoral"** (Hebrews 13:4).

You break it at your peril.

God's seventh law

Pastor Mark Jeske

The right of personal property is one of the most foundational building blocks of any sane and rational society. If people are not allowed to buy and own things, like horses, land, farm equipment, and a home, they lose any incentive for working. Why work and save to buy stuff that anybody who wants to can take? What business could survive for a week without guarantees of property ownership?

God carved into Moses' tablets an elegantly simple property law: **"You shall not steal"** (Exodus 20:15). I doubt if there are very many adults alive today who have not experienced the pain of theft or personal robbery. Next to the power of lust, Satan finds the human weakness of greed easily exploitable. It takes no stroke of genius to predict that stealing will be a feature of life on earth till Christ returns.

But God's people must have none of it. **"Keep your lives free from the love of money and be content with what you have, because God has said, 'Never will I leave you; never will I forsake you'"** (Hebrews 13:5). In this crooked age, honesty is a prized trait—in politics, in business, and in the church. Your personal honesty will be noted and valued. We honor our God not only by not stealing but by being appreciative of all the possessions he has generously given us and choosing to be content.

Say it with me: "Lord, if I have you, I have all I need."

God's eighth law

Pastor Mark Jeske

How old are children when they figure out how to evade responsibility by lying? Five? Four? Three? Jesus told the Pharisees once that when the devil lies, he is speaking his native language, for he is a liar and the father of lies. The sin we're all born with gives us that same fluency in the native language of liars.

Truth telling is learned behavior. It's hard work, because lying can be such a quick and easy way to shed blame, cover misdeeds, and make other people look bad. Lying is bad in and of itself, but it is especially evil when lies are used to damage someone else's reputation. God thought lying so dangerous that he built it into his ten laws: **"You shall not give false testimony against your neighbor"** (Exodus 20:16).

For this and every sin we sinful liars need a Savior, one who spoke the truth for all of us and bore the punishment for the lies of all of us. Joined to him now in faith, part of his holy body, called and empowered for new life, let's make a fresh start, and it all starts now: **"Do not lie to each other, since you have taken off your old self with its practices and have put on the new self, which is being renewed in knowledge in the image of its Creator"** (Colossians 3:9,10).

Even when the truth is hard, believers can handle it.

God's ninth and tenth laws

Pastor Mark Jeske

Both the ninth and tenth laws speak against the evil of coveting, which has led some Christians to number them together as law ten. **"You shall not covet your neighbor's wife. You shall not set your desire on your neighbor's house or land"** (Deuteronomy 5:21).

What really is coveting? It most certainly is not the same thing as wanting. There is nothing wrong with wanting a better life, wanting a raise, wanting to drive your own car instead of riding the bus, wanting a promotion, wanting to buy instead of rent a house, wanting to retire. Coveting is "bad wanting": wanting something that permanently belongs to someone else, like a spouse; wanting something badly enough to decide to steal it; wanting something evil, like a piece of the drug trade; wanting things to the point of greed; wanting more things so badly it makes you discontent with your life. A whole world of evil is hatched first invisibly in a covetous mind and heart.

Healing for a covetous heart comes from taking inventory of the rich blessings God has provided, cultivating a thankful heart, repenting of every evil desire, finding a fresh start for the soul in the forgiveness bought by Christ, and by turning covetous desires inside out and deciding to look out for other people for a change: **"In humility value others above yourselves, not looking to your own interests but each of you to the interests of others"** (Philippians 2:3,4).

Kept safe

Pastor Daron Lindemann

Have you ever led a tour? been responsible for a large group of people traveling a long distance? chaperoned a class trip, band trip, or sports traveling team? At the end of the day, what is your primary purpose?

You must return safely the same amount of first graders, hockey players, or adult day care residents with which you started. Start with 17. Return with 17. Not 14. Not 8.

That can be a challenge. Little kids get lost at parks. A car in the caravan doesn't make it through a red light. Inquisitive old folks can wander. My wife's high school class was stopped on their senior trip when a highway patrol officer with flashing lights pulled over their bus to deliver an embarrassed classmate left behind in Indiana (and they hadn't yet realized it). Thankfully, he was safe.

Your divine Guide has a primary purpose: to bring you safely to his heavenly kingdom. He watches you and protects you like a shepherd. He promises, **"My sheep listen to my voice; I know them, and they follow me. I give them eternal life, and they shall never perish; no one will snatch them out of my hand"** (John 10:27,28).

Lost or lonely? Listen to his voice. Underappreciated or overworked? He knows. You're safe. You're in good hands. Now follow where he leads and don't be afraid.

Being a tourist

Linda Buxa

As a military family, one perk of transferring was being tourists in each new location. In Alaska we hiked mountains, fished, saw whales and bears, and visited glaciers. After moving to Washington D.C., we took family pictures in the Rose Garden, Mount Vernon, every monument (multiple times), and numerous battlefields. Moving to California meant we explored places like Lake Tahoe, San Francisco, and all of southern California's theme parks.

Now that we've left military life and settled down, it's easy to get stuck in a comfortable routine of "been there, done that." Most cities recognize that most citizens succumb to this, so they offer a "tourist in your own town" promotion. For free or reduced rates, you explore the town to remember how many good things there are to be found among the familiar.

It's easy to take a "been there, done that" attitude when we hear old familiar Bible stories too. This is why we need to do a "tourist in my own Bible" promotion. Look with fresh eyes and rediscover the many good things among the familiar. Appreciate how each of these good stories led to the greatest part of the story: Jesus.

Rediscover the truth that **"the word of God is alive and active"** (Hebrews 4:12). Then close the book, being even more in awe of our God, who will take us to heaven where we will not be tourists but eternal residents.

May 20

Pray for your pastor

Pastor Mark Jeske

When you are new to the faith, it's understandable that you might be a little hesitant in explaining it to someone else. Everything is still so surprising and unexpected that you don't want to put your foot in something inappropriate, especially when what's at stake is people's everlasting destiny. It's expected that laypeople would want to work on their evangelism skills.

Does it surprise you to know that a famous pastor had some fears about being tongue-tied and afraid when gospel-sharing opportunities came up? No less a hero than the apostle Paul asked his friends and fellow believers in Ephesus to pray for him so that he would be ready when God sent people to him. He wanted to be able to make sound doctrine about Jesus Christ sound good to people: **"Pray also for me, that whenever I speak, words may be given me so that I will fearlessly make known the mystery of the gospel"** (Ephesians 6:19).

Amazing! Even St. Paul, teacher of all New Testament believers and missionary extraordinaire, feared being at a loss for words or saying the wrong thing at the wrong time. May I invite you today to pray for your pastor in the same way? Our training and experience are of great value, but we are vulnerable to the same limitations you are—faltering courage, mental confusion under pressure, indecisiveness, and procrastination.

Seriously—we need your help.

How do you make big life decisions?

Pastor Mark Jeske

The Bible over and over uses farm imagery to teach believers how to think about their lives, how God designed things to work, how to make big decisions. This not only made sense to Scripture's original readers, the majority of whom worked in agriculture-related jobs, but it still resonates today because there's no cheating and there are no shortcuts in farming.

If a farmer plants corn, corn there will be. He shouldn't expect a wheat crop. If he's too lazy to get going in April and doesn't get around to planting until July, there won't be any crop at all. St. Paul invites you to ponder farming as you think about your life priorities: **"Whoever sows to please their flesh, from the flesh will reap destruction; whoever sows to please the Spirit, from the Spirit will reap eternal life"** (Galatians 6:8).

Whom have you chosen to be your closest friends? I hope you've chosen wisely—you will become like them. On what do you spend your money? Are you serious about saving, arranging for education for your children, and investing in the ministries of your church, or do you love expensive vacations, gambling, and new cars?

To help you in your "sowing" (i.e., decisions on how you spend your time and money), imagine that your heavenly Father's eyes are on your credit card, checkbook, or smartphone as you do it.

Creation by committee

Pastor Mark Jeske

God gave us his Word to create and sustain our faith. Much of its content we can actually understand. Some of it remains a profound mystery, beginning with the very identity of God himself.

Already in the 200s A.D. Christians were using the term *Trinity* (tri-unity) to summarize this mystery. God's self-revelation in the pages of Scripture reveals a powerful unity of being, purpose, and action, but also three distinct persons with distinct minds and distinct functions. The Bible calls them the Father, Son, and Holy Spirit—each fully God, yet unique in how they relate to each other and what they do to bring about the rescue of the sinful human race.

The Trinity did not come into existence with the birth of Christ in Bethlehem or with the special outpouring of the Spirit on the day of Pentecost. Father, Son, and Spirit were at work together, a sort of divine committee for the planning, engineering, and construction of the universe from the very beginning: **"In the beginning God created the heavens and the earth. Now the earth was formless and empty, darkness was over the surface of the deep, and the Spirit of God was hovering over the waters. Then God said, 'Let us make mankind in our image'"** (Genesis 1:1,2,26).

On the annual feast day of the Holy Trinity, lift up your eyes to heaven and speak your worship and appreciation that you are allowed to be part of this absolutely marvelous enterprise.

Does God condone slavery?

Pastor Mark Jeske

The history of the "discovery" and settlement of North America celebrates great triumphs, but it also records dreadful abuses. Bringing Old World diseases to the New World killed off countless Native Americans. Periodic abrogation of treaties made Native Americans permanently suspect and scorn the integrity of the federal government. But the worst of all abuses was the widespread practice of race-based slavery.

Earnest Christians in slaveholding areas tried to justify slavery from passages in the Bible that urged slaves to work hard for their masters. Paul even wrote the epistle of Philemon to try to bring about reconciliation between a master and a runaway. But the fact that the apostles and missionaries in the New Testament era encountered slavery everywhere in the Roman Empire did not constitute divine approval. They were just helping new Christians deal with their reality, not approving of the ownership of human beings.

The fact is, God has always hated the slave trade. Listen to this list of examples of human rebellion against God's will: **"We also know that the law is made not for the righteous but for lawbreakers and rebels, the ungodly and sinful, the unholy and irreligious, for those who kill their fathers or mothers, for murderers, for the sexually immoral, for those practicing homosexuality, for *slave traders* and liars and perjurers"** (1 Timothy 1:9,10).

The slave trade continues today in various parts of the world. God hates it still.

Pecking order

Linda Buxa

We have ten chickens—and introducing new ones to the flock can be tricky. If we introduce just one chicken, it will likely get pecked to death. If we bring in a few, we need to separate them for a while so they get used to each other before they share a coop. Or we need to bring in a whole bunch to overwhelm them and so force them to create a new pecking order.

Sometimes it seems churches operate like a flock.

One person walking into church wonders if she will be welcomed or judged. Will she get pecked to death by rules? Some new members may feel as if a fence separates them from the long-time members—in the same space, but not quite welcomed. Or maybe your church is blessed with so many new members that you feel overwhelmed. At Pentecost, three thousand people joined the church, and the apostles had to correct behaviors and address arguments.

As we lovingly welcome new believers into our churches, we act less like chickens and more like the early Christians: **"All the believers were together and had everything in common. They sold property and possessions to give to anyone who had need. Every day they continued to meet together in the temple courts. They broke bread in their homes and ate together with glad and sincere hearts, praising God and enjoying the favor of all the people. And the Lord added to their number daily those who were being saved"** (Acts 2:43-47).

Surprise! Retaliation solves nothing

Pastor Mark Jeske

The criminal code that God set up for his brand-new nation of Israelites, newly freed from Egyptian slavery, was not intended for all people of all time. Israelite society was tribal. There were no civil institutions, no police, no government employees, no IRS, and no prisons. It would be decades before there were stable towns and actual houses for people to live in. The rough "frontier" justice that was provided for Israel circa 1440 B.C. was not a timeless model.

People love revenge fantasies, and so it's no shock to note that people at Jesus' time found justification in the old tribal code for private and personal vengeance. They liked the basic philosophy of "an eye for an eye." But Jesus said: **"You have heard that it was said, 'Eye for eye, and tooth for tooth.' But I tell you, do not resist an evil person"** (Matthew 5:38,39).

It's not that Jesus is allowing violent criminals to get away with their crimes. The Roman government would catch some of them and mete out judgment. But all evildoers will be judged in God's court, sooner or later. What Jesus discouraged was the popular justification for a personal vengeance crusade.

Jesus' advice is really helpful today. In our terribly secular and violent world, if everyone acted on "eye for eye and tooth for tooth," we'd all be blind and unable to chew our food.

Violent retaliation just begets more violent retaliation.

God works in you

Pastor Daron Lindemann

An executive assistant answers your e-mails, balances your calendar, and in general keeps you on top of your game. But he or she can't pry open the dark corners of your heart where sin hides and change your bad habits. That's a job for God. He not only works for you but in you.

"Now may the God of peace, who through the blood of the eternal covenant brought back from the dead our Lord Jesus, that great Shepherd of the sheep, equip you with everything good for doing his will, and may he work in us what is pleasing to him, through Jesus Christ, to whom be glory for ever and ever. Amen" (Hebrews 13:20,21).

God owns peace. And God's peace is always peace no matter what kind of storm rolls in, no matter which rumors spread, and no matter whose opinion differs from yours. His peace works in you.

His resurrection works in you too. You might drive by the wreckage of an accident, take a glance, and move on. And if you catch sight of blood splattered on the windshield, you might gasp!

God's blood was splattered on the cross, and it was not an accident. That blood works in you as an eternal covenant, unbounded and unbreakable in its commitment to save. No less available on bad days. No less effective on public sin. No less faithful to guilt-ridden Christians who know they should be doing better.

Let your life on the outside look like the work God is doing on the inside.

He's both a lion and a lamb

Pastor Mark Jeske

English majors and high school composition teachers know that it's considered bad form to mix metaphors. It's especially bad when you mix two metaphors that contradict each other.

How ironic that that's exactly what St. John saw in heaven when he was allowed to look at the risen, glorified, and ascended Christ. He saw a contradictory vision of the second person of the Trinity: **"Then one of the elders said to me, 'Do not weep! See, the Lion of the tribe of Judah, the Root of David, has triumphed. He is able to open the scroll and its seven seals.' Then I saw a Lamb, looking as if it had been slain, standing at the center of the throne"** (Revelation 5:5,6).

So—which is it? Is Jesus Christ a lamb or a lion? The answer is yes.

His Father chose him to complete and fulfill the Old Testament role of sacrificial lamb, an innocent victim who would die in place of the offender. He would shed his blood so that the worshiper (i.e., you and I) could go free.

But he is simultaneously a lion, roaring in power and authority, king of the forest, the jungle, the savanna, and more, king of all the earth. He will judge the world rightly and truly, and all things are subject to his authority. You ignore him and defy him at your peril.

He rules.

When can I get the glory?

Pastor Daron Lindemann

Getting all the glory means taking the stage, along with the spotlights, away from every other performer. The audience focuses nowhere else, and the world stops just for a moment.

It could be a masterful solo piece during a concert or a thunderous alley-oop dunk during a NBA playoff game.

The gospel writer John announces, **"We have seen his glory, the glory of the one and only Son, who came from the Father, full of grace and truth"** (John 1:14). He's talking about Jesus, who provided some world-stopping moments, to be sure.

But for Jesus, glory is not just about the thrill of a moment. All of Jesus' work and all of his person are the glory of God, including his most humiliating experiences. It's the glory that serves and saves sinners.

God's glory is found in the least who look to him for salvation and in the ill-equipped who believe against all odds that his words are true. If your career or other callings don't feel glorious, you're looking for the wrong glory.

God's glory is found in everyday things, the mundane, and in the unnoticed acts of your kindness. God's glory is found in your loyalty to your team, your determination to squelch gossip instead of spreading it, and even in the daily grind that most of the work world complains about but not you.

God's grace and truth, believed and practiced, take the stage away from everything else. How will you glorify him today?

Consider the cost

Linda Buxa

"Greater love has no one than this: to lay down one's life for one's friends" (John 15:13).

Nothing is free. A buy one get one free dinner means the restaurant is willing to take 50 percent for two meals. A free day off of work means the company is willing to absorb the loss of your hours. When you consider that, what's free to you actually has a cost. It makes a difference in your perception, doesn't it?

That's why the U.S. celebrates Memorial Day toward the end of May each year, to remember that what's free to us has had a high price for almost 240 years. Veterans' cemeteries are full of people—often teenagers—who decided they would sacrifice their personal comfort for me, for you, because they believed freedom is worth it.

This makes a difference in our perception, doesn't it? We don't take freedom for granted. Instead we consider the cost. We're thankful for and respectful of those who took their oath seriously and gave it their all.

We also pray for those who are left behind. Mothers and fathers miss their children, husbands and wives mourn their spouses, sons and daughters grow up without parents. Their sacrifice is not taken for granted either.

Memorial Day is a chance to remember that our spiritual freedom also came at a great cost. A Father sacrificed his Son, and the Son sacrificed his personal comfort so everyone—soldiers included—could be free. The only difference is that Jesus' cemetery is empty. Now you are not only free on earth, but you are free forever.

Spring cleaning

Pastor Mark Jeske

If you live in a part of our country where there is winter—I mean real winter, with snow and ice and subzero temps—one of the sweet rituals of spring is the sheer pleasure of opening the windows of your house. It is so wonderful to let the fresh air in and the stale air out. We drag the rugs outside and shake and beat five months of dust out into the free air. Carpets get shampooed and floors scrubbed. Everything smells *fresh!*

Our God understands that our spiritual progress is uneven. Sometimes Satan has us in his grip and we stall, making excuses for our compromises and halfhearted efforts. But sometimes the Word stirs us to action, real action. Spring is a great time not only to clean your house but to clean your *life:* **"Do not grieve the Holy Spirit of God, with whom you were sealed for the day of redemption. Get rid of all bitterness, rage and anger, brawling and slander, along with every form of malice. Be kind and compassionate to one another, forgiving each other, just as in Christ God forgave you"** (Ephesians 4:30-32).

Stop your life right here and now—you *know* what needs to change! What do you need to stop doing? What do you need to start doing? It's time to take out the trash. It's spring cleaning day in your soul.

Where do you start today?

Turn your life around

Linda Buxa

At age 15, Frank Abagnale started his six-year stint as a con man. (The movie *Catch Me if You Can* is based on his life story.) When he was 16, he posed as a pilot, passed the bar exam, masqueraded as a doctor, and became a master at forging checks and embezzling. After being caught at age 21, he spent six years in prison. He was paroled with the condition that he would turn his life around, using his powers for good to help the federal government.

His story is a lot like a man called Saul. He hated people who followed Jesus so much that he persecuted them. One day, Jesus met him on a road and turned his life around. (And even gave him a new name: Paul.) God used Paul's intensity and devotion for good—to teach others, to speak to government officials, to plant and encourage churches all over his part of the world.

Their stories are a lot like ours. We were born sinful and could do nothing about it. That's why God sent Jesus—to take our punishment and to give us credit for his perfection. He completely turned the trajectory of our eternal destination around. **"Very truly I tell you, whoever hears my word and believes him who sent me has eternal life and will not be judged but has crossed over from death to life"** (John 5:24).

You are no longer dead, but alive. And now you use his powers for his good and his glory.

june

"Start children off on the way they should go,
and even when they are old they will
not turn from it."

Proverbs 22:6

Planning for marriage

Linda Buxa

As many brides are putting the finishing details on their dream weddings, two economics professors from Emory University are sounding a caution. In their research, they discovered that people whose weddings cost $20,000 or more were 3.5 times more likely to end up divorced than those who spent $5,000 to $10,000.

Coauthor Andrew M. Francis said, "Industry advertising has fueled norms that create the impression that spending large amounts on the wedding is a signal of commitment or is necessary for a marriage to be successful."

Industry advertising has it all wrong.

The reality is that weddings are not fairy tales—and neither are marriages. When the ceremony becomes the focal point, preparing for marriage gets pushed to the side. When faced with the day-to-day realities of marriage that come up—paying the bills, caring for a sick child, and putting the other person's needs in front of yours—all those wedding day details suddenly seem insignificant.

In the Bible, God never talks about planning for one big day. Instead, he talks far more about how you make every day after the wedding the focal point. **"By wisdom a house is built, and through understanding it is established"** (Proverbs 24:3). Spend time privately praying for your marriage. Talk with each other. Worship together. Build understanding. Choose to forgive and love your spouse—every day, for the rest of your life.

That is what's necessary for marriage to be successful. That kind of success is priceless.

You'll make it

Pastor Mark Jeske

The incarnation of Jesus is the centerpiece of human history for many reasons. God taking on human flesh sends a powerful message of how valuable we are to our estranged Father, the lengths to which he would go to win us back. It honors our humanity that Christ now shares it and kept it via his ascension! Through his human body Christ lived for us, suffered for us, died for us, and rose again for us.

Through his humanity Christ also leads the way in how to live triumphantly in a broken and fallen world. He demonstrated how to overcome in adversity: **"Consider him who endured such opposition from sinners, so that you will not grow weary and lose heart"** (Hebrews 12:3). For example: he showed the value and power of prayer as he chose to spend time alone with his Father and dial into his will. He respected human authority even when it was wrong and abusive. He submitted rather than retaliating. He forgave rather than seeking revenge. He loved instead of hating. He stayed focused on what was important rather than becoming distracted by comforts, vanities, and pleasures.

Here is Scripture's promise for you: the more you read the four gospels and absorb Jesus' ways and words, the better-equipped you will be to follow in his steps . . . the more clearly you will understand your life's mission . . . the happier and more content you will be.

Hang on. You'll make it.

Adoptive placement courage

Pastor Mark Jeske

When some children learn at some point in their childhood that they have been adopted, there is bound to be some trauma. How could the child not feel some measure of rejection? The very word *adoption* has a negative vibe, and that's unfortunate.

Adoption is a marvelous solution to serious problems. If managed well, it can be win-win-win. A decent adoptive home provides a safe, loving, and secure place for a child at risk. It fills the empty arms of childless couples who have a lot to offer. And it provides relief for a desperate parent or parents who are willing to sacrifice their own emotional needs for the needs of the child.

When we think of heroes in the adoption process, let's remember the courage and sacrifices of a mother who is going through the hardest thing any woman could ever do—parting with a baby. The heroine for all such women is Jochebed, an Israelite slave in Egypt. It was her misfortune to give birth at a time when there was a death sentence on all the newborn Israelite boys. **"When she could hide him no longer, she got a papyrus basket for him and coated it with tar and pitch. Then she placed the child in it and put it among the reeds along the bank of the Nile"** (Exodus 2:3,4).

Her little boy was adopted by an Egyptian princess. Jochebed allowed him to call another woman Mama and allowed another woman to name him.

The Egyptian princess called him Moses.

June 4

Get a guide. Be a guide.

Linda Buxa

My husband and I took a bike tour in Chicago. On it, I learned how the neighborhood was formed, how Chicago reversed the ways its river drained, and how architects put their stamp on the area.

Now, I had been to Chicago before. It's a great city and a great place to explore, but not until I went with a guide did I learn some of the little details. Ultimately, I enjoyed the city more when someone explained it and pointed out what I would have missed on my own.

There was an Ethiopian man who was on a trip, and he needed a guide too—a Bible guide. When Philip, one of Jesus' disciples met him, he asked, **"'Do you understand what you are reading?' . . . 'How can I,' he said, 'unless someone explains it to me?'"** (Acts 8:30,31).

So Philip climbed up in the chariot and explained it.

Like the Ethiopian, we all could use a Bible guide. No matter how little or much we know our Bible, we can always discover new details that will make us understand it better, love God more deeply, and live it out more faithfully.

Find a pastor, teacher, mentor, or friend who tells you the truth about God (not just the stuff you want to hear). Learn from them. Read the Bible to make sure they are telling you the truth.

Then be a guide. Tell the people in your life the little details about how he works in your life. Don't let them miss out!

Ministry to the wealthy

Pastor Mark Jeske

Church workers tend not to have a lot of money, and so they are often uncomfortable around people of wealth. Jesus' teachings about mammon (filthy lucre) and camels going through the eyes of needles stick in people's minds. Some pastors have the philosophy that they should treat all members exactly the same, especially when it regards the subject of generosity.

St. Paul trained his younger pastors to have no such reluctance. In his view, people whom God had blessed with greater income and assets had a correspondingly greater platform for extraordinary service: **"Command those who are rich in this present world not to be arrogant nor to put their hope in wealth, which is so uncertain, but to put their hope in God, who richly provides us with everything for our enjoyment. Command them to do good, to be rich in good deeds, and to be generous and willing to share"** (1 Timothy 6:17,18).

Just because greed and materialism are pervasive and dangerous doesn't mean that money itself is evil or that all wealthy people are corrupt. In fact, some of God's greatest servants were very wealthy (such as Abraham or David). Church leaders can play a very valuable role by developing a ministry to the wealthy. They can bring significant investment to churches, schools, and Christian service agencies.

They can also bring enormous spiritual growth and blessing to the lives of the wealthy themselves.

Necessary résumé for church leadership

Pastor Mark Jeske

The quality of its leadership is one of the most important criteria for the growth and health of any organization, and that includes the church. St. Paul wanted congregations to be slow and cautious in lifting people up and investing authority in them. Bad leaders can damage an organization, perhaps cripple it permanently. Even worse are leaders who go off-message and spread false teachings. That can cause *eternal* spiritual harm to people.

St. Paul wrote three letters to some younger pastors whom he was personally training. These priceless New Testament documents are full of timeless wisdom for the church's permanent task of finding, recruiting, training, and equipping the best leaders possible. Paul's advice to congregations was to make sure to study a candidate's home life: **"He must manage his own family well and see that his children obey him, and he must do so in a manner worthy of full respect. (If anyone does not know how to manage his own family, how can he take care of God's church?)"** (1 Timothy 3:4,5).

If a dad gets ignored and pushed around by his teenagers, he won't be able to exert a firm hand in managing a larger group. If he makes his wife miserable, how do you suppose he will treat the women in the congregation? If he is in personal bankruptcy, how can he oversee the church's finances? This is no disrespect to people who struggle with the above three weaknesses. Jesus loves them too.

But they shouldn't be leaders of the church.

Better than they deserve

Pastor Mark Jeske

"It's nice to be nice to the nice." That little bit of folk wisdom comes from the great philosopher Frank Burns, surgeon with the 4077th M.A.S.H. unit. It's not too hard to sweeten up for people who treat you well. It's way harder to treat people better than they deserve.

And yet that's *exactly* what Christ asks us to do (for it's exactly how he lived his life, and exactly the concept behind his gospel mission to bring forgiveness to the world). Here is St. Paul's take on this: **"Make sure that nobody pays back wrong for wrong, but always strive to do what is good for each other and for everyone else"** (1 Thessalonians 5:15). That's hard! We all fantasize about payback when harm is done to us. We all know how to dish it back when some slight or insult is dished to us.

Kindness means treating the people around you *better than they deserve* (and doing it without bitterness, sarcasm, condescension, or anticipation of cashing in on possible heavenly rewards). *Kindness* means that you prefer to praise others than to be praised . . . that you let others go first . . . that you look for good in people who others say are failures . . . that you notice and acknowledge people low on the totem pole more readily than sucking up to the lofty . . . that you let go of yesterday's resentments and look for the good other people are doing today.

Kindness means that you find more joy in mercy than retribution.

Surprise! Oaths guarantee nothing

Pastor Mark Jeske

Why do you suppose that "adult" talk is so full of swearing? Simple. It's because people lie so much. They frantically embellish their statements and claims to try to get people to believe them this time.

Using an oath (e.g., "swear to God") suggests that the swearer is willing to submit to divine penalty for perjury, and thus the statement must be believable. Adding oathy intensifiers (e.g., "OMG") supposedly adds drama and emotion to the statement. Jesus asks you to rid your working vocabulary of both: **"You have heard that it was said to the people long ago, 'Do not break your oath, but fulfill to the Lord the vows you have made.' But I tell you, do not swear an oath at all"** (Matthew 5:33,34).

Even ceremonial oaths for certain government functions, like receipt of citizenship or entry into high office, are becoming meaningless because our society increasingly does not even recognize a higher Being and most certainly does not submit to the Bible upon which the swearer's hand is placed.

Jesus isn't commanding you to rebel against these government practices. He is urging you to avoid the practice of calling upon God to audit your spoken statements for veracity and to avoid the foolish invitation to God to smite you for lying. Thankfully God ignores most swearing. Good thing—not many swearers would be left standing if he didn't.

There are much better uses for God's holy name.

Shine brightly!

Linda Buxa

"Even after Jesus had performed so many signs in their presence, [the Jews] still would not believe in him. . . . Yet at the same time many even among the leaders believed in him. But because of the Pharisees they would not openly acknowledge their faith for fear they would be put out of the synagogue; *for they loved human praise more than praise from God*" (John 12:37,42,43).

Ouch. That sounds like someone familiar. It sounds like me—and possibly like you. We love Jesus, but sometimes it is tempting to downplay the hard things he says that might make others uncomfortable. Or maybe we don't want to be generous with our time, money, energy, and prayers. Then there are the times we don't want to stand up for what is right because it will cause trouble.

We have a ton of excuses for why we keep quiet about our faith, don't we? It's more comfortable. We fit in better. We risk far less rejection. Today is a day to get out of our earthly comfort zone and look for ways to openly acknowledge our faith. Speak boldly, act lovingly, shine his light brightly. And look forward to that day when we will hear God tell us, **"Well done, good and faithful servant! You have been faithful with a few things; I will put you in charge of many things. Come and share your master's happiness!"** (Matthew 25:23).

June 10

Hang on

Pastor Mark Jeske

"Things are not always what they seem." My mother told me that when I was a little boy, and I have found her words wise advice. They provide great spiritual insight too.

It may look as though Satan pretty much has won the battle for the hearts and minds of the people of the world. It may look as though greed and violence are the only way to get ahead. It may look as though you are doomed to a life of declining financial resources and declining health. It may look as though your family life is one big disappointment. But those things are *illusions*!

Satan has not triumphed. He in fact is mortally wounded and has had his power broken and his time to torment us shortened. He himself is going headfirst into the lake of burning sulfur and he knows it. He is in a rage, but believers in Christ are now out of his eternal reach. Christ Jesus won the great battle of Calvary, and his resurrection demonstrates that he now owns the future.

In the meantime, hang on! **"So do not throw away your confidence; it will be richly rewarded. You need to persevere so that when you have done the will of God, you will receive what he has promised. For, 'in just a little while, he who is coming will come and will not delay'"** (Hebrews 10:35-37).

Seriously! Just a *little* while.

Never unemployed

Pastor Daron Lindemann

Matthew left his job without a two-week notice—because he wanted to follow Jesus. If you need to leave your job in order to follow Jesus, then you have my blessing, but Jesus makes it clear that you can follow him *and* keep your job.

As a matter of fact, you can follow Jesus at your job, at the gym, in the classroom, where you hang out and go out, and everywhere in between. You see, for Christians, following Jesus *is* our job.

The Bible tells us that Jesus **"saw a man named Matthew sitting at the tax collector's booth."** Jesus didn't see a tax collector; he saw Matthew. He was a man, a soul to be understood and forgiven, to be empowered and employed. **"Follow me,"** Jesus said. **"And Matthew got up and followed him"** (Matthew 9:9). In Jesus, Matthew found mercy and meaning.

A survey revealed that 7 of the top 10 most gratifying jobs included pastors, firefighters, and then various kinds of teachers or therapists. The common denominator in these jobs: caring for people. Well, Jesus must really love his job because he cares about you. And he calls you to care about others. Anytime. Anywhere.

The next time someone asks what you do and you think about replying, "I'm in construction" or "I'm a financial rep" or "I'm unemployed," maybe you could say to that person, "I'm a follower of Jesus."

Then again, maybe they don't even need to ask.

Thanks, dads!

Linda Buxa

Father's Day is coming, but it seems like Dad will get the short end of the stick. Mother's Day is filled with ads reminding you to get flowers and buy presents! But dads get a silly card and a tie. (Though steak or burgers on the grill counts for something.)

Dads don't get nearly as much credit for parenting. But we all suffer the repercussions when men don't do the job God has given them. Children from fatherless homes are more likely to commit suicide, run away, have behavior disorders, drop out of school, and end up in jail than children from homes where Dad was active.

So, dads, as we look ahead to this Sunday, know that we notice what you do. We are thankful because you

- use your "Dad voice" when the kids disrespect Mom.

- make the kids finish the chores even when they are whining.

- run behind the bike until your firstborn finally masters the task.

- love the Lord your God with all your heart.

- tuck in your little ones (and not so little ones) and say a blessing over them.

- pray for your family while you are commuting.

- throw your kids up in the air while Mom closes her eyes.

- fight for full or joint custody against a court system that doesn't appreciate your worth.

- talk about God's commandments and **"start children off on the way they should go, and even when they are old they will not turn from it"** (Proverbs 22:6).

Early judgment day

Pastor Mark Jeske

Is God's patience unlimited?

In a sense it is. His mercy triumphs over judgment. Our Savior's blood washes even the dirtiest sinner clean. His open and welcoming arms have given hope even to such notorious rebels as King Manasseh and Saul the persecutor.

But when the repenting stops, when people stubbornly and persistently reject his grace and mercy, when they show by words and deeds that they want no part of a relationship with the God of Israel, the Lord pronounces the ultimate judgment—he lets people have what they want. **"Israel's arrogance testifies against them; the Israelites, even Ephraim, stumble in their sin; Judah also stumbles with them. When they go with their flocks and herds to seek the Lord, they will not find him; he has withdrawn himself from them. They are unfaithful to the Lord"** (Hosea 5:5-7).

The prophet Amos called it a "famine of hearing the Word of God." God essentially brings an early judgment day on people who have rejected him so persistently and so long that he hardens them in their attitude so that they can't change. They are frozen in their defiance. He actually takes his Word from them.

If that concept worries you, if you dread that it could happen to you, then it won't. Your heart is still soft; faith still lives there. Give all your sins to Jesus today, right now, and claim the forgiveness he bought for you.

Fly it proudly

Jason Nelson

My mother's birthday was June 14th. There were always flags and lots of bunting displayed on that day. There were even some small-town parades. My mom was a trustworthy woman, but she told her children it was all for her birthday. I think I was ten before I figured out there wasn't a national observance of the day my mother was born. It was Flag Day.

If the United States has a sacred artifact, it's our flag. It's right up there with the Constitution. The stars and stripes are symbols of our beginning and progress as a nation. I've pledged allegiance to it, raised it up a school-yard pole, seen it draped over coffins, watched it be planted on the surface of the moon, and cringed as it burned in protest. I'm always careful to fold it properly because it's the emblem of the country I love.

Symbols convey a message with straightforward power. Think of what a cross, a chalice, and an empty tomb mean to us as Christians. Appreciate what a red, white, and blue piece of cloth means to us as Americans. Brave people died under this banner. And countless others are still inspired by it. **"Blessed is the nation whose God is the Lord"** (Psalm 33:12). And especially blessed is the nation that flies Old Glory.

Status change

Pastor Mark Jeske

When a pro football player comes under contract with an NFL team, that team and its coaches and owners expect the player not only to wear the uniform but to absorb the culture of the organization. The player needs to master the playbook, perform in games, but also conduct himself properly with the press, represent the team well, and be active in the community.

Through your faith in Christ, you have changed teams. Instead of the rags of Satan's legions of the doomed you now wear the robes of holiness bought for you by Jesus Christ. Instead of wearing a toe tag for hell, you now are given Christ's halo to wear on your head. **"For you were once darkness, but now you are light in the Lord. Live as children of light"** (Ephesians 5:8). Your certainty of eternal life in heaven now changes how you act on earth.

God's Word helps you more clearly identify the works of Satan. Stop loving those things. Shun them. God's Word helps you see how precious and valuable other people are. Stop using people. Start helping them. God's Word helps you see how he is the source of everything good in your life and in the world. Stop avoiding him. Worship him.

Wear your new uniform with pride. Love your new philosophy. Live your new philosophy.

Better than birds

Pastor Daron Lindemann

We want to live like kings, not birds. So we worry, hoping to afford top-shelf brands or fussing to impress dinner guests with more time and effort then we offer the poor or irritated that the long line at Starbucks will disrupt our busy schedule. Like spoiled Israelites complaining about manna, we've turned up our noses at the basics . . . while the feathered birds do just fine without cupboards or closets.

"Therefore I tell you, do not worry about your life, what you will eat or drink; or about your body, what you will wear. . . . Look at the birds of the air; they do not sow or reap or store away in barns, and yet your heavenly Father feeds them. Are you not much more valuable than they?" (Matthew 6:25,26).

We are God's children; we *are* valuable to him. In the beginning God spoke and created the birds, but he created us by sharing his own breath. He then made us superior to all the animals. When our first parents sinned, God shed the blood of animals to provide garments for their shame, and he shed the blood of his Son to provide forgiveness for people, not birds.

Birds happily munch on seeds and berries, beautifully clothed in their colored feathers. God cares for them, but he cares "much more" for you and me. That's something to chirp about!

Strange agents of heaven

Pastor Mark Jeske

Christians could be forgiven for assuming that throughout the many centuries of Old Testament history the only believers in the true God were to be found within Israel. True—God did indeed lavish immense personal attention and care on that nation. But he had many other agents for his agenda, and some were even great "heathen" kings like Nebuchadnezzar of Babylon and Cyrus of Persia.

And Pharaoh Necho of Egypt, who ruled from 610 to 595 B.C. **"Necho king of Egypt went up to fight at Carchemish on the Euphrates, and Josiah marched out to meet him in battle. But Necho sent messengers to him, saying, 'What quarrel is there, king of Judah, between you and me? It is not you I am attacking at this time, but the house with which I am at war. God has told me to hurry; so stop opposing God, who is with me, or he will destroy you'"** (2 Chronicles 35:20,21).

At that point every Sunday school kid would expect to hear that good King Josiah's army attacked and repelled the Egyptians. In fact, Necho was right. He crushed the Judean army at Megiddo and Josiah was killed. God indeed had business for Necho at Carchemish way up north.

God is up to many things in many places. Let us not assume that we know his specific agenda; nor should we presume to tell him whom he can or can't use to accomplish those plans.

Who's the enemy?

Pastor Mark Jeske

One of the features of warfare in the 21st century is that a great deal of combat is between fighters who can't see each other's faces. Artillery, missiles, drones, and bombs deliver death from great distances, and when on target, the victims never knew what hit them.

You and I are combatants in a spiritual war with forces that we cannot see either. We are caught up in the titanic conflict between Christ and Satan, good and evil, that has been raging ever since Satan's rebellion and his expulsion from heaven. He and his fallen angels, also called "demons," "powers," and "authorities" in Scripture, have access to our lives. They seek to do us physical harm and whisper sweet temptations in our ears that can only cause harm to others and spiritual suicide to ourselves.

St. Paul has this wake-up call for all believers: **"Our struggle is not against flesh and blood, but against the rulers, against the authorities, against the powers of this dark world and against the spiritual forces of evil in the heavenly realms"** (Ephesians 6:12). Our armor is not Kevlar but the Word of God, which can protect our heads and hearts. You aren't in heaven yet. Don't dream that your spiritual journey will be easy. Don't be surprised by wounds and casualties. You are at war.

But you are in an army whose Commander has already dealt the deathblow to your worst enemy.

Can't buy me love

Pastor Mark Jeske

By my totally unscientific analysis, I'd say about 50 percent of the pop songs on the radio are about love in some way—longing for love, dreaming of love, exulting in the love someone is currently experiencing, or bitterly lamenting the love someone just lost. Love is the oxygen of the human spirit. Without it we die inside. So tell me—how would you define *love*?

You know you are being loved when someone makes you feel important . . . when someone does something for you "just because" . . . when someone consistently remembers your birthday . . . when someone will listen to your troubles without interrupting or changing the subject . . . when someone helps you out in a major way and expects nothing in return . . . when somebody shows up to be with you when you are stressed out and down.

The greatest love of all comes from God: **"This is love: not that we loved God, but that he loved us and sent his Son as an atoning sacrifice for our sins"** (1 John 4:10). Jesus was under no obligation to do the things he did. There is only one explanation as to why the Son of God went through the agony of his betrayal, unjust trials, condemnation, rejection, physical torment, crucifixion, and burial—to give forgiveness and life to you and me. He loves us! He loves us!

And by the way, **"Dear friends, since God so loved us, we also ought to love one another"** (1 John 4:11).

Let there be light

Pastor Mark Jeske

In a sense there was divine activity even before creation began—God must have made a gigantic mud ball in the dark. All of the elements were there, but they were all jumbled together. Matter existed, but it was in chaos.

And then came the moment when God decided to begin the process of bringing order of the chaos. The first thing that the world of dark mud needed was the presence of the glory of God himself. Before there were sun, moon, and stars, God brought the gift of light to the chaos, the light of himself: **"Now the earth was formless and empty, darkness was over the surface of the deep, and the Spirit of God was hovering over the waters. And God said, 'Let there be light,' and there was light"** (Genesis 1:2,3).

God had endowed matter with the ability to reflect light with different colors and hues, different depths and texture. Light itself is a stupendous work of his—acting like both wave and particle, it bolts through all creation at 186,000 miles per second, bouncing back when there is something there.

The people who appreciate light most are those from whom it has been taken. The blind will tell you how intensely they miss it and what a delight it is. When your eyes pop open tomorrow morning, whisper a little prayer, "Lord, how wonderful it is to *see* your world."

Let there be an atmosphere

Pastor Mark Jeske

Of the many branches of engineering, one of the most important is the science of how to move and control water—aqueducts, culverts, canals, locks, dams, levees, and just plain-old drainage ditches. Water is vital to human life: drinking, sanitation, farming, animal husbandry. Do you know who is the most astounding hydraulic engineer of all time? Yep. God.

On the second day of creation week, God looked at the enormous mud ball he had synthesized, lit now by the light of his glorious presence, and he spoke the words that set in motion the world's largest hydraulic project ever: **"God made the vault and separated the water under the vault from the water above it. And it was so. God called the vault 'sky'"** (Genesis 1:7,8). God thought, willed, and spoke, and now great amounts of water were extracted from the mud ball and suspended above the surface. He must also have created the atmosphere—the mixture of gases, especially oxygen, that together with the water would make plant, animal, and human life possible on his new planet.

Some of that water was suspended in the cloud canopy and some in the air itself—we call it humidity. The gravity force he invented would pull water down occasionally, and the surface would experience it as rain or snow.

I know, I know. We usually think of rain as a nuisance. Only when your region is experiencing a drought does the rain look like the gift of God that it is.

Let there be continents and oceans

Pastor Mark Jeske

Day 2: God moves some water up. Day 3: God moves some water sideways. He spoke, and although there was still a lot of mud on the earth, now there were clearly demarcated bodies of water and vast areas of dry land: **"God said, 'Let the water under the sky be gathered into one place, and let dry ground appear.' And it was so. God called the dry ground 'land,' and the gathered waters he called 'seas'"** (Genesis 1:9,10).

The concentration of all that water in the oceans (71 percent of earth's surface) gives our planet its distinctive look from space. *Apollo* astronauts in orbit, gazing at earth from their capsule, started calling it the "blue planet." Oceans are busy places, always in motion above and below the surface.

The land masses were busy places too, for God's creative word caused every manner of flora to burst forth. Each species had its own way of producing seeds so that there would be a next generation. Each species was suited to the climate God had put there. Each species added to the shade, food, and beauty of the new land mass. God's unique design put fresh water within the land masses in the form of lakes and rivers, while the vaster oceans are salty. Both types of water are home to their own abundance of aquatic plants.

God liked what he saw and called it good. Do you like it too?

Let there be sun, moon, and stars

Pastor Mark Jeske

Day 4 saw a massive demonstration of God's unlimited power and brilliance. There was now a universe full of stuff surrounding our planet! **"God said, 'Let there be lights in the vault of the sky to separate the day from the night, and let them serve as signs to mark sacred times, and days and years'"** (Genesis 1:14).

Our sun—source of warmth and light, God's chosen instrument for replenishing the earth's energy, driver of the solar convection cycle that moves water around and up, powerful gravitational pull that keeps the earth and other planets slinging around in their elliptical orbits, marking the passages of years by our orbit and the passing of days by its rise in the east . . .

Our moon—just a big rock ball orbiting around us but with wonderful reflective ability, bouncing the sun's light back to us in pale white beams, a lesser light marking out months with its crescents, using its own smaller gravitational pull to move our tides in and out . . .

Our stars—oh my, the stars, each one a sun, so unbelievably far away that their light takes many years just to reach us, billions of stars in billions of galaxies, glittering above on a clear night, moving on a set track above us each night but predictable enough to guide navigation for those wise enough to study them . . .

When you have the slightest, teeniest doubts about God's power, wisdom, and love, go outside and look up.

Let there be animals

Pastor Mark Jeske

There is almost no place on earth where God's animals haven't found a way to thrive. They're everywhere! Day 5 was the day when God made animal creatures that could go where humans can't—he made creatures with wings that could defy gravity and soar and dart through the air, and he made creatures with fins and tails for rapid swimming and gills to extract oxygen from water. **"God said, 'Let the water teem with living creatures, and let birds fly above the earth across the vault of the sky'"** (Genesis 1:20).

Should we be surprised that a God who is generous, a God of abundance, should have made so many of these flying and swimming creatures that the very air and water *teemed* with them? That exuberant abundance characterized God's entire creative week, and it has characterized his continuing creative activity ever since. He commanded them to be fruitful, i.e., reproduce like crazy, filling the water and skies.

So elegant is God's design of his air and sea creatures that engineers who dared mechanical flight and sailing carefully studied birds and fish to see how they do it. Read a little on the history of heavier-than-air flight to see what people learned from bird's wings about the concept of "lift."

Oh, by the way, isn't it a joy also that many of the birds and fish are so tasty?

Let there be people

Pastor Mark Jeske

God began his work on the sixth day with the creation of land animals, both the wild ones and those intended for domestication (livestock). They too were given the ability to reproduce, as with everything else in God's brilliant design "according to their kind."

And then came his masterpiece, the crown of his creation—the human race. People, intended to be God's children, were made in his image, i.e., with desires and values just like his, made to love and carry out his agenda. They were holy, just like God, and charged with management of all creation: **"God created mankind in his own image, in the image of God he created them; male and female he created them. God blessed them and said to them, 'Be fruitful and increase in number; fill the earth and subdue it'"** (Genesis 1:27,28).

Adam was made of dust, and that is the meaning of his name—*Adamah* in Hebrew means "earth." From his rib God made a woman, who would be the mother of the human race. That is what her name means—*Chavah* (Eve) means "living." She was exactly what he needed, someone who corresponded to him, someone suitable for him. There they were, just those two, looking at their paradise in Eden, smiling up at their God, looking at each other in wonder.

And then came the wedding. And the wedding night.

When you thought I wasn't looking

Pastor Daron Lindemann

Sometimes it's fun being a dad, like when you're firing up the grill or taking the perfect dad nap. Sometimes it's not that fun, like house repairs that never end.

Being a dad, however, is a 24/7 job. Dads can't just flip a switch and take a break when the going gets tough. And all the while, someone is watching.

There's a Bible verse in Proverbs that says, **"My son, give me your heart and let your eyes delight in my ways"** (23:26). A father who wants the heart of his child wants his child to always watch and learn.

"Dad, when you thought I wasn't looking . . . I saw you repair my pinewood derby car and I learned that love is often in the small things. . . . I saw you pray and I learned I could talk to God and trust him. . . . I saw tears in your eyes when Grandma died and I learned it's okay to cry. . . . I watched the person you are and realized that I wanted to be like you."

Fathers, take heart that even though your example of Christian faith and love has, at times, faltered, God still wants you to be a protector, provider, and Christian role model for your children. God is the perfectly faithful Father to you and your children, and they see him through you.

And you through him.

Personalize your work

Pastor Daron Lindemann

You receive a card in the mail. You curiously open the envelope, glancing at the card, which says something nice like, "Congratulations, graduate!" or "Friends are like rainbows."

Then you open up the card and see two different types of writing on the inside. One is preprinted, and the other is scribbled by the sender. Which attracts more of your attention?

Even though a paid professional created the preprinted message, with a symmetrically balanced font and letters spaced to perfection—the personal note is more meaningful.

At your workplace, nobody else can do the job that you do. Your fingerprints on your keyboard, your traces of coffee or coconut water that have smudged the papers, your passwords, these are uniquely yours. Someone else could perform the job description, but they'd do it differently. A proven expert higher up the professional chain could come in, but he or she still wouldn't be you.

Your name, your reputation, and the way that you smile or serve or handle stress, these personalize your position in a way that honors your Savior. And shares the gospel. The apostle Paul wrote, **"What has happened to me has actually served to advance the gospel . . . because of my chains, most of the brothers and sisters have become confident in the Lord"** (Philippians 1:12,14).

We personalize everything these days: phone cases, license plates, and tattoos. Your job is personalized, and because of it *you* make a difference—for Jesus.

Personal makeover

Pastor Mark Jeske

Deep down inside, people are not all that proud of their houses, automobiles, bodies, and faces. That's why the reality TV industry finds such a ready audience for its many "makeover" shows. You know the drill—professionals in home remodeling, auto restoration, or personal beauty parachute into somebody's life and in a short time, shazam! A whole new you!

Something like that is happening with you in your spiritual life. You were born a mess—selfish, lazy, materialistic, and wired to agree to Satan's temptations already as an infant. But at some point in your life God did an intervention. His Holy Spirit planted faith in your heart through Baptism and the Word and awakened a new self inside you.

Now it's time for you to claim that awakening and develop it: **"You were taught, with regard to your former way of life, to put off your old self, which is being corrupted by its deceitful desires; to be made new in the attitude of your minds; and to put on the new self, created to be like God in true righteousness and holiness"** (Ephesians 4:22-24). The Bible is both your energy sourcebook and values guidebook. It prompts you to care what God thinks about your decisions and values, shows you what he values, and powers you up to act.

Here's God's bonus—putting on the new spiritual self not only glorifies him, but it is the path to a happy life for you.

Angel of light

Linda Buxa

Acceptance. Love is love. Love wins. Pick your slogan, and Satan is doing an outstanding job of making his lies about marriage, family, and sexuality seem lovely and full of light. In reality, **"the god of this age has blinded the minds of unbelievers, so that they cannot see the light of the gospel that displays the glory of Christ, who is the image of God"** (2 Corinthians 4:4).

The problem is that a culture of acceptance in this world will not actually bring peace to anybody—because every single person's greatest problem is the darkness caused by separation between themselves and God. As Christians, our job is to speak the truth *in love*. (*In love* is critical!)

All those blinded by the devil's lies still have time to learn about the real Light of life. Look at the people around you, fighting so vehemently, and see them as Jesus did: **"When he saw the crowds, he had compassion on them, because they were harassed and helpless, like sheep without a shepherd. Then he said to his disciples, 'The harvest is plentiful but the workers are few. Ask the Lord of the harvest, therefore, to send out workers into his harvest field'"** (Matthew 9:36-38).

Millions and billions of people need to hear about Jesus, whose eternal love is the only love that actually wins. Don't simply pray for "other" workers. Be a worker. Get out into the harvest field. Talk to the people in your life one-on-one. Listen to them. Love them. With compassion. With truth. With grace.

June 30

Threefold blessing

Pastor Daron Lindemann

The triune nature of God remains a mystery. We admittedly trust and worship a God whom we don't completely understand. Yet he isn't eons away from our lives. He comes close and gets real with us.

"The LORD bless you and keep you," God's Word promises you in his blessing, knowing that you need the Father's care that he gives to his children.

He gives care like sunshine and rain, farmers and crops, health, a functional government, paychecks, doctors, and unseen angels delivering you from evil you don't even realize could have happened.

"The LORD make his face shine on you and be gracious to you," God's Word promises you in his blessing, as the Son smiles at you with forgiveness and delight.

He gives delight like a teacher smiling at her students as they walk out of the classroom at the end of another year. They tested her patience quite often. They let her down again and again. But she knew it would work like it always does. Because of her expert knowledge and firm but gentle encouragement, they now walk into the world better prepared.

"The LORD turn his face toward you and give you peace," God's Word promises you in his blessing, assuring the attention of the Holy Spirit's peacefulness. You need not be afraid. And when you're not afraid, you are more gentle with others, kinder, wiser, and happier.

These are the words from Numbers 6:24-26 that we commonly call the *benediction*, which means "good words."

july

"Blessed is the nation whose God is the Lᴏʀᴅ,
the people he chose for his inheritance."

Psalm 33:12

God plays a long game

Pastor Mark Jeske

Try as we might, we can't see into the future. We can guess, plot probabilities, and make predictions, but our ideas could be totally wrong.

So can our analysis of what is going on around us and what God is up to. The few Israelites left in Judah after the Babylonian army ruined and plundered the land would have thought that all was lost. They would have concluded that God was powerless or that he had lost his love for and loyalty to the Israelite people or that the Israelite nation would now cease to exist. They might have feared that worship of the true God would cease on earth. And they would have been wrong on all counts.

In fact, the captivity was part of God's plan for healing and restoration of his people: **"The land enjoyed its sabbath rests; all the time of its desolation it rested, until the seventy years were completed in fulfillment of the word of the Lord spoken by Jeremiah"** (2 Chronicles 36:21). It was a 70-year time-out. God permitted the Jews to return, and in the fullness of time, Jesus Christ, the Savior of the world, was born in the very land God had promised to Abraham two millennia earlier. God plays a long game. Cut him a lot of slack. Not all bad news is truly a defeat. He can turn even disasters like the Babylonian captivity inside out and make them bless his people.

Don't you wonder what he's up to in your life?

Choose your spouse carefully

Pastor Mark Jeske

Why do people get married? Usually it's because of how their potential partner makes them feel—important, excited, secure, desirable. People usually get married for what they think they're going to get out of it. They generally aren't thinking too much about how their new spouse is going to change them.

I wonder if King Jehoram of the southern kingdom of Judah had any idea of what he was getting himself into when he married Athaliah, daughter of the evil royal couple Ahab and Jezebel, how she would change him, how she would change the spiritual character of his kingdom: **"He followed the ways of the kings of Israel, as the house of Ahab had done, for he married a daughter of Ahab. He did evil in the eyes of the Lord"** (2 Chronicles 21:6).

The cost of that poor marital choice? As the prophet Elijah foresaw, Jehoram would suffer extreme dysentery and a massive bowel prolapse, dying in excruciating pain. The chronicler states that his death was to no one's regret. After he was dead, Athaliah established a six-year reign of terror, murdering all but one of her own children.

You may be seeking someone who's good-looking, has a reliable income stream, and who's fun to be with. Make sure you also find a biblical Christian who knows and lives the faith. If you're going to be changed by your spouse, you want to be changed into a better Christian.

Lord of the weather

Pastor Mark Jeske

The ancient Semitic peoples of the eastern Mediterranean region—the Canaanites, Amorites, and Arameans (Syrians)—lived in constant need of water for their animals and their crops. They knew that they needed divine help for their survival, so they developed an elaborate mythology about a god they named Baal. Baal would give the rainfall that they needed, and his sister/wife Asherah would grant fertility to the earth and livestock if they were properly appeased.

I used to wonder why Baal worship was so durable in the Old Testament era and why it was so intriguing to the Israelites. Easy for me to say—my region gets 35-40 inches of rain a year, not 8 inches. The Lord's prophets had to remind the Israelites constantly that it was not Baal who kept them alive: **"Ask the Lord for rain in the springtime; it is the Lord who sends the thunderstorms"** (Zechariah 10:1).

Today Satan doesn't bother tempting people with Baal mythology. He's getting a lot of mileage from encouraging people to venerate the god Science and see our planet as our Mother—you know, as in Mother Earth. When you see heavy clouds gathering above you, feel the barometric pressure changing, sense the wind picking up, and smell that pre-rain smell, look up and thank the God of heaven who is going to keep us alive another day. Water still is life for the people of the earth.

He and he alone is the Lord of the universe, and that includes the weather.

July 4

Dual vision

Linda Buxa

I'm not quite ready for bifocals, so my eyes have separate purposes. My left eye has a fairly minimal prescription, which makes it my "close" eye for reading and computer work. My right eye has a stronger prescription, making it my "far away" eye for driving and watching my kids' activities. Because I am fearfully and wonderfully made, my eyes work together, but my brain knows which eye needs to take over in which setting. Amazing!

Because you are fearfully and wonderfully made too, you also have dual vision. Today your "close" eye is focused on your earthly country. As the United States celebrates Independence Day, we thank God for the people who were willing to lose their lives because they believed so strongly in freedom. We praise him that people are still willing to die to defend our freedoms. We also pray and intercede for **"all those in authority, that we may live peaceful and quiet lives in all godliness and holiness"** (1 Timothy 2:1,2).

Our "far away" eye is working too because we know there is no complete freedom and independence until we get to heaven. Today we thank God that he believed so strongly in freedom from pain, sadness, mourning, and death that he was willing to sacrifice his Son for us. So even as we celebrate with our "close" eye, our "far away" eye is **"longing for a better country—a heavenly one. Therefore God is not ashamed to be called their God, for he has prepared a city for them"** (Hebrews 11:16).

Happy Independence Day!

A new thing

Jason Nelson

Sometimes I would just like to ride it out and not learn one more new thing. But I want to try to stay current for a lot of reasons. I don't want to become the grumpy, old Caucasian gumming up the works.

I have a very strong bias that the future belongs to those who not only know and believe in what God has done in the past but also perceive what God is doing right now. I got this idea from him. **"See, I am doing a new thing! Now it springs up; do you not perceive it? I am making a way in the wilderness and streams in the wasteland"** (Isaiah 43:19).

If you can be the kind of leader who perceives what God is doing, you will make a way in the wilderness for your family, business, and church. If you can see through the tangled underbrush and find the open areas, you will be able to seize new opportunities. That kind of vision is developed by paying close attention to everything, gathering lots of information from credible sources, and connecting many data points so you can point the way forward. A clear focus comes out of a broad view. A sense of direction is God's gift wrapped in a hunch. Go ahead and take the way he is making for you.

God does new things. God blesses new things. When you can show others the streams of salvation in the wasteland, they will follow you because everyone needs to be refreshed.

Answer to prayer

Pastor Matt Ewart

Have you ever said that something was an "answer to prayer"? That phrase is freely used to refer to any number of situations where things happened to turn out favorably. I've probably attached that phrase to situations that I didn't even pray about.

But think about what that phrase really means.

If something was an answer to prayer, it means that things would have turned out differently had it not been for prayer. A single prayer or a series of prayers affected the outcome of the situation. An intercession to God moved him to redirect things in a specific way. Now this would be an absurd assumption were it not for God's open invitation through the psalmist: **"Call on me in the day of trouble; I will deliver you, and you will honor me"** (Psalm 50:15).

There are some troubles going on in your life right now, and tomorrow will add more troubles on top of them. Make a list of the troubles, whether they feel big or small. List all the things you are afraid of because you have no control over them. What is it that you completely depend on God to handle?

When these things come up, give them the name Trouble and call upon God with them on your heart. In his own way and in his own time, he will deliver you from them. When he does, honor him with a simple yet profound thought: *That was an answer to prayer.*

Choose to be generous

Pastor Mark Jeske

You don't have to go to clinics and workshops to learn how to be a taker. You don't have to go to grad school to study selfishness. You don't have to send your kids to summer school to help them work on their greed. All those things come naturally. Way too naturally. It's cultivating a generous spirit that takes the energy.

Think how stunned you feel when somebody actually gives you something—with no expectation that you must now reciprocate. It is the way of God himself: **"You will be enriched in every way so that you can be generous on every occasion, and through us your generosity will result in thanksgiving to God"** (2 Corinthians 9:11). Do you get the picture? God's mercy and power and resources are looped into a giant convection system that is always moving in circles. Once you let go of your cramped, little, selfish universe, you tap into the mighty and limitless river of God's blessings.

Generosity is learned behavior. You have to learn it yourself, and it's your job to teach it to your kids. Generous people are God's agents of mercy in a broken and suffering world. God has blessed you richly so that you in turn can bless other people with your unique skills, time, energy, and money. It was God's intent to send all those things *to* you so he could get something done *through* you.

Don't wait till you feel it. Go first.

Self-made man

Pastor Mark Jeske

The American Revolution took place in part to get rid of the aristocracy, i.e., inherited titles, privileges, and money. We love stories about people who made it big on their own talent, grit, and hard work—we call them self-made men. Well, talent, grit, and hard work are all good things, but the truth is that all of us, without exception, have benefited from the work of others—from mothers and fathers, teachers and pastors, mentors and business partners, critics and adversaries.

And from God. To a remarkable degree we are what God has shaped us to be: **"Then the word of the Lord came to me. He said, 'Can I not do with you, Israel, as this potter does?' declares the Lord. 'Like clay in the hand of the potter, so are you in my hand, Israel'"** (Jeremiah 18:5,6). Our bodies are his design and execution. Our talents are his gifts. Our accomplishments were made possible by opportunities that he sent. Our membership in his family is the gift of Christ.

Adversity that he sent sanded off some of our rough spots and tenderized our hearts. Friends that he provided give us joy and encouragement. Sexuality and marriage, his inventions both, give us intimacy and emotion and human bonding. The Word that he sent explains the meaning of life and gives us purpose.

It is good to be clay in the hands of a skillful Potter.

They won't know for sure

Jason Nelson

When I was teaching, I had to cowboy up for a consultation with a mama bear who was pretty tough on her cubs. We were meeting to discuss why her boys weren't doing better in school. The one in my class compensated for insecurity with passive-aggressive negligence in schoolwork. I had a theory. I told her bluntly, "Troy doesn't think you love him." She growled, "That's ridiculous. Of course I love him. He should know that. Why, I have given him . . ." And then she listed all the expensive toys and gadgets that filled their home. When I could get a word in, I asked, "Have you ever told him?" Dead silence.

I'm not sure that actions always speak louder than words. Actions can hint at love's existence. But should anyone have to work hard to come to that conclusion? And I am a little suspicious of the actions of folks who just won't say the only words that matter. The people we love won't know for sure unless we tell them.

I don't know what girl Solomon was thinking about in his Song. But she felt secure in his love because he expressed it clearly: **"My beloved spoke and said to me, 'Arise, my darling, my beautiful one, come with me.' My beloved is mine and I am his"** (Song of Songs 2:10,16). She knew for sure he loved her because he told her. So I'm going to put this right out there: Beloved in the Lord, I love you.

Listen to your conscience

Pastor Mark Jeske

Even non-Christians know that they have a conscience. In popular imagery they may feel that there is a good angel sitting on one shoulder and a little demon in a red suit sitting on the other. Each whispers contradictory instructions in the nearest ear.

There is such a thing as natural knowledge of God. People know that there is a higher Power of some kind, and they know that this Power has established good and bad, right and wrong. Even people who have never cracked a Bible have a pretty good grasp of God's moral law. It's what keeps all societies on earth from tearing themselves apart, putting some brakes on the mad impulses of the evil one in us.

People listen to the "little devil" at their peril: **"For although they knew God, they neither glorified him as God nor gave thanks to him, but their thinking became futile and their foolish hearts were darkened"** (Romans 1:21). Yielding to sin contrary to one's conscience is addictive, and slowly the good voice gets softer and softer. In judgment God gives people over to their evil desires and all the terrible consequences that ensue.

God expects people to listen to the "good angel" (i.e., our conscience). Anyone eager to hear the voice of the true God behind the voice of conscience can hear him speak in the pages of Scripture. It is there that people will find the answer to life's riddle that even conscience cannot provide: Jesus Christ.

Don't call me Naomi

Pastor Mark Jeske

Nobody is lonely his or her entire life. What creates inner bleakness, however, is when things you love are taken away from you. When people you trusted betray you. When people you depended on take advantage of you. When people you loved die on you.

In a time of famine, an Israelite woman named Naomi, along with her husband and two grown sons, needed to emigrate temporarily to find food. They found food in the land of Moab, and the boys found Moabite wives. Then— in a ten-year span, all three men died.

A sad widow told her daughters-in-law that she had decided to go back to Israel: **"'Don't call me Naomi,' she told them. 'Call me Mara, because the Almighty has made my life very bitter. I went away full, but the LORD has brought me back empty'"** (Ruth 1:20,21). The rest of the book tells the powerful story of how one of those daughters-in-law, Ruth, stayed with the older woman, who in time got to hold a grandson on her lap.

Sometimes we are so full of our own troubles that we have no ears to hear the sighs of loneliness and pain from people around us. Ruth had her own sorrows—she was a widow too—but she spent some energy on the older woman. God loves it when broken people serve other broken people. That's how he heals the broken. That's how he fills the hearts of the lonely with joy.

Today is National Cheer Up the Lonely Day. Who needs you to do just that?

What's holding you back?

Pastor Mark Jeske

When people say they're "ADD," some are kidding and some are serious. Attention Deficit Disorder is a quick and easy way to blame something else for your laziness and carelessness, but it is also a real mental problem that cripples people's ability to concentrate and focus on what's important.

Do you know people with spiritual ADD? They mean well. They really intend to get back to church, really, one of these weeks, seriously, but life just keeps intervening. Birthday parties and family brunches and vacations and soccer tournaments and exhaustion from work and home repairs and a Sunday golf league and work brought home and a sick kid and a houseful of Sunday midday guests just keep pushing that church attendance day farther and farther until the original intent and resolution fade into the rearview. Spiritual inertia carves ruts so deep that it would take divine dynamite to blast them out.

What's holding you back from a more joyful faith, a more visible faith, a more energetic faith? Scripture gives many examples of people who overcame despite suffering far worse problems than you ever did: **"Therefore, since we are surrounded by such a great cloud of witnesses, let us throw off everything that hinders and the sin that so easily entangles"** (Hebrews 12:1).

What are your top three distracters?

(I mean it—make a list right now and look at those items. What needs to change? Today?)

I'm tired and thirsty

Pastor Mark Jeske

There's a reason why blues music is so enduring.

Look around at the office, in your classroom, on the streets where you are driving—you are looking at tired people. The daily struggle to survive is exhausting. Disappointments and setbacks sap your strength and make you weaker for the next one. People are weary.

They're thirsty too, thirsty to be reinvigorated, thirsty for the Water of Life. Thirsty to feel that things are working for them in their lives again, thirsty to feel good again, thirsty to be loved, thirsty to like themselves again. The common denominator—people are thirsty for God: **"You, God, are my God, earnestly I seek you; I thirst for you, my whole being longs for you, in a dry and parched land where there is no water"** (Psalm 63:1). When Jesus described himself to a Samaritan woman as the Water of Life, he was offering her not only the endless delight of heaven but the secret to a happy and fulfilling life *right now.*

Through Christ we have the assurance of worth and value. We have his promise for spiritual strength and relief from suffering, forgiveness of our sins, protection from the evil one, and hope for a future way better than our past.

Lord, I believe you. In the meantime, how about a little sip of heaven, just to keep me going? Please?

A better way

Jason Nelson

You can tell from his writing that the apostle Paul was fluent in the ideals of great civilizations. Being from Tarsus, he knew of the Greek ideal of freedom. Being a Jew, he could speak of the Hebrew ideal of peace. Being a Roman citizen, he benefited from their ideal of justice.

There is controversy and conflict because no one lives up to the ideals. So the critics corner becomes a crowded place. You can elbow your way in there if you want. I go there myself. But I am thinking there is more room to flourish if we go light on proving people wrong and just show them a better way.

Being a Christian, Paul added the missing ideal and showed us a better way: **"I may speak in the languages of humans and of angels. But if I don't have love . . . none of these things will help me"** (1 Corinthians 13:1,3 GW). No vote, no covenant, no law will matter without love. **"Love is patient. Love is kind. Love isn't jealous. It doesn't sing its own praises. It isn't arrogant. It isn't rude. It doesn't think about itself. It isn't irritable. It doesn't keep track of wrongs. It isn't happy when injustice is done, but it is happy with the truth. Love never stops being patient, never stops believing, never stops hoping, never gives up"** (verses 4-7).

I think God has our civilization where he wants it. Hallelujah! What a great time to show people a better way.

A heart for God

Pastor Mark Jeske

I'll admit it—I'm a sucker for church architecture. I'm drawn to big and ornate houses of worship like a moth to a flame. When I see them as I'm driving, my head swivels. When I see them while walking, I try to get in. I love to look at pictures of them. I love to work on ours to make it even more beautiful than it is now.

God loves his houses of worship. He loves it when people gather for singing, prayer, study of the Word, generosity of giving and service, and fellowship. He loves to hear his praises, and he loves to feed his people with Word and sacrament. But we should be under no illusions that these man-made structures contain him: **"'Where is the house you will build for me? Where will my resting place be? Has not my hand made all these things, and so they came into being?' declares the Lord. 'This is the one I look on with favor: those who are humble and contrite in spirit, and who tremble at my word'"** (Isaiah 66:1,2).

In a way it's a little absurd to dedicate a church to God. He already made and owns every stick of wood and piece of stone in the place. But there's a place he doesn't own, where he would *really* like to live, and that is in your heart. The ones he likes best are humble and contrite.

Only you can give yours to him.

Beat the system

Pastor Matt Ewart

For just about any system out there, you can find a book that claims to help you beat it. The system could be taxes, card games, or the stock market. To beat it means you found a way to make things work in your favor.

Can you beat the devil at his system? He uses sin to destroy relationships and cut us off from God.

You might think that as long as you avoid immediate consequences of sin, you can beat the devil at his own system—you can "enjoy" sin without the negative results.

But the devil isn't always going for the immediate win. Quite often he is looking for a little foothold that will undermine you in the long run.

Guilt is his favorite foothold. Excusing your sin rather than repenting of it will cause your guilt to grow and grow. Given enough time it will suffocate your relationship with God to the point where prayer becomes awkward and personal study of his Word is nonexistent.

"Do not give the devil a foothold" (Ephesians 4:27).

Only God could beat the devil's system. He did that by putting your sin with its guilt onto Jesus. That was the only way to spare you from sin's eternal consequence.

Today do not let guilt run your life, and do not use guilt to manipulate others. The system of guilt has been defeated. Your life now runs on something much more powerful: grace.

July 17

It's time

Pastor Mark Jeske

Our world offers you many choices, many temptations, many causes, many philosophies. What do you want? What's important to you? What do you care about? Where do you see the biggest payoff? What are you chasing? Whom do you trust? Whose approval do you crave? How do you know what success looks like?

Here is the prophet Hosea's challenge: **"Sow righteousness for yourselves, reap the fruit of unfailing love, and break up your unplowed ground; for it is time to seek the LORD, until he comes and showers his righteousness on you"** (Hosea 10:12). Wow—there's no other choice in life that yields greater satisfaction, that has a bigger payoff, that can satisfy your soul than to pursue the way of the Lord.

So what does that mean? It means listening to the Word so that you know what's truly valuable; so that you know what lies are coming at you from hell; so that you can tell the truth when you hear it; so that you will be able to tell who are your true friends and who are dead weights that will drag you down; so that you know what to pursue that will bring you a lasting, honorable, and righteous reward.

The Word tells you that there is no meaning, forgiveness, or true love outside of a relationship with Jesus Christ. The Word calls him the central organizing principle of all human existence.

It's time to seek the Lord!

He knows everything about you

Pastor Mark Jeske

Libertarians in our country regularly sound agitated alarms about government surveillance, secret wiretaps, data mining, and spy drones. We *love* our privacy in this country. Technology companies don't ever want to let government agents into the data in their smartphones.

Do you know that God knows absolutely everything about you? Does that creep you out, or does that reassure you? His eyes see it all, his ears hear it all, and his infinite RAM capacity is greater than all the server farms on earth linked together. He remembers it all.

That's actually good news for believers. You may think of yourself as pretty small and insignificant, just another grain of sand on the seashore. Compared to 50+ billion stars in each of the 50+ billion galaxies in the limitless and expanding universe, you and I are, well, pretty microscopic indeed. But we are not insignificant! God pays close attention to everything about you.

He planned you from all eternity. He designed your adult shape, loaded gifts and abilities into your DNA, placed you in a unique location on earth, chose you to be his, washed you of your evil residue through your baptism, and lives in you personally. He watches everything you do and say and takes immense delight in your growth and development. **"See, I have engraved you on the palms of my hands"** (Isaiah 49:16).

You matter that much to the supreme Lord of the universe.

In an age of openness

Jason Nelson

Not since Adam and Eve's first date has there been this much openness in society. People reveal almost anything on social media. One celebrity posted a selfie while she was in the shower. This is a shocker to those of us who were told "never let 'em see you sweat."

Millennials are masters of social media. Your native transparency has a huge upside for spreading Christianity. The gospel is not an encrypted message. Jesus had this in mind when he said, **"In the same way, let your light shine before others, that they may see your good deeds and glorify your Father in heaven"** (Matthew 5:16).

People are recruited to all kinds of movements from what they see via social media. My young friends, could you use it to let your light shine so that others may glorify God? I'm not thinking of staged religious demonstrations. That's not your style. Rather, would you be willing to reveal your personal relationship with Jesus Christ? Would you be willing to let the world see your reverence when you bow your head and listen in real time when you pray? Could you use new platforms to show others the power of the cross in your life? I'd upload a video of you singing an original Christian song. Maybe you could crowdsource the next iteration of the one holy Christian and apostolic church. You can tell I am running out of ideas. But I'm very confident you will be able take it from here.

Ahem—did you consult me?

Pastor Mark Jeske

The most fundamental principle of prayer is the one we forget the quickest—that God is holding gifts and blessings in his heavenly arms, ready to drop them on our lives, *and he's just waiting to be asked.* Some argue, "If he knows everything, then he knows what you need and should just give it right away." The reality is that God likes the experience to be interactive. He wants us to feel part of the solution. And so he waits: **"You do not have because you do not ask God"** (James 4:2).

You don't have to try to justify yourself. Jesus Christ's perfect life and innocent death have already justified you. You don't have to argue with God—he knows everything about your life. You don't have to be afraid—he's not a distant, aloof, mysterious power. He is your Daddy. You don't have to feel embarrassed at your stuttered, mumbled prayers. The Spirit edits everything you say into the proper form. You don't have to beg. As God's child you have the privilege of stepping directly into his royal throne room.

What things do you lack in your life? Bring them to him. Has it been a while since your last serious prayers? Don't stay away—he loves to hear from you no matter what. What is hurting your heart or your body right now? Talk to him. Who among your friends needs his help? Bring their needs to him. What does your church need? Just ask.

He's waiting . . .

Balance the here and now with the there and then

Pastor Mark Jeske

Do any of your relatives spend money "like there's no tomorrow"? Everybody knows how tempting that is. It is so easy, so really easy, to borrow a lot of money, rack up big balances on the charge card, and live high in the here and now. Tomorrow seems a long way away. Perhaps a day of reckoning will never come.

What a disaster it would be if you got so absorbed in the struggle for survival that you forgot to look up. The life we are living on earth right now will soon be over. If you are young, you think that statement foolish—young folks think time passes soooo sloooowwwly. Ask senior citizens, and they will tell you that their lives seem to have flashed by in a blink.

Soon comes judgment day. If that day is today, will you be ready? **"Let us run with perseverance the race marked out for us, fixing our eyes on Jesus, the pioneer and perfecter of faith. For the joy set before him he endured the cross, scorning its shame, and sat down at the right hand of the throne of God"** (Hebrews 12:1,2). Fix your eyes on Jesus while you live—he gives you the forgiveness, strength, and hope that you need right now.

Fix your eyes on Jesus even more as your life fades away. Through him you will get it back in a glorious eternity.

Shoes off

Pastor Matt Ewart

Think about two places where you are most likely to be barefoot. I bet I can predict where they are. Ready?

The first place is probably your home. The second place is probably a beach. *How did I know?*

The other thing I know is that most people prefer to be barefoot. When you don't have shoes on it means you aren't hard at work. You're not in a rush to go anywhere. You're in a comfortable environment. You're relaxed.

The interesting thing is that the Bible mentions a place where God takes off his shoes and walks around barefoot. The prophet Ezekiel was given a vision of God's temple that God had abandoned due to Israel's unfaithfulness. But then God returned with this good news: **"He said: 'Son of man, this is the place of my throne and the place for the soles of my feet. This is where I will live among the Israelites forever.'"** (Ezekiel 43:7).

God was home. He wasn't in a rush to go anywhere. He was in a place that he wanted to be—with his people. The ultimate fulfillment of this was when the Son of God came and dwelled among us. Look at his bare feet and his hands for the proof of how much he desired to be with you.

The next time you find satisfaction in kicking off your shoes, remember what love your Savior showed by dwelling with you and walking in your place.

Why do you want to do this alone?

Pastor Mark Jeske

Life is hard. The law of entropy says that everything is in a state of breaking down. You may assume that everything positive you try to do will encounter resistance; you may equally assume that trouble is going to come and find you. Here's the question: Is it your plan to tackle everything all by yourself? Are you open to letting God into your game plan?

Does that sound like a dumb question? Maybe, but even believers have to figure it out one person at a time. Are you going to hold onto your troubles and hide them? Why do you want to do this alone?

King Asa knew he had to change the culture of his realm. The priesthood was weak and the Word of God was not being taught. Violence was everywhere—it was so bad that the Bible says it was not safe to travel about. **"The Spirit of God came on Azariah son of Oded. He went out to meet Asa and said to him, 'Listen to me, Asa and all Judah and Benjamin. The LORD is with you when you are with him. If you seek him, he will be found by you'"** (2 Chronicles 15:1,2). Asa listened to that great advice and sparked a nationwide spiritual renewal. The Bible tells how the people did seek God eagerly *and he was found by them.*

God doesn't play hide-and-go-seek. He wants to be found.

Suffering for others' evil

Pastor Mark Jeske

Children have an intense appreciation for fairness of treatment by their parents. They want an immaculately consistent system of rewards and punishments, and they strenuously protest when they believe that they are falsely accused. And they really, really hate blanket punishments when only one little sinner was at fault.

Well, they probably better get used to it. One of the features of our broken world is that innocent people get dragged into the painful consequences of the evil deeds of others. An abusive father or alcoholic mother will leave a lot of collateral damage on others in the family. A poorly run tavern can attract drunkenness, fighting, gambling, drugs, and prostitution, which blight the whole neighborhood. On a grand scale, governmental leaders like Hitler and Hussein can drag their entire country into reckless and destructive adventures.

Even King David, "a man after God's own heart," by his own selfish blunders caused a season of suffering for his beloved Israel: **"So the Lord sent a plague on Israel, and seventy thousand men of Israel fell dead. David said to God, ' . . . I, the shepherd, have sinned and done wrong. These are but sheep. What have they done?'"** (1 Chronicles 21:14,17).

What will you do when these things happen to you? 1) Choose not to hate the person(s) who dragged you into their consequences, and 2) think about other people who may be hurt when you are attracted to risky life choices.

Is your worship really for me?

Pastor Mark Jeske

When I gave my wife jumper cables as a Christmas gift one year, she didn't look particularly touched. Truth be told, those cables were more for me—to give me peace of mind. She had no interest in learning how to use them. And when she "gave" me a new grill for Father's Day one year, she would cheerfully admit that *she* wanted a new grill.

If we are 100 percent honest with ourselves (and with God), our religious practices and observances might sometimes be more self-serving than God-worshiping. The prophet Zechariah spoke God's words of warning: **"Then the word of the Lord Almighty came to me: 'Ask all the people of the land and the priests, "When you fasted and mourned in the fifth and seventh months for the past seventy years, was it really for me that you fasted? And when you were eating and drinking, were you not feasting for yourselves?"'"** (Zechariah 7:4-6).

When you go to church only to hang out with friends or just to hear music you like or out of boredom or habit or to get attention or power for yourself, the worship value shrivels up. The motions and the actions and the rituals have no value in and of themselves. Here's what matters: Did the Word hit your heart? Did the Word change your heart? Did the Word change your life?

Were you seeking to please and honor your Savior by what you said and did?

Just relax

Pastor Matt Ewart

It's funny when you consider the difference between relaxing and being lazy. A snapshot of one can easily be mistaken for the other. Only the context of what happened beforehand can determine the difference between the two.

While the Bible speaks against laziness, it also cautions those who are over busy. People who never take time to relax are not only doing themselves a physical disservice, but they also might be reflecting a spiritual misalignment.

If the devil could have his way, he would have you constantly busy. If you are always worrying about what you need to do next, you are never able to pause and reflect on what it means that God is in control of all things.

In Christ, the context of your life has changed dramatically. God's snapshot of you will always show the work put in by Jesus on the cross. It took his whole life and even his death, but he was able to make you holy. That's how God sees you.

Take time to rest in the context of Jesus' work. Relax as you meditate on all God has done. Trust that he forgave yesterday and will work all things out for your good—even the things you don't have time to get to today.

"I gave them my decrees and made known to them my laws, by which the person who obeys them will live. Also I gave them my Sabbaths as a sign between us, so they would know that I the Lord made them holy" (Ezekiel 20:11,12).

YOLO

Pastor Mark Jeske

Know what a *meme* is? It's a belief or philosophy that gains acceptance rapidly horizontally, peer to peer, usually through social media, rather than through formal education. One that everybody younger than 30 knows is "YOLO," i.e., "You only live once." It is a standard excuse for doing something lame or stupid, like having your fourth shot of Jack in an hour or taking a total stranger to your apartment, the rationalization being that life is short and you have only a very limited time to do exciting and risky things.

One of the great benefits of believing the Christian gospel is being relieved of the terrible pressure that you have to get it all now before the final gong goes off. Life on earth is indeed short, uncertain, full of trouble, and hard, but life in heaven is endless, secure, amazing, and fulfilling. Just before a great persecution of Christians broke out in Rome, Paul wrote these words of encouragement and comfort: **"I consider that our present sufferings are not worth comparing with the glory that will be revealed in us"** (Romans 8:18).

What that means is that you can say no to Satan's temptations and not feel cheated. It means that whatever you have forgone or sacrificed for Jesus will be repaid many times over. It means that in heaven God will finally make all things right.

~~YOLO~~ YGTLT—"You get to live twice."

The spotlight

Pastor Matt Ewart

John the Baptist had the important job of clearing the way for Jesus. To drive home the importance of repentance, he regularly made use of something called Baptism (thus his name). People flocked to see this unusual yet authoritative prophet who defied mainstream teaching methods.

But one day someone stole his popularity. Someone else set up shop down the river in a better location and began to employ his trademark Baptism techniques.

That someone was Jesus.

John's disciples got quite upset that the crowds were now going to Jesus, so they alerted John to this troubling news. Here's how John responded: **"A person can receive only what is given them from heaven"** (John 3:27).

Translation: God gave John time in the spotlight, and it served a good purpose. Now God was giving that spotlight to Jesus for an even better purpose.

While it was tough for him to lose popularity, John recognized that God's plan required him to take second place. Jesus had to become greater, and John had to become lesser.

You naturally want to react like John's disciples did. You want to protest when God decides to take the spotlight away from you. But remember that it's always a good thing when God shines the spotlight on himself. No matter how popular or unpopular you become in the world, what really matters is that Jesus forgave you to make you God's child.

Let him adjust the spotlight to best testify to that truth.

Teach your kids about drugs

Pastor Mark Jeske

Why would anybody inject recreational drugs for the first time?

I can understand how an addict would feel the compulsion, but why would you start in the first place? Do people not fear the enslavement? impoverishment? destruction of relationships? physical emaciation? risk of overdose and death?

Those miserable outcomes sadly may be the very reason some people find drugs so attractive. People who are miserable; hate their lives; feel really rebellious, angry, depressed, or alienated may actually find a thrill in an activity so dangerous, so full of risk, so exciting, so bad. Smoking or injecting opiates may express people's self-hatred or even a death wish, and it happens in Christian families too.

Have conversations with your kids about drugs. Don't say it could never happen to us. One of my sons has lost a high school friend already to a heroin overdose. Encourage your kids to see that they have great value to you and their family and to God himself. The Father who was willing to sacrifice his own Son to win back the human race expresses his passionate love for people with these encouraging words: **"Do not fear, for I am with you; do not be dismayed, for I am your God. I will strengthen you and help you; I will uphold you with my righteous right hand"** (Isaiah 41:10).

Men and women

Jason Nelson

I listened to a young, Iranian, Christian woman describe how difficult her life had been in Iran. As is the case in many despotic societies, she had little value. She didn't have equal protection under the law. She didn't have the educational or financial opportunities men had. Because all women are inferior to all men there, she was always in danger. She faced the risk that any evening she could get into a taxi with a male driver and even though she was married she could be raped and nothing would be done about it. She had no self-esteem and no hope.

This message drew her to Christianity: **"In Christ Jesus you are all children of God through faith, for all of you who were baptized into Christ have clothed yourselves with Christ. There is neither Jew nor Gentile, neither slave nor free, nor is there male and female, for you are all one in Christ Jesus"** (Galatians 3:26-28). It changed her life. In Christ she had equality with men. In Christ she had human dignity. In Christ she had an equal share of redemption and eternal life. And if it came to giving up her body rather than giving up that faith, she was prepared to do it.

High on the list of things that must distinguish Christianity from other religions, or no religion, is the way Christian men treat women. In Christ, Christian men honor women. Christian men respect women. Christian men advocate for women as equals.

I'm nobody

Pastor Mark Jeske

"I'm a loser, and I'm not what I appear to be." If the super-talented, superego John Lennon could sing that in 1964, where does that leave the rest of us ordinary mortals?

I never cease being surprised to hear painfully self-deprecating remarks from people whom I admire for their talent, achievements, and charm. Satan must have a field day working on people's self-hatred. That sinful weakness in us all must be the gift to him that keeps on giving. Here is the superhero King David's cry of heart pain: **"You know how I am scorned, disgraced and shamed. . . . Scorn has broken my heart and has left me helpless; I looked for sympathy, but there was none, for comforters, but I found none"** (Psalm 69:19,20).

You can plan on those low feelings coming over you at times. Expect them and be ready for them. They are not real though. They come from Satan's distortions of God's reality. They come from fear over unconfessed and hidden sin, so repent anew and believe in Christ's free and full forgiveness. They come from insecure people trying to be taller by pounding on you. Ignore it. Let God's words of favor and approval over you have the last word. Those low feelings come from personal vanity and selfish ambition. Live within your capabilities and talents and find joy in helping other people use theirs. Take pleasure in others' gifts and achievements.

If there are super talents around you, don't hate on yourself. Clap and cheer for them.

august

"It was you who set all the boundaries of the earth; you made both summer and winter."

Psalm 74:17

Children are God's agents too

Pastor Mark Jeske

Adults have a thousand ways to make children feel small. We mean well. We want to protect them, prevent them from hurting themselves or others, let them grow and mature. We want to do all the teaching, sharing with them our vast learning and life wisdom. We want to prepare them for service to the Lord someday. Well, children are God's agents too, and occasionally he will use them for extraordinary service right now.

"Josiah was eight years old when he became king, and he reigned in Jerusalem thirty-one years. He did what was right in the eyes of the LORD and followed the ways of his father David, not turning aside to the right or to the left. In the eighth year of his reign, while he was still young, he began to seek the God of his father David. In his twelfth year he began to purge Judah and Jerusalem of high places, Asherah poles and idols" (2 Chronicles 34:1-3). Think of it—a second grader became king of Judah, and at the age of a college sophomore he was ready to lead a spiritual reformation that changed the entire country and brought a generation of peace and prosperity from God.

A servant girl led the chief of the Syrian general staff, Naaman, to the prophet Elisha. What can your children and grandchildren teach you? How are they changing the world around them? How is God using them to bring love and understanding to your world?

Are you watching? Are you listening?

Does God's patience have limits?

Pastor Mark Jeske

As a father to my kids, I am a mixture of attributes. I am partly stern, partly easygoing. I am partly demanding, partly forgiving, partly insistent, and partly tolerant.

It would be a mistake to project our mind-set onto God. The Bible describes a God who both punishes sin and forgives sin. But he's not half-and-half. He's 100 percent of both (at the same time!). Is he patient? You bet. But there are limits to his patience: **"'When I called, they did not listen; so when they called, I would not listen,' says the LORD Almighty"** (Zechariah 7:13). Does his willingness to judge and punish negate the gospel's good news? Not at all.

It's a paradox. Scripture's descriptions of God exist not so much for you to understand as to believe. The extreme proclamations of God's law, such as the prophet Zechariah's above, are to teach us humility and respect in his presence. Don't push him off till later. There may be no later for you.

But God's precious gospel message is extreme too. God laid on the back of his Son, Jesus, all his anger and punished him in full for all our sins. His mercy is far greater than all our sinful failings. So how do you know which applies to you? *The key is repentance.* When you approach the Father with a repentant heart, honestly aware of and ashamed of your inner evil but also trusting in your Savior Jesus, you will always find a smiling face on your Father.

The true source of our prosperity

Pastor Mark Jeske

My dad was a doer, and he taught me to be a doer. He taught me to value being self-reliant, curious, hard-working, thrifty, quick to save, and slow to spend. I am grateful for that wonderful guidance. But there's a risk there—the risk that I might be foolish enough to suppose that I am the source of my personal prosperity.

Here's where farmers still have much to teach us. Even in this age of technological miracles, farmers know that their crops are at the mercy of forces that no farmer can control. Even when they obey all the laws and rhythms of the seasons, even when they do everything right and in the right order, they must watch and wait and pray. Insects, hail, plant disease, drought, floods, and early frost can destroy a whole season's work in a hurry.

It is my personal belief that it's much harder to be an agnostic or atheist farmer. Farmers just *know* the true Source of their prosperity: **"The seed will grow well, the vine will yield its fruit, the ground will produce its crops, and the heavens will drop their dew. *I will give* all these things as an inheritance to the remnant of this people"** (Zechariah 8:12). Without God's smile and blessing, nothing will work for you.

Take inventory of everything good in your life and thank the Source. Think of everything you're struggling with and striving for right now, lift your eyes up to heaven, and entrust it all to the Source.

Leaders go first

Pastor Mark Jeske

Possibly when you think of leadership you think exercise of power. Possibly you think authority, telling others what to do, command and control. Other words that come to mind—*Privilege? Elite?*

Leadership in Christ has a different flavor. Leadership within the church of God should not be about power and commanding the obedience of others. Leadership is about persuasion, inspiration, teaching, tone, empowerment, modeling, and service. Christian leaders don't tell others what to do; they don't sit on their thrones and expect the little people to do the work and make the contributions.

Look at the example of the capital campaign for the construction of the Jerusalem temple. Leaders go first. **"Then the leaders of families, the officers of the tribes of Israel, the commanders of thousands and commanders of hundreds, and the officials in charge of the king's work gave willingly. They gave toward the work on the temple of God five thousand talents and ten thousand darics of gold, ten thousand talents of silver, eighteen thousand talents of bronze and a hundred thousand talents of iron. Anyone who had precious stones gave them to the treasury of the temple of the Lord"** (1 Chronicles 29:6-8).

Sacrificial leaders are fun to follow. They release energy in people. They inspire trust. They don't tell the way to; they show it. They don't ask people to do anything they wouldn't also do.

First.

Something to offer

Pastor Matt Ewart

Sometimes you might feel like you have nothing to offer people, or you feel like you can't serve in a meaningful way. Do other people even *want* your help?

Depending on the day, I can land on either side of that question. Some days I feel like I'm absolutely no help to anybody. Other days I'm convinced that the world would stop turning were it not for my awesomeness. Both reactions are wrong, and the account of Jesus feeding the five thousand tells you why.

"When Jesus looked up and saw a great crowd coming toward him, he said to Philip, 'Where shall we buy bread for these people to eat?' He asked this only to test him, for he already had in mind what he was going to do" (John 6:5,6).

What could the disciples possibly do to feed all these people? Nothing. There was no way they could provide an impromptu catered meal for thousands and thousands of people. They had absolutely nothing to offer. Or did they?

While Jesus provided the amount of food needed for those people, he depended on the disciples to distribute it. Without their help, the people would have gone hungry. And in the end, the disciples who started with nothing ended up gathering basketfuls of leftovers.

To this day, God provides what is needed. From forgiveness in Jesus to the fruit of the Spirit, he provides it all. Think of how he might use you today to bring these blessings to others. You have everything to offer.

Let your word be your bond

Pastor Mark Jeske

If you have any ideas about taking out a home mortgage, your lender will obtain your FICO credit score to gauge your financial capability and track record for debt repayment. Your credit score doesn't tell the lender everything, but it is a reliable way to reduce the lender's risk. Once your credit reputation is shot, it gets really, really hard to borrow money.

There's no rating agency for truth telling, but after a while the people with whom you associate will have a pretty good sense as to how much truth is in your words. Every time you are caught in a lie your "rating" goes down, and you have to protest and embellish and intensify your statements more and more. The more words you have to add to your basic statements, the more people will suspect that you are faking or hustling them.

Jesus has a simple solution: **"All you need to say is simply 'Yes' or 'No'; anything beyond this comes from the evil one"** (Matthew 5:37). Simple: develop a reputation for telling the truth. Simple: Look people right in the eye without wavering and tell the truth. Simple: say it one time and then fall silent because there's nothing more that needs to be added.

That way you never have to wonder which version of the story you've told. Because there is only one version.

Facebook friends: What's the point?

Diana Kerr

Have you ever heard of Friendship Day? You get one guess who created this holiday—yep, Hallmark! Shocking.

Sorry, Hallmark, but I have no plans to send your greeting cards to my friends on that day. There are just way too many: 1,337 to be exact.

I'm talking about my Facebook friends. Yes, I know, that seems like an excessive amount. Honestly, I actually know all those people.

Still, that is *way* too many friends to maintain relationships with, which makes you wonder, *What's the point of all those Facebook friends?* Most people's instinctive answer would be, "To keep in touch." But is that *really* our goal?

Have you realized how easy it is to let the devil suck you into comparison on social media and in wanting to make yourself look good? Envy, jealousy, pride, and boastfulness all show up *so* easily, tainting our friendships in real life and online.

For me personally, it takes conscious effort to use social media as a tool for *good* instead—for encouraging and for sharing my faith. When you're about to post something on Facebook for your friends to see, ask yourself *why* you're doing it. Are you doing this to build people up or to bring them down? to encourage and inspire or to make them feel jealous or lesser than you? **"Do not let any unwholesome talk come out of your mouths, but only what is helpful for *building others up according to their needs*, that it may benefit those who listen"** (Ephesians 4:29).

The trump card

Pastor Matt Ewart

Some card games can be tricky to learn, especially if trump cards are in play. The trump cards have special value based on their suit. So if spades are trump, a low spade can beat a high card of any other suit. Until you figure out how trump cards work, the card game won't make much sense.

That's why I gave up on euchre and sheepshead.

The Bible is similar. There can be parts of it that don't make much sense. In some places we might have questions about why God does the things he does, and we might worry that his character isn't what we were told to believe.

But things can be quickly sorted out once you figure out what is trump. No matter what section you are wrestling with, there's always one sure thing you can take away from it—one unbeatable truth.

The trump card is a Person.

While God communicated many things in many ways through several prophets, God laid down his trump card when his Son became flesh. Everything in the Bible points to him. No matter what, everything written somehow testifies to his existence or his role in your salvation.

So when there are challenging things in the Bible you might not understand, ask yourself this question: What does this section teach me about Jesus? When it comes to the Bible, the trump card is a Person. Once you know that, everything else falls into place.

Jesus said, **"These are the very Scriptures that testify about me"** (John 5:39).

I hurt

Pastor Mark Jeske

Have you ever noticed how exhausting physical pain is? Not only are your nerves all jangled and fried after a day of constant pain, but you have no energy. Steady pain drains you, and so does steady emotional pain. You don't sleep well, if at all, and that leaves you in a semi-zombie state.

When part of you hurts all the time, all of you hurts: **"My back is filled with searing pain; there is no health in my body. I am feeble and utterly crushed; I groan in anguish of heart. All my longings lie open before you, Lord; my sighing is not hidden from you. My heart pounds, my strength fails me; even the light has gone from my eyes"** (Psalm 38:7-10).

One of God's goals for your life is to discourage you from falling in love with life on earth. This is not our final destination. We're not home here—the Bible calls us pilgrims and wanderers. From God's point of view, our pain is not disastrous if it relaxes our grip on our money and our stuff (which we'll have to leave behind anyway). Pain also lifts our faces up to heaven to call to our greatest physician. When he comes with deliverance, we will then know who helped us—we won't just shrug or call it coincidence or luck.

Pain is so much more bearable when you're not alone. How wonderful of God to send us people to help bear the load. Do any pain sufferers need you today?

The common good

Jason Nelson

A blessing from my early years in public school is remembering the preamble to the Constitution: *"We the People of the United States, in Order to form a more perfect Union, establish Justice, insure domestic Tranquility, provide for the common defense, promote the general Welfare, and secure the Blessings of Liberty to ourselves and our Posterity, do ordain and establish this Constitution for the United States of America."*

This introduction was added *after* the framers outlined the most promising form of government in human history. The Constitution gets debated, interpreted by the courts, and amended by Congress. But the preamble hasn't been touched. It stands to declare that the sacred purpose of American government is the common good.

A blessing from my later years in Christian school is remembering these words of God: **"Let each of you look not only to his own interests, but also to the interests of others"** (Philippians 2:4 ESV). The ultimate expression of faith in Jesus is concern for others that supersedes concern for ourselves. It is such a privilege to live in a nation where practicing our citizenship lines up so nicely with practicing our faith.

Agreeing on the common good is challenging in a big, diverse nation like America. We are in the process of deciding what the common good should be. Our democracy leans different directions after the votes are counted. But it hasn't fallen. It won't fall as long as one thing we have in common is concern for each other.

I've been cheated

Pastor Mark Jeske

If you manage to stay alive for any length of time, you will have been taken advantage of, probably numerous times. Maybe you were cheated out of a father in your home. Maybe a friend conned you into making a loan that was never repaid. Maybe you were set up as a sacrificial lamb in something that went badly at work. Maybe you are unjustly excluded and estranged from family members.

King David, when he was just the future king, posed no threat to the current king, Saul. He never lifted a hand against him, never aroused a rebellion against him. But Saul was so insecure and paranoid that he led repeated violent assaults against the young man. David keenly felt the injustice: **"Those who hate me without reason outnumber the hairs of my head; many are my enemies without cause, those who seek to destroy me. I am forced to restore what I did not steal"** (Psalm 69:4).

Does it come as any surprise that our Savior Jesus' path also led through unjust hatred? David's words were prophetic for him, even quoted in John's gospel in the upper room on Maundy Thursday evening. They are prophetic for us as well. All who follow Christ can expect to experience the same injustices and hostility he did.

Fear not. There is nothing taken from you in this life that God cannot and will not restore to you a hundred times over in the next.

God loves you

Pastor Matt Ewart

"To love at all is to be vulnerable. Love anything, and your heart will certainly be wrung—possibly be broken."—C. S. Lewis

Lewis spoke with great eloquence about something that modern musicians still sing about: love hurts. It's bound to hurt because of the world we live in. Love binds you together, but that bond will eventually be broken by separation. Sin is the cause. Death is the guarantee. Love anything, and your heart will certainly be wrung.

With that in mind, consider what it means that *God* loves *you*. For God to love sinful mortals seems foolish. This would certainly leave him vulnerable because it would only be a matter of time until we would be separated from him—sin being the cause and eternal death the guarantee.

But because his love is so persistent, he pursued a path that would not leave his love for you unfulfilled. It was a path that required the Son of God to become the vulnerable victim. His love demanded something extraordinary from him.

"This is love: not that we loved God, but that he loved us and sent his Son as an atoning sacrifice for our sins" (1 John 4:10).

Love might require something extraordinary of you today. It might require vulnerability and the potential for heartbreak. But the reason you don't hold back love is because of Jesus. He forgave sin. He overcame death. He is the cause and the guarantee of this truth:

God's love never fails.

Friends don't let friends drift away

Pastor Mark Jeske

Everybody has a circle of influence. You can't change the world or the country or your entire city, but you can make a difference in how certain people think and act. You are probably more influential than you think you are. People in your circle watch you all the time. They listen to how you talk, they watch what you do, and they allow you to offer advice on their lives. That doesn't mean they always do what you recommend, but they will think about what you say.

You can't believe in God for somebody else. But you can make Jesus look good to people. You can remind them of the shortness of life, the reality of hell, our need for a Savior, and the wonderful and complete work that Jesus did on our behalf. **"Encourage one another daily, as long as it is called 'Today,' so that none of you may be hardened by sin's deceitfulness"** (Hebrews 3:13).

You can be there for people not just on days of celebration, but even more important, on days of loss. Pull, not push. Say, "Come with me," rather than "You oughtta . . ." You can be respectful, compassionate, and attentive. People get tired; they get distracted; they let disappointments beat them down; they get depressed and give up. You might be God's personal agent to give hope.

The Lord Jesus is going to return to earth at any minute. All of a sudden Today is going to become Eternity.

God bless the pendulum keepers

Jason Nelson

The march of time is kept with a pendulum. Its swinging keeps things interesting, challenging, and moving forward. History teaches that trends run out of steam when they reach their limits and some very brave soul begins pushing back. Eventually a few other pendulum keepers join in. Momentum accelerates as lots of folks jump on. A counter trend dominates until some equally brave pendulum keeper on the other end sees the risks of extreme movement and exerts a lot of energy trying to push it back. God bless the pendulum keepers.

For Christianity to be taken seriously, Christians need a reputation for being thoughtful about everything. **"Let your reasonableness be known to everyone."** There is an existential reason for us to remain levelheaded: **"The Lord is at hand"** (Philippians 4:5 ESV). But it seems like moderation is a place we visit only briefly as society lurches from one extreme to another. God is coming to restore order. He depends on wise people to neutralize extremes that conflict with the gospel. **"Come now, let us reason together, says the Lord: though your sins are like scarlet, they shall be as white as snow; though they are red like crimson, they shall become like wool"** (Isaiah 1:18 ESV). God bless the pendulum keepers who give us pause so we can concentrate on this extraordinary message.

Don't panic when we get so far out you can see over the edge. God will continue to raise up pendulum keepers until he makes the pendulum rest.

Free at last

Pastor Mark Jeske

Not long after St. Paul moved on from the Galatian cities with his message of freedom in Christ, good old boys moved in and tried their best to reimpose Old Covenant rules about food, restricted social contact, ceremonial circumcision, and religious observances.

I think I know why church leaders do that. They like rules. They don't trust people. They mean well, sort of. They love the Word of God so much that they want to build a wall around it to protect it. They like being in control. Traditions become traditionalism; laws become legalism. They like being the priests, the go-betweens, and aren't sure that the believers are ready to be God's royal priests. And so they make rules. To "help."

Paul heard about what was going on in Galatia, and since he couldn't be there in person, he wrote a furious letter: **"It is for freedom that Christ has set us free. Stand firm, then, and do not let yourselves be burdened again by a yoke of slavery"** (Galatians 5:1). It is the solemn task of congregational and denominational leaders to lay on the people's consciences no less than what God's Word says, but also *no more* than what God's Word says. It is not enough to mean well. Mandating man-made laws is not spiritually healthy. It is legalism, poison for the soul.

Christians, do not let anyone take away your freedom in Christ. While you can learn from your sisters and brothers, ultimately you are responsible for your own spiritual care and feeding.

I hate my workplace

Pastor Mark Jeske

I love my job. Honestly. I have never second-guessed my life's work. But I know many people who are miserable in their jobs, not so much because of the work they do but because of the people they have to do it with. Is your workplace dysfunctional? Do you have an overcritical boss? spiteful coworkers? Does this sound like what you head into each day: **"My adversaries pursue me all day long; in their pride many are attacking me"** (Psalm 56:2).

Obviously if you could have left easily, you would have by now. So you need the job and have no good options at present. What to do? You can pray for God's strength and mercy to help you be like Jesus, willing to bear abuse from other people without retaliation. You can choose not to bring that anger and stress home and take it out on your family. You can choose to confuse the mean people in your workplace and treat them with forgiveness, grace, and patience. You can do good work, and then quietly assure yourself that the problem is not you.

You can give your problems and griefs to God and ask for relief. You can find happy places to recharge, surrounding yourself with positive people and drawing affirmation and strength from them. You can do things for other people so that your world won't close in around you and your problems.

When all else fails, take a deep breath, look up to heaven and pray, "Come soon, Lord Jesus."

Livin' small

Pastor Mark Jeske

What kind of life do you expect as a child of God? Do you feel you should be riding in a Porsche? Have granite countertops? Have a country club membership? Own a summer cottage? Vacation in Paris?

You may have been given some of these treats by your exceedingly generous Father, or you may never experience them. Or perhaps they still lie in your future. But even if your whole life will be Formica and Chevys, when you're connected to Christ, life is good. It is no shame to live small. The life lessons you learn in your times of hardship and poverty teach you the true value of things, and may also teach you the true value of people.

Jesus and his disciples lived small. So did John the Baptist and Elijah. And so did David, years before he had his own palace: **"David left Gath and escaped to the cave of Adullam"** (1 Samuel 22:1). David's years in the wilderness of Judea in some ways were the best years of his life. He was totally dependent on the Lord's protection. He had little and was running for his life. He was not distracted by luxuries or the burdens of paying for them, protecting them, and caring for them.

I will tell you from my own experience that my poorest days economically were also the times in my life when I read Scripture most avidly, prayed most intensely, and was most aware of my need for God.

A little bit of heaven

Pastor Mark Jeske

Everybody knows somebody who has "dropped out." You do too—people who have dropped out of school, dropped out of the workforce, dropped out of their marriages.

And dropped out of church. That's the worst of them all, because it has eternal consequences. But it's never too late to come back. Feeling guilty? You will find God's forgiveness there. Feeling confused? You will hear God's clear words explaining both your origin and his will for your life. Feeling burdened? You will find a holy place to pray. Feeling anxious? The Lord's Supper will feed your soul and calm your fears. Feeling angry? You will find peace for your heart so that you can let it go. Feeling aimless? You will find service teams that will welcome you, and you will find the thrill of making somebody else's life better.

Feeling lonely? A congregation is a great place to find new friends. Social capital is capital too. St. Paul spent almost the entirety of Romans chapter 16 listing and thanking dear friends in the congregation there: **"Greet Ampliatus, whom I love in the Lord. Greet Urbanus, our fellow worker in Christ, and my dear friend Stachys. Greet Apelles, tested and approved in Christ. Greet those who belong to the household of Aristobulus"** (verses 8-10).

Feeling lost? Church is home. God's home. Your home.

One of them has to be right

Jason Nelson

As an American Christian, I unequivocally defend the right of people to practice the religion of their choosing. I am depending on non-Christian Americans to defend my constitutional right to do the same. I am comfortable with that ambiguity. I get very concerned about any political discussions that even hint at favoring one religion over another. That threatens the very religious liberty I cherish. Majorities can change, and there must always be due respect for the minority in this great land.

But religious liberty doesn't mean all religions are right because people have a right to practice them. Religions other than Christianity have some admirable tenets. And every human being deserves respect because they are just that. But accepting a religion as valid as long as it works for the individual defies the laws of the universe and the claim of exclusivity that all world religions make. One of them has to be right. No matter how sincerely a person may believe otherwise, jumping off a cliff always ends the same. People can be sincerely wrong.

I believe Christianity is right because of God's fearless invitation to put it to the test. **"Do not quench the Spirit. Do not treat prophecies with contempt but test them all; hold on to what is good, reject every kind of evil"** (1 Thessalonians 5:19-22). With life's great questions in mind, test the Bible's teachings and God's plan of salvation against all others. Nothing else compares.

Back to school

Linda Buxa

It's back-to-school shopping season. Whether their babies are leaving for preschool, kindergarten, high school, or college, parents around the country are feeling a combination of excitement and dread, pride and angst.

As we make sure we have everything on our children's school supplies lists, we remember that our kids should always be learning. And what's on God's always-in-school list is our priority: **"He decreed statutes for Jacob and established the law in Israel, which he commanded our forefathers to teach their children, so the next generation would know them, even the children yet to be born, and they in turn would tell their children. Then they would put their trust in God and would not forget his deeds but would keep his commands"** (Psalm 78:5-7).

It's your option how you educate your children, whether public school, Christian day school, or home school. But God has not given you an option when it comes to teaching your children about him; he has *commanded* it. It is your job to consistently tell your children about Jesus, that he lived and died for them, that he subtracted all their sins and added all his holiness to their lives. Now they get to take his perfect report card and proudly show it to their Father as if it were their own.

That is the best lesson they will ever learn!

Listen to the elders

Pastor Mark Jeske

Senior citizens suspect that nobody in our culture wants to be like them. TV commercials for Caribbean vacations, fashionable clothes, beer, and fast cars feature the young and beautiful, not the old and saggy. It seems like senior TV actors are needed only for companies selling walk-in bathtubs, medical-alert necklaces, catheters, and final expense life insurance.

Younger folks who neglect the wisdom of the seniors, however, are wasting a huge asset. Ignoring his older advisors cost King Rehoboam 80 percent of his kingdom and launched decades of civil war: **"Then King Rehoboam consulted the elders who had served his father Solomon during his lifetime. 'How would you advise me to answer these people?' he asked. They replied, 'If today you will be a servant to these people and serve them and give them a favorable answer, they will always be your servants.' But Rehoboam rejected the advice the elders gave him and consulted the young men who had grown up with him"** (1 Kings 12:6-8).

Seniors, we need you! Your decades of accumulated life wisdom really matter! You know money and people's behaviors better than young folks do. Retired people also have the time to do what working-aged people can't— volunteer. Our society depends on social networks and organizations of volunteers that help people. They are one of society's essential glues.

If only Rehoboam had listened to the elders. If only we would listen to the elders.

Choose to be kind

Pastor Mark Jeske

How many weddings have you attended in your life? It's likely that a third of them incorporated some of the verses of 1 Corinthians chapter 13 in some way—you know, the famous "Love Chapter" of the Bible. It is the perfect wedding Scripture because it provides a beautiful and clear picture of what a happy home looks like. **"Love is kind,"** says St. Paul (1 Corinthians 13:4). It sure is. The real question: are *you* kind? Kindness is learned behavior; it doesn't come naturally. It is a mind-set that has to be chosen. Kindness means that you treat people better than they deserve to be treated.

Our fuel for this impossible task is our awareness of the kindness with which our Lord Jesus has treated us. He has lifted from your shoulders forever the impossible task of earning his approval. He gives it freely and pours more blessings on your head than you know what to do with. He invites you, challenges you, *commands you* to show that same kindness to the fools and sinners who surround you each day.

Go ahead—shock people with kindness. In a dog-eat-dog world you will stand out like a shining beacon. Pick up someone else's mess. Do little acts of service that only God will see. Take an elderly person to the doctor. Buy flowers for someone recently divorced. Send a card to a sad person "just because."

Don't wait till you feel it. Go first.

Perspective 101

Jason Nelson

One of the trade-offs made in order to emphasize science, technology, engineering, and math (STEM) in schools has been teaching less history and good literature. To get more of one thing in a crowded curriculum, students will learn less of another. STEM-related subjects help young people get good jobs in their world. History and literature help them keep perspective on it.

History is the play-by-play on human events, and literature is the color commentary. One reason for hysterical reactions to traumatic events is that citizens have lost perspective. Tragedies invite a Twitter storm from commentators who blurt out the worst case in 140 characters but don't offer perspective. They fuel paranoia because people can't remember that we have been through worse before and survived.

People unite when they see themselves as part of the same running narrative. That is why the imperative to *remember* occurs so frequently in the Bible: **"Remember how the Lord your God led you all the way in the wilderness these forty years, to humble and test you in order to know what was in your heart, whether or not you would keep his commands"** (Deuteronomy 8:2). God's people held it together when they remembered their own history and got into all sorts of trouble when they forgot it and failed to teach it to the next generation.

So **"remember the wonders he has done, his miracles, and the judgments he pronounced"** (Psalm 105:5). Then we can keep everything in perspective.

You have changed

Pastor Matt Ewart

Have you noticed that a place you knew well as a child looks much different when you revisit it as an adult? Rooms are smaller. Walls are shorter. You notice things that you didn't notice as a child. In reality, this place from your childhood didn't change one bit. You did.

In a similar way, the more your faith grows, the more your perspective on life changes. There's no better example than what happened in the lives of Jesus' disciples the day of his death. The world looked very scary to them on that day. They locked themselves in a room because they didn't want to face the dangers of being associated with Jesus.

But after the resurrection, the disciples were unleashed. They began to publically preach the gospel of Jesus and would rather face death than hide their faith. What started it all was a visit from Jesus on Easter Sunday when he said these words: **"Peace be with you! As the Father has sent me, I am sending you"** (John 20:21).

Once this peace settled into their hearts and minds, the world looked like a very different place. The resurrection didn't change the danger of the world around them. The resurrection changed *them*.

Just like it changes you. Today there will be things that make you sad, hopeless, or fearful. When those things come up, look at them from the viewpoint of Jesus' empty tomb. With death defeated and sin left powerless, the things that used to seem so daunting become quite small. Not because they have changed. *You* have.

Choose to care

Pastor Mark Jeske

I know why Christians often have trouble sharing their faith.

I know because I sometimes have trouble sharing *my* faith. For one, who wants to risk rejection? We all have to eat a lot of rejection and disappointment each day—why ask for more? For another, I stress over not having the right words to say at the right time. For another, the task of fulfilling Jesus' Great Commission to bring the gospel to the ends of the earth seems so daunting that I don't even start. But the biggest reason? I don't love such people enough.

Caring about other people's spiritual condition and destiny is learned behavior. It also requires effort, a conscious choice to spend time and energy and love on people. We need to *choose to care.* Somebody exerted himself or herself on my behalf—that's why I am a believer. I can do that for someone else. **"Be merciful to those who doubt; save others by snatching them from the fire; to others show mercy, mixed with fear"** (Jude 1:22,23).

People may look totally fine with their Christ-less lives. Do not believe it. People have nowhere to go with the guilt their consciences lay on them. People have no answers if there is hope for them after death. Christians can share the good news of the One who snatched us from the fires of hell; Christians can shows others the same love and mercy that Christ showed us.

Don't wait till you feel it. Go first.

Such an angel

Pastor Matt Ewart

When I was in college, I donated a week of spring break to help out a church with some canvassing. Not only was it an opportunity to serve, but it was also a free plane ticket to a warm, sunny place.

While there I visited hundreds of houses and invited dozens of people to the local church. I am told that one of those people thought I was an angel. (People who know me know better than to make such a comparison.)

That person was in a season of life where God seemed distant, and she sincerely wanted to find a church to get connected. She just didn't know where to start. That's when she heard a knock on her door and found me on the other side of it. To her, it was like an angel of God had appeared at just the right time.

Have you had moments where the perfect stranger appeared at the perfect time? Perhaps you concluded that this stranger could be none other than an angel sent by God.

Maybe God does send angels. Or maybe he just sends out his sons and daughters with the good news of Christ that can dispel any darkness.

You might have a chance today to be someone's angel. You have news from God that can bring light to someone in darkness.

"The people walking in darkness have seen a great light; on those living in the land of deep darkness a light has dawned" (Isaiah 9:2).

The terror of terrorism

Pastor Mark Jeske

There have always been acts of sensational violence and terrorism in America, but the sad events of 9/11 changed our national psyche forever. Instantaneous worldwide digital media make all of us aware all the time of all the ways violent predators stalk their prey. How can that not leave you with a deep sense of fear and insecurity?

Violent crime and near-constant warfare were part of people's lives in biblical times as well. Terrorists don't need guns, bullets, and suicide vests to terrify people. Knives, swords, and arrows cause terror too: **"They shoot from ambush at the innocent; they shoot suddenly, without fear. They encourage each other in evil plans, they talk about hiding their snares; they say, 'Who will see it?' They plot injustice and say, 'We have devised a perfect plan!' Surely the human mind and heart are cunning"** (Psalm 64:4-6).

This side of heaven such human cruelty will always be with us. Satan enjoys human suffering and will goad people on to attack one another. But our God sees, cares, acts, protects, remembers, and will bring justice sooner or later.

Our military, CIA, FBI, state troopers, and local police are some of God's answers to our prayers for security. Thank you, Lord, for these brave men and women. Protect them as they protect us. Send also your holy angels to keep each of us in your care. We trust that we are untouchable until we have finished our earthly work for you.

The scent of the Savior

Pastor Mark Jeske

Mary Kay Ash, the founder of the immense cosmetic network, was legendary for training her salespeople always to present the company in the very best light—she wanted the Mary Kay brand to shine from them. Her reps were to look like proper ladies—in the beginning they were to wear white gloves, and there was never any alcohol served at any corporate events. From humble beginnings in Texas in 1963, Mary Kay is now a global cosmetics empire.

Can people in your world detect any Christianity in you? Does your life exemplify the "brand"? Do you look (and smell!) like Jesus? **"But thanks be to God, who always leads us as captives in Christ's triumphal procession and uses us to spread the aroma of the knowledge of him everywhere. For we are to God the pleasing aroma of Christ among those who are being saved and those who are perishing"** (2 Corinthians 2:14,15).

Do you like being thought of as one of Jesus' sales reps? Do you like being told what the "brand" ought to look and sound like? Do you know that Jesus has no other plan for spreading his gospel of forgiveness and immortality to the ends of the earth? He has decided to limit himself to people, people like you and me. For better or worse, you and I are all there is.

I want to bring the pleasant aroma of Jesus to my world tomorrow. You?

Jealous love

Pastor Mark Jeske

Which are your personal top five adjectives to describe God and his relationship with you? You might list *patient, forgiving, generous, all-powerful, wise, kind,* or *eternal.* One you probably wouldn't list is *jealous.*

Jealousy is bad, isn't it? It means consumed with envy, unhappy, bitter, resentful of what someone else has, discontented, and devious. Does that sound like the God you know? Does it surprise you to hear these words coming from God's mouth? **"This is what the LORD Almighty says: 'I am very jealous for Zion; I am burning with jealousy for her'"** (Zechariah 8:2). This isn't envy-jealousy. This is intense love-jealousy.

"Zion" refers to the heart of Jerusalem, the people of God. It is God's special metaphor for believers, for you. He wants you to know that he's crazy in love with you, that he is thinking about you all the time and consumed with a desire to have a fatherly relationship with you. He's eager to bless you, loves to spoil you, and is willing to take extreme measures to build a relationship with you. He hates Satan's lies and seductions and groans when we fall for them.

He pours out his words through speaking and writing prophets, fulfills his promises, intervenes invisibly and sometimes visibly in our lives, accomplishes miraculous things, breaks the laws of nature when he needs to, and stops at nothing to win and keep your love.

Let your love for God be just as hot.

We don't know what to do

Pastor Mark Jeske

Some problems are smallish and don't task your brain too much—the water pump on your car breaks down . . . you have a leaky pipe in your basement . . . you find some rotten wood under a window sash in the dining room.

And then there's massive invasion by Moabites and Ammonites from your southern border. King Jehoshaphat of Judah heard alarming news of a vast army coming for Jerusalem apparently unprovoked, and he feared it would overwhelm his defenses. He did just the right thing—he consulted the Lord: **"We have no power to face this vast army that is attacking us. We do not know what to do, but our eyes are on you"** (2 Chronicles 20:12).

There is no shame in admitting that some problems are just too big for you. Stage 4 pancreatic cancer is like the invasion of the Moabites. So is a marriage breakup, being fired at age 60, discovery of major embezzling by your business partner, or the death of a child. Sometimes you are just so stunned that there is nothing to do but pray to the Lord, "We don't know what to do, but our eyes are on you."

God was so pleased with Jehoshaphat's prayer that he simply turned Judah's enemies against one another, and they slaughtered one another until none was left. It just may be that God has a solution for your troubles that only he could think of and that only he could pull off.

Fill them in

Jason Nelson

I've met some pastors who are frustrated that younger adults know so little about the Bible. Their unhappiness shows. They sound angry with people because they don't know better.

The world has changed. It's a done deal. The church is struggling to catch up. My parents' generation made their kids go to church whether they liked it or not. And whether we liked it or not, we sat there and absorbed a lot of what the Holy Spirit was dishing out. But many avant-garde parents of my generation didn't force the issue. And now we have wave after wave of people who just don't know any better. They don't have any pew calluses to remind them of what they once heard.

So **"how, then, can they call on the one they have not believed in? And how can they believe in the one of whom they have not heard? And how can they hear without someone preaching to them?"** (Romans 10:14). The challenge of our time is figuring out how to get an audience with people who are not predisposed to hearing the message. But that has always been God's challenge to his church: reach people who don't want to be reached with the gospel that they don't know they need to hear. The passion of the Christ for all people is made known through the compassion of his messengers. **"How beautiful are the feet of those who bring good news!"** (Romans 10:15). Let's start by remembering what the message is called.

september

"Jesus said, 'Let the little children come to me, and do not hinder them, for the kingdom of heaven belongs to such as these.'"

Matthew 19:14

Praying at our wits' end

Jason Nelson

We hit our limits by getting ahead of ourselves: stretching, trying, straining, falling, adjusting, and trying again. We gain wisdom from overreaching. We learn humility from what we don't understand or can't do. We don't have to fake it anymore. There is a curious satisfaction in realizing our own limitations. Take a cleansing breath. Heave a sigh of relief. Be yourself. Offer a nice little prayer.

"My heart is not proud, Lord, my eyes are not haughty; I do not concern myself with great matters or things too wonderful for me. But I have calmed and quieted myself, I am like a weaned child with its mother; like a weaned child I am content" (Psalm 131:1,2).

God is beyond us and in us and with us. Our limitations are never the end of the story. He doesn't honor barriers and tugs us past them kicking and screaming. When we settle down, we realize that he pushed us past ourselves to make us grow. He teams us with people whose limits are different from ours so we accomplish more together than we ever could alone. He redeemed us out of a love that is beyond our capacity to grasp it. He gave us faith in Jesus because we could never save ourselves. That is our confidence. We don't need to make any excuses. We can offer a nice little prayer: **"Israel, put your hope in the Lord both now and forevermore"** (Psalm 131:3).

A God of unlimited resources

Pastor Mark Jeske

Every Christian pastor knows of the growing plague of young people just moving in with each other without the benefit of marriage. We've heard all the rationales, justifications, excuses, and dodges. What's just as shocking is the number of older couples who are moving in with each other and sharing a bedroom. "We don't want to lose our social security and retirement benefits by marrying," they say. "We can't afford to get married."

Arrgh! Think of the message these fearful people are sending God—"We can't afford to do what you want. What you ask will impoverish us." King Amaziah of Judah really wanted to take some military action with people who had no use for the Lord. **"A man of God came to him and said, 'Your Majesty, these troops from Israel must not march with you, for the LORD is not with Israel—not with any of the people of Ephraim. Even if you go and fight courageously in battle, God will overthrow you before the enemy, for God has the power to help or to overthrow.' Amaziah asked the man of God, 'But what about the hundred talents I paid for these Israelite troops?' The man of God replied, *'The LORD can give you much more than that'"* (2 Chronicles 25:7-9).

Our God is a God of unlimited resources. When people do what is right in his eyes, he throws open the gates of heaven and pours out all they need and more.

Sacrifices for the truth

Pastor Mark Jeske

We all like to be comfortable. As the saying goes, nobody wants change except for a baby with a wet diaper. Even if we don't like our life situation, inertia keeps us static, pushing off the problem, hoping that it will get better.

But sometimes you just gotta make a change. Sometimes your environment has gotten so toxic that you fear harm to your family or to your soul. Sometimes you have to sacrifice some personal comfort or convenience or tradition to get yourself and your family closer to God.

Like the Levites who lived in the northern kingdom of Israel did when they saw that the new king, Jeroboam, was setting up a heathen and pagan state religion in their land: **"The Levites even abandoned their pasturelands and property and came to Judah and Jerusalem, because Jeroboam** [king of Israel] **and his sons had rejected them as priests of the Lord when he appointed his own priests for the high places and for the goat and calf idols he had made. Those from every tribe of Israel who set their hearts on seeking the Lord, the God of Israel, followed the Levites to Jerusalem to offer sacrifices to the Lord"** (2 Chronicles 11:14-16).

Sometimes you need to change churches when you realize that your pastor or denomination is out of sync with what you know to be scriptural truth. Maybe you need to change schools when you feel that you can no longer trust the professors.

Let Scripture and your conscience be your guides.

Choose to be patient

Pastor Mark Jeske

One of the reasons marriages fall apart is seeing too much of one's spouse. Seriously! When you're dating, you see the other person only for limited time spans. Then you go home. You only see each other when you are at your best. When you're married, you see each other all the time, and you soon figure out that your spouse has a long way to go in certain departments. Well, what do you do when those hard realizations dawn on you?

First conclusion: humility. Realize that you're not always a prize to be with. Second, your spouse is a work in progress. Cut him or her some slack. You are God's agent to help your spouse grow and develop. **"Love is patient,"** said St. Paul (1 Corinthians 13:4). It sure is. The question is, are *you* patient?

Patience means that you take the time to explain your point of view to your spouse. Patience means that you take God's view of time and play the long game. Think how long God has been working on you. You probably don't see eye to eye with your spouse on money management, rate of saving, time management, defining what is "clean enough" and what is "tidy enough."

Take the time to explain patiently what you want and expect. As you wish to be heard, so open your heart to let your spouse straighten you out on a few things—your spouse just may be God's change agent in *your* life!

Don't wait till you feel it. Go first.

Work isn't a four-letter word

Jason Nelson

A teacher, a nurse, a lender, and a welder. This isn't the punch line to a joke. These are the occupations of my children. I'm proud of the work they do. I preached often, "Any job they pay you to do is a good job." I thank God they find their jobs fulfilling and don't go thinking, "It's a dirty job."

Here is what the Feds say about Labor Day:

"Labor Day constitutes a yearly national tribute to the contributions workers have made to the strength, prosperity, and well-being of our country" (U.S. Department of Labor).

I say, "Amen, brother." I didn't fully appreciate the blessing of going to work until I couldn't do it anymore. No doubt the Great Recession renewed appreciation for a good job in many Americans. Our job titles are always much more than ways to support ourselves. They are expressions of who we are and the biggest contribution we make to our society. The reward of work is partly what we get out of it, but also in what we give through it.

Christians always have another motivation to work hard. It is our routine way of serving the Lord. It is the call of God we answer every time the alarm goes off. So, **"whatever you do, work at it with all your heart, as working for the Lord"** (Colossians 3:23).

No room for pride

Pastor Matt Ewart

"I got this."—Every guy who ever lived.

Why are guys so afraid to ask for help anyway? And it isn't just refusing help from human beings. They refuse help from sheets of instructions. Don't they know that it would be much easier and much more efficient to just ask for help every once in a while?

Females have the same flaw, but for them it takes a different form that goes something like this: "Awww, you shouldn't have." Ladies, you know you say it. But why do you say it? Here's why. When someone does something really nice for you, there's a small feeling of guilt if you didn't do something nice for them. Part of you wants to give back whatever they gave you so that things will be even.

For both men and women, the root of all this is pride. Pride refuses help from others. Pride wants things to be even.

With Jesus there is no room for pride. He taught a very important lesson when he washed the disciples' feet. He is the one who must help you. He is the one who must give you forgiveness.

With your new life in him secured, he wants the abandonment of pride to be a regular exercise in your life. While you serve others out of love for God, give others the opportunity to serve you too.

"Carry each other's burdens, and in this way you will fulfill the law of Christ" (Galatians 6:2).

Recognize your idols

Pastor Mark Jeske

The word *idol* today has a pleasant connotation. In today's lingo it means a star, a great performer, someone who can wow and dazzle a crowd, somebody who has hundreds of thousands or maybe millions of Twitter followers. Television pumps out idols by the dozens for us to fawn over and applaud.

In biblical times the term referred to an image or statue representing a heathen god or goddess. Satan made sure that the Old Testament Israelites saw much to like in the worship of deities other than the God of Abraham. The prophets' spoken and written messages for many centuries railed on the people for losing their love for the Lord and trusting in idols, which is to say, trusting in a nonexistent fantasy. Not all paths lead to heaven. Idol worship is spiritual suicide.

King David, sacred poet, knew and respected his own sometimes wandering heart. He consciously strove to get rid of his own idols and repledge himself to the Lord: **"Those who run after other gods will suffer more and more. I will not pour out libations of blood to such gods or take up their names on my lips"** (Psalm 16:4). So which idols do you chase? Where is your trust? Your own ingenuity? Quick tongue? Stock portfolio? What's on your life agenda? What excuses do you make for shorting the Lord of honorable worship time and offerings?

What do you need most in your life to make you happy?

Everybody is warped

Pastor Mark Jeske

All sin is bad. No sinners are any better than any other, but you wouldn't know that from some of our national "Christian" dialogue on the homosexual lifestyle. For some reason, this particular sin strikes some people as worse, more disgusting, more insidious than all the others. Gay people feel singled out and shunned by Christian communities, as though they were the lepers of today.

Living a gay lifestyle is indeed forbidden by God's Word. But so is living an adulterous heterosexual lifestyle and, for that matter, quite a few other life choices: **"Do you not know that wrongdoers will not inherit the kingdom of God? Do not be deceived: Neither the sexually immoral nor idolaters nor adulterers nor men who have sex with men nor thieves nor the greedy nor drunkards nor slanderers nor swindlers will inherit the kingdom of God"** (1 Corinthians 6:9,10).

Everyone is warped. Everybody is broken. All the sinners mentioned above, plus those who offend God in all the other ways that there are to sin, need God's Word, need the sharp knife of the law, need repentance, need hope, need the gospel message of God's unconditional love, need the assurance of Jesus' forgiveness, need the Spirit's new mind, need the Spirit's infusion of strength. Our church communities should be places that uphold God's high standards but also places that extend welcome and warmth to people who know they need a Savior.

No loathing, no hate, no bitterness, no selective indignation, no fear.

Where does your compass point?

Pastor Mark Jeske

If you are a fan of the movie series *Pirates of the Caribbean,* you know all about Captain Jack Sparrow's magic compass. His compass did not point to magnetic North. It pointed toward the thing your heart most wanted at the time.

How appropriate for our age, the Age of Me. People today don't want a moral compass to tell them the truth about their Creator's behavioral expectations. They want shortcuts to get them what they want. Rejecting the idea of absolute truth, people today prefer relativism, i.e., each person can work out his or her morals, values, and "truth." There is no True North anymore, only many desires and many opinions.

It is radical and countercultural that the Bible should claim to be the vehicle of absolute truth. It reveals the mysteries of human existence—where we came from, what we're doing here, and where we're going. Unlike Captain Jack's compass, it doesn't pander to whatever an individual wants it to say. It is an infallible guide to right and wrong human behaviors as well as the main power source for living a godly life: **"Your word is a lamp for my feet, a light on my path"** (Psalm 119:105).

No pirate captain ever found the fountain of youth. Arrgh! Scripture alone reveals our Savior Jesus Christ, who not only gives us the daily forgiveness of our sins that we must have but who also unlocks the gates of heaven for all who believe and grants us a drink of the Water of Life.

Cover this

Jason Nelson

The prophet Jeremiah has a reputation for being very unhappy. He was dealt a lousy hand, and his audience regularly played the victim card. But tucked in among Jeremiah's laments is a challenge for disgruntled believers to get off their backsides and act in accord with their own history. **"Stand at the crossroads and look; ask for the ancient paths, ask where the good way is, and walk in it, and you will find rest for your souls"** (Jeremiah 6:16).

Sometimes Christians gripe about the way we are portrayed in the media. We cringe every time it is reported that a psychopath committed an inexcusable crime because *God told him to do it.* And we know we bring more to the table than "moments of silence" when something bad happens. But others can only define us if we haven't clearly defined ourselves.

Rather than bicker with the press, let's invite them to cover this: Cover the historic mercy of Christians who established world class hospitals. Cover the intellect of Christians who founded great universities. Cover the adventurous spirit of Christians who discovered new worlds.

Cover the expertise of Christian teachers who are educating disadvantaged students in Christian schools. Cover the compassion of Christians who are using their church facilities to minister to people others leave on the streets. Cover the outpouring of humanitarian aid Christians are offering around the world. Cover the healing work of Christian nurses and doctors. Cover the consistent way Christians serve others in Jesus' name.

Can you believe it?

Diana Kerr

Among my friends, the same topic comes up every year around this time. The friends who are teachers bring it up the most: *Can you believe how many kids know nothing about 9/11? My students weren't even born when it happened.*

My husband's grandma says the same thing about D-Day. She mourns the fact that many in our country don't even remember what date it was. Same thing with Pearl Harbor. So many tragic, life-robbing days in our country's history quickly become distant memory.

The United States has, for the most part, moved on since 9/11. What happened on that horrific day doesn't carry the same weight and emotional pain for most of us as it did 14 years ago unless we lost someone close to us.

We can view that fact as a sign of historical indifference or ignorance, but maybe there's a positive way to view it. Maybe we can be thankful that the Great Restorer has brought healing to our nation. We can be thankful that God came beside our country in those dark days and helped us band together to initiate repair and to fight back against the pain. We can be thankful that many of our country's children have never experienced a terrorist attack with the magnitude of 9/11. Most of all, we can be thankful that God is a good God in good times and in bad: **"Though he brings grief, he will show compassion, so great is his unfailing love"** (Lamentations 3:32).

The role of rules

Pastor Matt Ewart

Every family has its own set of rules:
• Rules that dictate proper behavior.
• Rules that govern the use of electronics.
• Rules that establish a general daily schedule.

Each family is a little bit different, but every family has rules.

Here's a silly question: *How long did you have to keep the rules before you were brought into your family?*

You know that the role of rules is not to bring people *into* a family. Rules indicate you are already *in* the family, and they provide a baseline for showing respect to everyone in the house.

Here is the same question but on a spiritual level: *How long did you have to keep God's rules before you were brought into his family?*

Well, that's not what his rules are for either. His rules were not designed to bring people in. Before God gave a single commandment to the Israelites, he established the basis for his relationship with them: **"I am the Lord your God, who brought you out of Egypt, out of the land of slavery. You shall have no other gods before me"** (Exodus 20:2,3).

God puts his act of redemption before mentioning a single rule because rules don't bring you into God's family. Only Jesus does.

The Son's obedience and the Spirit's adoption sealed your place with God. The rules remind you that you are there by grace, and they provide guidance for showing love to everyone in the house.

Teach your kids how to be happily married

Pastor Mark Jeske

I do not have good news. The perception of the value of marriage is on the decline in our country. Even when they weary of casual hookups, young adults today are much more likely just to move in with each other. Just in my lifetime the average age of marriage has climbed from 22 to 28.

But I also bear good news. There is a growing body of research to show that getting married and staying married is a powerful wealth builder. Children in an intact marriage show huge social and educational advantages over children of single parent homes. Marriage provides the only God-approved way to have a sex life.

So how do you have such a great home life that your kids will joyfully look forward to getting married? Here's a powerful principle: **"Husbands, in the same way be considerate as you live with your wives, and treat them with respect"** (1 Peter 3:7). Husbands, family leadership means you go first in studying your wife and attuning yourself to her needs. Husbands, you may crave respect, but leadership means that you go first in showing it. One of your most important jobs is creating a home culture where your wife feels precious, important, of great worth in your eyes. Christian fathers and mothers need to model affirming behaviors, not just to make their own lives better but also because they are being watched.

The best marriage teaching is shown, not preached.

All is well

Jason Nelson

There are things that go *bump* in the night that disturb our sleep. There are things that go *bump* in the daytime that disrupt our plans. There are things that go *bump* in our immune systems that weaken our health. There are things that go *bump* through our connected devices that cause slowdowns and flash crashes. We need to watch out for all the things that go *bump*.

There is so much we can't see coming. Darkness provides cover for evildoers. A lack of visibility into our own bodies and equipment hides weaknesses that could cause a breakdown. So we depend on others to watch over us, and others depend on us to watch over them. God assigns vigilant people to do different kinds of watching. They *de-bump* things before they cause harm. **"I have posted watchmen on your walls, Jerusalem; they will never be silent day or night. You who call on the Lord, give yourselves no rest"** (Isaiah 62:6).

Brave public servants answer alarms at all hours and rush in when angels step aside. They may not even realize they are God's watchmen. Emergency rooms are staffed with people who are always ready. Someone is always watching a radar screen somewhere. The list goes on. And there are dedicated watchmen who keep an eye on God's promises. They pray over us and call out his name to us so that when things go *bump* in our souls, we can rest assured that all is well.

Teach your kids to choose friends carefully

Pastor Mark Jeske

Parents like to think that their children's growth and education come primarily from their teachers at school. Would that 'twere so. Our kids' education is derived to an astonishing extent from their peers, from the people they hang out with. Each year you will have less and less influence on the people they choose as their friends. Each year you will be less and less aware of the conversations and culture that they are part of.

It is important that you have the "friends" talk with them early in life. **"Walk with the wise and become wise, for a companion of fools suffers harm"** (Proverbs 13:20). Some young people despise education. They can become a boat anchor to your kids. Some despise their parents or truth telling or the law or the Christian faith. They take foolish risks; they love danger; they breathe rebellion. There have always been plenty of people like that—the book of Proverbs calls them "fools."

Try to create a culture in your home where your kids are comfortable bringing their friends over (so that you can have a look at them and listen to them talk). Don't let your kids be evasive or mumbly about who they're hanging out with or where they are going. Show an interest. Ask questions. Watch for behavioral changes. Stop grumbling about being their personal taxi driver and welcome those times when you're in the car with them.

Make them take out their earbuds and actually talk with you.

Our streets are so violent

Pastor Mark Jeske

The human race just can't get over having been expelled from Paradise. We just cannot shake the illusion that there should be heaven on earth. Ever since our first parents decided that Satan's way of life sounded exciting, we, their descendants, have to live in Satan's war zone.

One of its trademarks is human cruelty and violence. The "good old days" in biblical times were not always so good: **"Lord, confuse the wicked, confound their words, for I see violence and strife in the city. Day and night they prowl about on its walls; malice and abuse are within it. Destructive forces are at work in the city; threats and lies never leave its streets"** (Psalm 55:9-11). Sound familiar? There is plenty of evil in small towns and leafy suburbs, but cities are huge concentrations of humanity, and the very scale attracts and intensifies people who decide to enrich themselves by preying on others. What to do?

For one, give up the illusion that there can be heaven on earth. Crime and violence are not aberrations. They are "normal" in a world where the prince of darkness still wields so much power and influence. Second, it is the work of Jesus to create countercultural communities (a.k.a., churches) that show unconditional love for people and can tend to the wounded. Third, pray continually that our Lord would restrain Satan and those who do his violent and evil work. Deliver us from evil indeed!

As your time comes to leave this earth behind, let go without regret.

Make a plan

Pastor Matt Ewart

Do you wish you were more generous? Sure you do—who doesn't? *How* to become more generous is the question.

You might think that more money would make you more generous. That sounds good at first, but between the lines you are actually blaming God for your lack of generosity: until he gives you more money, you can't be generous.

Since blaming God never seems to end well, let's think through this a different way. God's greatest act of generosity did not require money. It required a plan and a sacrifice. Might the model of generosity he wants you to follow be similar?

Make a plan. Throw away the list of everything God *hasn't* given you and replace it with an inventory of what he *has* given you. Then the first thing you do is decide how much to give back to him through an offering.

So how much should you give? That's a fair question, but there's actually a better one that you can ask. It might scare you, but it goes like this: How much money do you have to sacrifice before you are forced to trust God with what's left?

"Each of you should give what you have decided in your heart to give, not reluctantly or under compulsion, for God loves a cheerful giver" (2 Corinthians 9:7).

Having a plan insulates you from giving reluctantly or out of compulsion. A plan that includes sacrificial giving moves you to trust in God every day. Generous people don't make more money. They make a plan.

Worship is praising

Pastor Mark Jeske

What is worship?

Okay, I suppose that sounds like a dumb question. It's what we do in church, plus a little bit at home and privately, isn't it? Most of us have "worship habits" grooved pretty deeply in our lives, so we don't think about it much anymore. It's possible to keep repeating familiar and comfortable phrases and songs by rote. But what is worship really?

Worship is how we express our relationship with our God. It is our joyful, grateful, appreciative response to God's great person and astonishing works: **"Sing to him, sing praise to him; tell of all his wonderful acts"** (1 Chronicles 16:9). Worship is praise—publicly acknowledging God's greatness, shining your personal spotlight on God, using speech and music to extol and exalt (i.e., lift him up high in our lives).

You can't give God any more glory than he has already—how could your little voice add anything to the vast chorus of praises of the heavenly host? You can't make God any more glorious than he is already—his light fills the heavens as he reigns in majesty over all. But in our little hearts, often clogged with other idols, he is not always supreme. Only we ourselves can lift him up in our own lives. He thought you important enough to send his Son, his dearest treasure, to win you back. Think of him as important enough to give him the praise he deserves.

Start now.

Choose to praise

Pastor Mark Jeske

When I was a teenager, it seemed to me that everybody else pretty much had it going on and I was on the outside looking in. Only much later in life did it dawn on me that everybody else was struggling just as much as I was. They were just better at pretending self-confidence.

People are cruel. Children are cruel. Teenagers can be especially cruel. They are masters of mockery, cliques, exclusion, castes, boasting, gossip, and sarcasm. All these things just cover for their own inner fears and depression.

Do these teen dysfunctions sound like your adult world? Rise above it and shock people by being different. Let your Jesus show and change the culture. Choose to praise instead of belittle: **"We who are strong ought to bear with the failings of the weak and not to please ourselves. Each of us should please our neighbors for their good, to build them up"** (Romans 15:1,2). Anyone can mock somebody else. It takes a Christian to look for good in people and praise them out loud.

People are starving for affirmation. Most people I know are running on fumes, burdened with health problems, money stress, family troubles, and self-doubt. Looking for things to praise in other people *costs you nothing* and might lift someone out of a huge hole. Tomorrow pick one person just because and choose to praise him or her.

Don't wait till you feel it. Go first.

Just a spoonful

Pastor Matt Ewart

You know those big spoons that are in your kitchen silverware drawer? I'm not talking about the soup spoons. I'm talking about the BIG serving spoons. On a few occasions, I've had to use the big spoon to eat cereal because all the other spoons were dirty. With the big spoon you can't help but deliver generous amounts of food to your mouth.

What size spoon do you use to deliver forgiveness to other people? Peter thought he was being generous when he said this to Jesus: **"Lord, how many times shall I forgive my brother or sister who sins against me? Up to seven times?"** (Matthew 18:21).

He grabbed the BIG spoon right away. Seven is a pretty generous number . . . **"Jesus answered, 'I tell you, not seven times, but seventy-seven times'"** (Matthew 18:22). . . . Or not.

We tend to think that setting a high limit on the forgiveness we dish out is the right thing to do. We think of forgiveness in terms of the big spoon. But we shouldn't.

God set no limit on the forgiveness he gives to us. He doesn't administer grace with a spoon, but with a shovel. Every day you need loads of grace and forgiveness from God.

Someone in your life needs more forgiveness from you than can fit on a spoon. You know because you've tried. So forget about the spoon. Break out the shovel and forgive them just as God forgave you.

Rise of the nones

Pastor Mark Jeske

I am of the Baby Boomer generation. We have much to be proud of, but much also of which to be ashamed. Our parents believed in institutions—they were joiners. We were rebels and were skeptical about institutions. We began the drift away from church. Our children, the Millennials, have adopted our ideas with a vengeance. According to social researchers, one-third of the Millennial generation has left the church and may never come back. The most rapidly growing religious preference in America today is "none."

Some of that is the church's own fault. We are slow, too slow, to adapt to people, preferring instead to make people conform to our traditions. We are too wired for institutional preservation and not enough about meeting people where they are. But much of this phenomenon is simply Satan's work. And while church skeptics and skippers may feel smug about sleeping in on Sunday and dawdling over a late brunch, cutting yourself off from Word and the Lord's Supper is ultimately spiritual suicide: **"'I gave you empty stomachs in every city and lack of bread in every town, yet you have not returned to me,' declares the Lord. 'Therefore this is what I will do to you, Israel, and because I will do this to you, Israel, prepare to meet your God'"** (Amos 4:6,12).

Let's listen to the new generations. Let's learn from them. And let's love them enough to tell the urgent story of Christ in terms that make sense to them.

Teach your kids how to worship

Pastor Mark Jeske

One of the most sickening experiences Christian parents undergo is the realization that your young adult kids don't want to go to church anymore. What fear, what hurt, what guilt washes over you! Where did I go wrong? What did I fail to do? What's wrong with them?

Age 18 is too late to start cultivating a love for worship. It starts 18 years before that. It starts with a plan for a worship life in your home—thoughtful shared meal prayers, family Bible stories around the table, singing, interactive intercessory prayer, and bedtime devotions. It starts with a joyful Sunday attitude by the parents and an intentional plan to explain worship forms to kids. It continues with involving older children in age-appropriate church activities, just like a Passover festival long ago: **"Every year Jesus' parents went to Jerusalem for the Festival of the Passover. When he was twelve years old, they went up to the festival, according to the custom"** (Luke 2:41,42).

Kids need God in their lives too. They need his forgiveness, guidance from his Word, a value system to armor their minds and hearts against the evil one, a listening ear for their prayers, and a high view of the worth of their lives to live up to. They need Christian friends in their lives who will reinforce, not ridicule, their faith.

Most of all they need to see how much your faith matters to you, how you talk it and live it.

God works; we work

Pastor Mark Jeske

What causes things to happen?

Does that sound like a dumb question? Seriously—has God ordained everything and we are just going through the motions, or is he just watching as *we* act out human history? How do you fit into the scheme of the universe? Are your deeds your free choice, or is God controlling everything? Do you have marionette strings attached to your hands and feet? Or are you on your own?

The answer is yes to all of the above. There is a double causality to everything that happens, and we do not have the vantage point or ability to navigate time and eternity to keep them apart. Both God and we interact in earth's history. Here's an example: **"When the Arameans of Damascus came to help Hadadezer king of Zobah, David struck down twenty-two thousand of them. He put garrisons in the Aramean kingdom of Damascus, and the Arameans became subject to him and brought him tribute. The Lord gave David victory wherever he went"** (1 Chronicles 18:5,6).

So—did David win the victory or did God win the victory? The answer is yes. David's courage and military skill and God's sovereign will and almighty power were all at work. Can you abide this paradox? God is at work in your life, leading and guiding and protecting and nudging and compelling. You are an independent agent in your life. Your words and deeds matter. Your choices have real consequences.

God works. We work.

Have some peace when it makes no sense

Jason Nelson

I'm starting to get how this blessing works: **"The peace of God, which transcends all understanding, will guard your hearts and your minds in Christ Jesus"** (Philippians 4:7). Because I'm a Christian, I've been expecting some peace. But I still have trouble sleeping. I still don't have everything done. I'm still concerned about so much violence in our world. I still bounce my foot up and down constantly. But I see this blessing isn't about the peace of Jason. It's about the peace of God. It's about God remaining perfectly calm as he deals with things that cause our innards to roil because they are out of our control. The apostle could have said, *"Here you go. Have some peace when it makes no sense."*

God never gets rattled. He is *Jehovah Adonai.* He has always been here and always will be. He has seen it all, sees what's coming, and is unmatched in directing how it will play out. Even when hell breaks loose, he doesn't get rattled. He is *El Shaddai.* He shatters satanic revolts against his authority with his power. He is the wonderful Counselor, mighty God, everlasting Father, and the Prince of *shalom.* Nobody gives peace like he does. No matter what, he guards our hearts and minds through faith in Jesus Christ. Because God says, **"I AM WHO I AM"** (Exodus 3:14), we can have some peace when it is what it is.

Having hope

Pastor Matt Ewart

Job suffered in a way that I can't imagine.

He lost everything in a matter of minutes. His livestock. His livelihood. His house. His family. Everything was gone. Then he lost his health as painful boils covered his body.

When Job's friends looked at the method and timing of his misfortune, they determined that Job did something so evil that God had to immediately bring down violent judgment on him.

Job knew better. He knew that God was not punishing him for something, but at the same time, he couldn't prove it. In that moment, Job said this: "[God] **is not a mere mortal like me that I might answer him, that we might confront each other in court. If only there were someone to mediate between us, someone to bring us together"** (Job 9:32,33).

In those words, Job expressed an expectant hope that yearned to be fulfilled.

He hoped for one who could bridge the gap between himself and God. He hoped for one who could prove that God was not punishing him. He hoped for one who could vouch for him while representing the interests of God.

The One Job hoped for has come. His name is Jesus Christ.

Jesus' empty tomb is evidence that the punishment for your sin was paid in full on the cross. God already inflicted punishment for your sin once, and he will not do it again. Jesus now sits in heaven to guarantee the work he did for you. You have what Job hoped for.

September 26

Oh, grow up!

Pastor Mark Jeske

Don't you hate it when your kids *settle*? Know what I mean . . . when they settle for Cs when they could get As . . . when they settle for second team when they could start . . . when they stay a peon at work when they could be a manager?

How do you suppose God feels? He has provided a great wealth of spiritual information in the Bible to help us understand the great arc of human history and the bright thread of his plan of salvation weaving through it all. He has revealed deep secrets of what is going on behind the scenes, of spiritual warfare, of angels and demons. He has given peeks into life in heaven and the very throne room of God. He has laid out a life plan for every one of his believers. *And then they don't even read it!*

The Hebrew Christians got a spanking from one of the apostles for settling, for staying spiritual babies when God had prepared them for so much more: **"We have much to say about this, but it is hard to make it clear to you because you no longer try to understand. In fact, though by this time you ought to be teachers, you need someone to teach you the elementary truths of God's word all over again"** (Hebrews 5:11,12).

Are you hungry for the Word? Do you pursue its knowledge? Are you just riding on the wagon pulled by someone else or are you eager to be useful to God's agenda? Would the angels call you a spiritual baby or spiritual grown-up?

Chariots of fire

Pastor Mark Jeske

Gehazi, servant to the prophet Elisha, had no difficulty seeing his problems. Ben-Hadad II, the evil king of Aram, had sent an entire company of infantry with chariot support to surround the town of Dothan and seize Elisha, whom he blamed for passing military secrets.

As Gehazi looked out early that morning, he must have assumed that it would be the day of his death. **"'Oh no, my lord! What shall we do?' the servant asked. 'Don't be afraid,' the prophet answered. 'Those who are with us are more than those who are with them.' And Elisha prayed, 'Open his eyes, Lord, so that he may see.' Then the Lord opened the servant's eyes, and he looked and saw the hills full of horses and chariots of fire all around Elisha"** (2 Kings 6:15-17).

Classic military strategy is to isolate and overwhelm the enemy with vastly superior numbers. Satan and his demons knew that strategy long before military textbooks were written. He whispers to us that we are alone and friendless, that no one must know of all our problems and failures, that resistance is futile, that his forces rule the universe, and that no one will ever come to help.

In fact, those who are with us are more than those who are with them. Your faith in Christ connects you to the might, wisdom, and compassion of the Almighty God himself. You cannot see the legions of angels at work for you behind the scenes.

But Satan can.

On God's side

Linda Buxa

During the Civil War, one of President Lincoln's advisors said he was grateful God was on the Union's side. Lincoln told him, "Sir, my concern is not whether God is on our side; my greatest concern is to be on God's side, for God is always right."

Joshua, the leader of the Israelite army, was about to battle Jericho, and he fell into the same trap as Lincoln's advisor. **"He looked up and saw a man standing in front of him with a drawn sword in his hand. Joshua went up to him and asked, 'Are you for us or for our enemies?' 'Neither,' he replied, 'but as commander of the army of the Lord I have now come.' Then Joshua fell facedown to the ground in reverence, and asked him, 'What message does my Lord have for his servant?'"** (Joshua 5:13,14).

We could use the same reality check. Sometimes we're surprised that our plans just don't seem to be working out for us. "Why isn't God blessing me the way I thought he would?" Maybe it's because we made our decisions all wrong. We came up with our plans without consulting God—and yet we still expected him to fall in line with our ideas.

It goes a whole lot better for us when we first fall facedown and ask, "What message do you have for me?" That's when his goals become our goals and our plans and priorities become a whole lot clearer.

Make it your greatest concern to be on God's side, for God is always right.

Sins of the sons

Jason Nelson

I know about pain that doesn't go away. I wrote a book about it. I'm writing about it again, but not because of my miserable back. This is about the pain of having a child with pain that doesn't go away.

I have a son suffering from mental illness, homelessness, addictions, and legal trouble. I have overreacted, underreacted, and not reacted at all. I facilitated court orders and devoted energy and resources to treatment for him with no lasting benefit. Doctors and police officers have told me they are seeing this more and more in young men. I'm telling you because I know I'm not alone.

I can't describe the burden of sadness and responsibility I feel. I'm a Christian father. And I thought going to church and a Christian upbringing would inoculate my children from such consequences of sin. But, mental illness is in our family history. That was a risk factor for my son. He made it six times worse through alcohol and drug abuse. People have assured me that the sins of the sons may have nothing to do with the sins of the fathers. But that is not consoling.

My prayers are insistent: *"Lord, you made your own promises to my son at his baptism and many times since. Please preserve the shred of faith he still has, and keep this one."* **"Start children off on the way they should go, and even when they are old they will not turn from it"** (Proverbs 22:6). I ask for your prayers as well.

Look in the windshield, not the rearview

Pastor Mark Jeske

Is a sharp memory good? Depends. It's good when you remember names, birthdays, anniversaries, appointments, and promises. It's bad when you remember past slights, insults, failures, injuries, mistakes, faux pas, other people's faults, and every embarrassing and humiliating thing that's ever happened to you.

Even worse than remembering those negative things is stressing over them, obsessing over them, fuming over them, hating on yourself over them, consumed in ancient resentments, trapped in an endless memory loop in which you are the fool.

It's time to let go of your pain memories. They don't define you. In Christ you are a new creation every day. Washed by his grace, honored with a new identity, loved by your Father, empowered by the Spirit, you can choose your self-image. You are walking toward an endless future in heaven; you are Satan's slave no more: **"Not that I have already obtained all this, or have already arrived at my goal, but I press on to take hold of that for which Christ Jesus took hold of me. Brothers and sisters, I do not consider myself yet to have taken hold of it. But one thing I do: Forgetting what is behind and straining toward what is ahead, I press on toward the goal to win the prize for which God has called me heavenward in Christ Jesus"** (Philippians 3:12-14).

Take out the trash and leave it out there. Look in the windshield, not the rearview.

october

"He gives strength to the weary and increases
the power of the weak."

Isaiah 40:29

Angels: God's messengers

Pastor Mark Jeske

It is our joy (and burden) to live in an age of multiple means of communication. You can get your thoughts to another person through speech, handwritten note, snail mail, e-mail, tweet, social media, text, and phone call.

It pleases God to reveal information to people in quite a variety of ways as well—the spoken word directly, prophet spokesmen and women, dreams, and written text. Once he had a miraculous, mysterious hand write a message on a wall. He also liked to use angels on really significant occasions. In fact, that's what their name means—the Greek word from which *angel* comes from (*ággelos*) means "messenger."

The very first words spoken as the New Testament era dawned were from one of these heavenly messengers to a priest on duty in the temple: **"Then an angel of the Lord appeared to him, standing at the right side of the altar of incense. When Zechariah saw him, he was startled and was gripped with fear. But the angel said to him: 'Do not be afraid, Zechariah; your prayer has been heard. Your wife Elizabeth will bear you a son, and you are to call him John'"** (Luke 1:11-13). That special son would be charged with nothing less than the ministry of preparing the entire world for the coming of the Savior in human flesh.

Pay attention to these angelic visitors. Their words are for you too.

Angels: God's child protectors

Pastor Mark Jeske

Some of the sweetest religious art depicts winged angels hovering over children walking or sleeping in their little beds. Those images are not just pious fiction or romantic projections, as it were, from the imaginations of anxious parents. They represent an important truth about God's care for little ones whom he thinks belong to him too. When our children were baptized, God put his claim on them and assumed the responsibility and obligations of Fatherhood.

Angels do God's bidding for the care and protection of all his believers. But they have a special role in the lives of children (a role that we would love to know a lot more about). Jesus just hinted at this mighty comfort for every believing parent: **"See that you do not despise one of these little ones. For I tell you that their angels in heaven always see the face of my Father in heaven"** (Matthew 18:10). Although Jesus' main point was for grown-ups to treat children with respect, sharp-eyed parents quickly spot an important word in Jesus' remark. That word is *their*. Yes, our kids apparently have their own protecting angels.

How wonderful of Jesus to show that we have help in our parenting. The world is full of dangers that threaten us all but especially our little ones—disease, injury, violent people, Satan, and death stalk children too. How good it is to know that their own angels have to appear before God personally for reporting and instructions.

Angels: God's bailiffs

Pastor Mark Jeske

Judgment day will be a very busy time for God's holy angels.

Half of them will be appointed to serve as God's bailiffs, arresting and arraigning unbelievers to stand trial in God's solemn final court proceedings. Jesus gave an earnest warning to all who had ears to hear that on the last great day you can run but you can't hide from these swift heavenly agents: **"As the weeds are pulled up and burned in the fire, so it will be at the end of the age. The Son of Man will send out his angels, and they will weed out of his kingdom everything that causes sin and all who do evil. They will throw them into the blazing furnace, where there will be weeping and gnashing of teeth"** (Matthew 13:40-42).

Weeping and gnashing of teeth indeed. Can you imagine the regrets of all the people who had no time for God during their lifetimes and now realize their terrible mistake? Can you imagine their terror as angels come for them, not gentle and sweet but menacing and inexorable? Can you imagine the endless loop running in their brains of "coulda, shoulda, woulda"?

It is our sacred duty as individuals and as congregation members to present the message of our Savior as clearly and as winsomely as possible. We can't predict what people will do with the gospel of Christ, but we can tell the story and let the Word do its work.

The blazing furnace of hell is real.

Angels: God's limos

Pastor Mark Jeske

What's the best ride you ever had? A big touring motorcycle? Luxury coach? Hot air balloon? Wedding party bus? Stretch limo? First-class cabin on a big plane? Nothing you have ever experienced before will compare to the ride you will get from God's angel limos.

When a believer dies, Jesus says that the angels will carry the soul straight to heaven: **"The time came when the beggar died and the angels carried him to Abraham's side"** (Luke 16:22). And then when judgment day comes, while some flee in terror, the believers will look up longingly and welcome their angelic escorts. We will be **"caught up . . . in the clouds to meet the Lord in the air"** (1 Thessalonians 4:17). What a thrill!

These angels will enjoy their work. They are rooting for us—they rejoice over even one sinner who repents. Although their speed and power make them seem like our bosses, in fact they were made to be ministering spirits, serving God by serving the people God made. How wonderful it will be when we can finally see them, learn their names, and thank them for their millennia of work on behalf of the human race. The stories they will be able to tell!

For now they toil on, invisible to us, battling the evil one and his legions of demons. Soon, soon, comes the Day. Lift up your heads in the confidence of Christ and be ready.

One way

Sarah Habben

"There couldn't possibly be just one way to God. There are billions of people in the world!"

"What about Jesus?"

"What *about* Jesus?"

So went a 2008 interview with Oprah, who feels every religion beats a path to the same bliss. Heaven is for anyone who lives with love and generosity. Jesus is optional.

But Oprah doesn't get to make the rules for heaven. God has his own rules for reaching his heaven—Option A: through Jesus. Option B: be perfect.

Heaven is accessible if we show *perfect* love and generosity toward *every* person (telemarketers and tailgaters included), in *every* thought, at *every* moment.

Are you perfect? Me neither.

I can't earn heaven by my own innocence. But what about Jesus? As a man who is also God, he lived under God's law without ever sinning.

I can't pay for my own sins, let alone someone else's. What about Jesus? As God who is also man, Jesus' holy death paid for the sins of all people of all time. His resurrection is proof of that.

I can't reach heaven by following the Way of Good Deeds. That just puts me on a collision course with Satan and hell because I'm not good enough. What about Jesus? He says, **"I am the way and the truth and the life. No one comes to the Father except through me"** (John 14:6).

Billions of people. Billions of lifestyles. Billions of ways to hell. Only one way to God and eternal life in heaven.

Option A: *through Jesus.*

We've never stopped dating

Jason Nelson

My wife and I had a milestone wedding anniversary. It's one that makes you wonder how you made it this long. There has been the better and worse, sickness and health that seemed unlikely when we made the promise to endure it all together. There has been the grit and grind of building a long life together. How did we make it this long? I think it's because we never stopped going on dates. We got married, but we never stopped dating. My pick-up line still needs work, but our dates usually begin when I ask, "So what do you want to do today, Dear?" And she usually responds with a sigh, "I dunno." Then we decide to do something jazzy like grocery shopping. But it's fun because we are doing it together. And we have learned how to make it an event.

God's brilliant **"one flesh"** (Mark 10:8) concept of marriage entails much more than fitting complementary body parts together so you can make love and babies. It implies a preference for each other over any available option for any possible activity. I hope we never stop dating. Other companions are good to be with. There are nice people available to my wife who like to shop more than I do. And there are nice people available to me who might like to sightsee more than she does. But she gets in the car for a drive, and I push the cart because in our bones we want to be with each other more than anybody else.

The best part of heaven

Linda Buxa

"Jesus answered him, 'Truly I tell you, today you will be with me in paradise'" (Luke 23:43).

My kids and I often talk about heaven. It started with my girls when they were toddlers. When little girls in princess costumes hear that there are streets of gold and lots of gems, well, heaven sounds pretty great. As they got a little older, their idea of perfection involved wondering if they could eat all kinds of candy and not get sick. Other times they'd have a rough day at school and just wanted to be in heaven. (We get that, right? Imperfect relationships on earth are hard!) My son is fascinated by thinking about sports in heaven. My daughter loves to declare which people she hopes will be in the rooms next to her. Adults do this too. The first thing people say after Grandpa dies is that he gets to see Grandma now.

All of our conjuring glosses over the best part. In heaven we will be physically reunited with Jesus—the transfigured Jesus who Peter, James, and John got to see on earth while he talked with Moses and Elijah. He is the Lord of the universe, sitting at the right hand of God and interceding for us.

So we keep talking to the kids about heaven, but our conversations will start with celebrating that we get to be with Jesus, God's Son. Because, ultimately, no matter what the other side benefits are, the best part of heaven is that we'll be with Jesus in paradise.

Safe in God's hands

Linda Buxa

We live in a near-constant state of panic for kids' safety. Some schools have banned kids from playing tag, and all balls have to be made of foam. Others won't let kids walk home from school until they are in middle school. It seems we no longer let our children play, take risks, or explore life without adequate adult supervision.

It's almost as if we believe that to be a good parent you must always be in control, manage every situation for your children, and never allow them to feel pain or adversity. Really, though, this makes us slaves to fear, which means we have forgotten God's promises. We forget that he knows the plans he has for our children, that he is the one who carries lambs in his arms, that he loves them more than we do.

True, God's love isn't some magic bubble; it doesn't make children emergency-room-visit proof. They will get stitches, break bones, and get sick. They will have their hearts broken.

That's when we remind ourselves that God's love gives us the right to go to him with our fears—and leave them with him. **"Do not be anxious about anything, but in every situation, by prayer and petition, with thanksgiving, present your requests to God. And the peace of God, which transcends all understanding, will guard your hearts and your minds in Christ Jesus"** (Philippians 4:6-8).

You go first

Jason Nelson

An important safety tip for early season ice fishing is to politely tell your fishing buddy, "You can go first. I'll be right behind you." Then if you fumble a bit with your equipment, you can buy some time and keep an eye on him as he heads out on the ice. Soon enough you will know if it is safe to follow.

Everything about our lives is venturing out on thin ice. The ice is treacherous. There is always the risk of breaking through and going down, way down. I guess we could just stay off the ice. Or we can follow the One who has tested what lies ahead and knows where it's safe. If I can mess up my metaphor, where us sheep may safely graze.

Our heavenly Father saw from above that the ice was really thin.

He spoke to his beloved Son:
"'Tis time to have compassion.
Then go, bright Jewel of my crown,
And bring to mankind salvation.
From sin and sorrow set him free;
Slay bitter death for them that they
May live with you forever."—Martin Luther

God said to Jesus, "You go first." Jesus obeyed his Father's will. He was born of a virgin mother and came to be our brother. In his everyday, perfect life; substitutionary death; and victory-sharing resurrection, Jesus went first. We call after him, "Wait up! Savior, we follow on, guided by you."

Too much? Too little?

Pastor Mark Jeske

Everybody would like to strike it rich. From the gold fevers of the mid-1800s to today's sophisticated investors like arbitrageurs of Wall Street, from the tulip investors in Holland in 1637 to Carlo Ponzi in the 1920s to real estate speculators in 2006, people have dreamt and grasped and cheated and prayed for wealth.

Not Agur, son of Jakeh, author of the marvelous 30th chapter of Proverbs. In fact, he prayed to God to keep him not only from poverty (understandable) *but also from becoming wealthy.* Seriously! **"I ask of you, Lord . . . give me neither poverty nor riches, but give me only my daily bread. Otherwise, I may have too much and disown you and say, 'Who is the Lord?' Or I may become poor and steal, and so dishonor the name of my God"** (Proverbs 30:7-9).

Wise words. Agur realized that desperate people sometimes throw away their morals to survive. He feared that kind of desperation. But he was also insightful enough to know that money has a terribly corrupting power that is potentially just as destructive of your morals. In practical terms, he was inviting God to send some investment and business setbacks periodically so that he would not accumulate so much money that it would go to his head. He wanted both to love God and need God.

What is your personal financial level right now? Are you struggling and broke? risking idolatry with significant financial resources? Or like a spiritual Goldilocks, right in the Agur sweet spot?

The smell of Jesus

Sarah Habben

I remember a time I walked into my high school dorm room with a greasy bag of leftover French fries. My roommate—fresh off a shift at McDonalds—just about gagged. But the same smell drew hungry, hopeful friends from halfway down the hall.

Believers who "smell" like their Savior get a mixed reaction too. To some, we stink. To others, we couldn't smell sweeter. **"We are to God the pleasing aroma of Christ among those who are being saved and those who are perishing. To the one we are an aroma that brings death; to the other, an aroma that brings life"** (2 Corinthians 2:15,16).

When I share the truth that Christ is the only way to heaven, I cause a division. A few are drawn to the cross like hungry kids to a bag of fries. But many more wrinkle their noses in disgust. And that is hard. I sometimes feel lonely in the shadow of the cross. I am sometimes tempted to water down my witness so as not to offend.

That's when I need to unwrap God's Word. To soak up the aroma of Christ that rises from its pages. To lick the plate of his delicious promises. To be so delighted by the meal that I must share it with others.

The smell of French fries can fill a hallway. We believers can fill our homes and schools and cities with the smell of Jesus—the aroma of life everlasting.

Simple. Powerful.

Sarah Habben

Should I do it now? Is now the right moment to share my faith? No . . . I'm so bad at explaining things. She'd probably take offense. Or worse, she'd scoff.

Have those thoughts ever flashed through your head during that suspended moment after an unchurched friend vents about some mess in her life?

Perhaps, like me, you've chosen to murmur words that steer clear of anything too theological, afraid that you lack the wisdom and eloquence to do your faith justice.

The apostle Paul wants to convince us otherwise. The philosophers of his time delighted in clever oratory. Paul, however, spoke the simple message of the cross: **"For Christ** [sent me] **to preach the gospel—*not* with wisdom and eloquence, lest the cross of Christ be emptied of its power"** (1 Corinthians 1:17).

Paul knew it wasn't his cunning choice of words that would bring anyone to faith. It wasn't *his* words at all. It was the work of the Spirit in the message of the cross.

It's a simple message, but it's packed with the power to quell fear, anger, and grief. It's the message that Jesus is the Son of God. He knows the sin that crouches in every heart, wounding every life. And so he chose to be born as a human baby, to live perfectly in our place, to pay for our sins with his life, to rise again and rule on our behalf.

Now is the time. Fill that silence. Speak of Christ's cross. It's simply powerful.

Stripping away pretense

Jason Nelson

That tearing sound you hear is God stripping away pretense. He allows only so many layers to build up before he rips them off our politics, our piety, and our personas like grimy old bandages. It hurts when God strips away pretense because we have to look at our own delusions and rev up our consciences to leave the gravitational force of groupthink. God strips away pretense so we can be wise and recognize that the truth is staring back at us. **"Wisdom is directly in front of an understanding person, but the eyes of a fool are looking around all over the world"** (Proverbs 17:24 GW).

Pretenders double down on lies. Fallacies become a twisted orthodoxy reinforced with predictable rhetoric and sketchy logic. But God's Word clears things up for us, and its truth is as plain as the nose on our face. We can stop pretending and trust his wisdom.

God gives us the wisdom to accept Jesus as our Lord and Savior. Where two or three are gathered in his name, he is in the midst of them. Where more than two or three are gathered for some other reason, there is going to be some pretending going on. It is not our responsibility to unmask every pretender. It is our duty to recognize pretense in our own lives and confess it before God. And it is our calling to be honest brokers of the light and truth that will never fade away.

Your bucket list

Linda Buxa

Do you have a bucket list? My kiddos make one each summer, and we complete about 75 percent of it. Not bad, considering we have diverse personalities and interests. We watch movies, paint faces, have water fights, and go to the beach. Most grown-ups set their sights higher: swim with dolphins, visit European cathedrals, see the majesty of Alaska.

God has a bucket list for his family members to do on this earth too.

"Now we ask you, brothers and sisters, to <u>acknowledge those who work hard among you</u>, who care for you in the Lord and who admonish you. <u>Hold them in the highest regard</u> in love because of their work. <u>Live in peace</u> with each other. And we urge you, brothers and sisters, <u>warn those who are idle and disruptive</u>, <u>encourage the disheartened</u>, <u>help the weak</u>, <u>be patient with everyone</u>. Make sure that <u>nobody pays back wrong for wrong</u>, but always <u>strive to do what is good for each other</u> and for everyone else. <u>Rejoice always</u>, <u>pray continually</u>, <u>give thanks in all circumstances</u>; for this is God's will for you in Christ Jesus. <u>Do not quench the Spirit</u>. <u>Do not treat prophecies with contempt</u> but test them all; <u>hold on to what is good</u>, <u>reject every kind of evil</u>" (1 Thessalonians 5:12-22).

Thanks to the God of peace who sanctifies you, you can complete 100 percent of these!

Lift us up

Jason Nelson

The mark of good coaches is that their teams get better the more coaching they do. Not perfect, just better. They see potential in each player and *coach 'em up* to get better individual performance and good team results. Effective parents, pastors, instructors, directors, managers, and other shepherding types have the same knack for upping people's game through the way they interact with them. They know that everything they do has the potential to elevate admirers whose silent plea is "please say or do something to lift us up."

That yearning is in all of us whose existences are typically inclined to the downside. We want our children to leave home in the morning happier than when they came in the night before. I want my wife to wake up and look at me with a smile. I wanted my students to walk out of every class feeling better than when they walked in. I want to leave church more hopeful than when I rolled up because I encountered an uplifting God in Word, sacrament, and song. And I want you to be more devoted to him by the end of this little reflection than you were a dozen lines ago.

Jesus lifts us up. There is a powerful updraft that flows out of his Word, his work, and his presence in our lives. Playing for him **will renew our strength so we can soar on wings like eagles, run and not grow weary, walk and not be faint** (Isaiah 40:31).

What does God want of you?

Pastor Mark Jeske

Remember the old WWJD rubber bracelets that people used to wear? "What Would Jesus Do?" Those bracelets served a good purpose if they kept people more mindful of God in their lives. But they could also provide a lazy person's shortcut to behavior decisions.

Can I be a little direct? I think it's hazardous to assert that you know what Jesus would do in all situations. In the three years of their ministerial training, Jesus' disciples were astounded over and over at the things the Master said and did. They could not predict his behaviors and in fact repeatedly and wrongly tried to talk him out of the unpleasant *but absolutely necessary* parts of the Father's plan of salvation. And herein lies the danger—with only WWJD as your moral compass, you might be tempted to call on your Jesus-guesswork to justify what you've already decided you really want to do.

You need surer ground than your own imagination. Go to the Book. The Bible is an absolutely reliable guide to your decision-making and not subject to Satan's whisperings. But take it straight up—do not adulterate with your own notions, philosophies, feelings, and secret wants: **"Every word of God is flawless; he is a shield to those who take refuge in him. Do not add to his words, or he will rebuke you and prove you a liar"** (Proverbs 30:5,6).

A better bracelet behavior reminder? How about WDJS (i.e., "What Did Jesus Say?")?

His eyes are on the workplace

Pastor Mark Jeske

Where does worship happen? Well, in church, of course. In your home, when you sing and pray together. In your quiet place, when you read Scripture and talk to God. But don't forget about your workplace.

Seriously—God is intensely interested in what goes on in your place of employment. He wants to see how you treat your customers and your fellow employees. He wants to see how you treat your boss and the quality of your work when nobody is watching. **"Whatever you do, work at it with all your heart, as working for the Lord, not for human masters, since you know that you will receive an inheritance from the Lord as a reward. It is the Lord Christ you are serving"** (Colossians 3:23,24).

Those promises are a great comfort when you work at a place that isn't fun anymore. Maybe it never was, but it can still be a place of worship for you. Anybody can complain and grumble and mail in a performance. A worker who has decided to be positive and happy and cooperative can infect everybody else to be positive and happy and cooperative.

So whatever you do, work at it with all your heart. Know that God is watching you, smiling at your efforts. You can smile too, since you know that you will get two paychecks—one on payday and one in heaven.

The eyes of your heart

Sarah Habben

Richard Peck's novel *A Year Down Yonder* is set during the Great Depression. Fifteen-year-old Mary Alice is sent downstate to live with Grandma Dowdel while Ma and Pa scratch out a living in Chicago. Problem is, Mary Alice's grandma is tough as nails.

Turns out, though, that Grandma Dowdel's crusty exterior hides a tender wisdom that allows her to see her granddaughter with the "eyes in the back of her heart."

It's a poignant phrase, isn't it? The eyes in our head gather essential information. But the eyes of our *heart* grasp what is hidden.

The apostle Paul had something to say about the eyes of our heart too. In his letter to the saints in Ephesus, Paul describes the invisible riches we have in Christ. And then Paul prays for his readers: **". . . that the eyes of your heart may be enlightened in order that you may know the hope to which he has called you, the riches of his glorious inheritance in his holy people, and his incomparably great power for us who believe"** (Ephesians 1:18,19).

Through Baptism and the Word, the Holy Spirit has pried open our spiritual eyes. The merest squint reveals the search beam of Jesus' love. But let's not be satisfied with a peek. Let's make it our life's ambition to open wide the eyes of our heart, to know God better. Let's linger over his Word, the better to see what is invisible: A call to hope. A heavenly inheritance. God's power.

What a wonderful view.

Revelation benediction #1: Read, hear, believe

Pastor Mark Jeske

The last book of the Bible intimidates Bible rookies. It is couched primarily in the language of visions and dreams and needs some care in interpreting and understanding. And the content of those visions is so scary! Things do not look good for the church until Jesus comes back. Even the rookies, however, can see that there is an unbelievably happy ending for Christians.

In the meantime, to give encouragement and hope to the believers as we struggle along, waiting for our final redemption, the Lord gave seven "benedictions" or "blessed statements." These statements describe happy outcomes for the people who do certain things. Here's #1: **"Blessed is the one who reads aloud the words of this prophecy, and blessed are those who hear it and take to heart what is written in it, because the time is near"** (Revelation 1:3).

The Bible, including its priceless Revelation at the end, does not self-read or self-hear or self-believe. It is a stunning gift of God, but that gift needs to be received gladly and thankfully and then *used*. It is not intended as a decorative object in homes and churches. It is a working document, living and breathing, pulsing with spiritual energy, and deep with wisdom for the Christian life. It reveals Satan for the ugly terrorist that he is but reveals Christ our Savior in his sacred and triumphant glory.

You will be blessed when you read it and hear it. You will be blessed even more when you believe it.

Revelation benediction #2: Blessed dead

Pastor Mark Jeske

In the circles in which I move, nobody much envies dead people. "Poor Benny," they say. "He was sick for so long." "Poor Louise. She had a hard life."

Actually you would do well to be one of the Christian dead. If you died a believer in Jesus Christ, the book of Revelation calls you blessed: **"Then I heard a voice from heaven say, 'Write this: Blessed are the dead who die in the Lord from now on.' 'Yes,' says the Spirit, 'they will rest from their labor, for their deeds will follow them'"** (14:13).

Labor in and of itself isn't a bad thing. In fact, we will have plenty of work to do in heaven—interesting, challenging, creative, fulfilling work. It's the *dreariness* of our labor here on earth that is so draining, labor that's unappreciated, mindlessly repetitive, pointless, misused, insufficiently compensated, and criticized. How blessed are they who are finally done with that phase of their existence—finally set free for joyful service!

It gets better for the Christian dead—their deeds follow them, that is, the good things they did on earth will finally get recognized by Christ himself! We all (quite rightly) expect to get yelled at when we appear at the Pearly Gates. In fact, on the day of judgment, the only thing you will hear from the King is, "Well done, good and faithful servant! Come and share your Master's happiness."

Revelation benediction #3: Stay alert!

Pastor Mark Jeske

I'm a little paranoid when I'm on the road and have an early business meeting. If I forget to bring my personal alarm clock, I will try to set the alarm on the contraption next to the bed, but to be safe I will have the front desk give me a wake-up call as well. I don't want to miss the meeting.

Jesus will return to earth without warning. Of all the metaphors that he might have chosen, are you surprised that he chose that of a *thief*? You get the point—thieves have the nasty habit of breaking and entering when you least expect it. They always seem to catch you by surprise. Jesus' return is going to catch a lot of people by surprise. They will be thinking that they have plenty of time to get their spiritual act together. They will think that they will see the signs of the end time long in advance and have plenty of time to repent. They will think that they can stall God's judgment day legal proceedings the way they have been working the legal system here on earth.

Wake up! Stay alert! **"Look, I come like a thief! Blessed is the one who stays awake and remains clothed, so as not to go naked and be shamefully exposed"** (Revelation 16:15).

On judgment day, you will either be found wearing the robes of Christ's holiness or you will be found naked.

Revelation benediction #4: You made the guest list

Pastor Mark Jeske

Everybody in Los Angeles loves Hollywood parties. That's where deals get hatched, that's where the beautiful people go to be seen, and that's where up-and-comers try to get noticed by people who make things happen in show business. But woe to you if you are a "B" trying to get into an A-list party. "I'm sorry, sir—your name does not appear to be on the guest list. Vinnie, would you escort this gentleman to the gate?"

Here's good news—the Bible delivers your invitation to the wedding supper of the Lamb of God, delivers it to you *personally*: **"Then the angel said to me, 'Write this: Blessed are those who are invited to the wedding supper of the Lamb!' And he added, 'These are the true words of God'"** (Revelation 19:9). You made it! You made the list! God actually wants you to join him and all the saints at the great feast.

Your body will be restored from all ailments and aging. Your loved ones who died in the Lord are now alive in the Lord! There is no trace of Satan, sin, or sadness. You can finally see all the angels who have been helping and protecting and attending you your whole life. They are smiling, glad to see you. You finally actually get to see Jesus face-to-face, still in his human flesh, scars on hands and feet still visible.

Oh—one thing. One very important thing. You need to RSVP.

So—are you in?

Revelation benediction #5: You're immortal

Pastor Mark Jeske

Pretty much everybody knows what it's like to be mocked, shamed, humiliated, and ridiculed. Sometimes those things come because of your faith. Persecution of Christians began soon after Christ ascended into heaven, and in one way or another it hasn't stopped. People today still suffer for their Christian faith.

The book of Revelation reveals that all Christians are winners. Those who came to faith in Christ have arisen from the spiritual death into which they were born; they have already undergone the "first resurrection": **"Blessed and holy are those who share in the first resurrection. The second death** [that is, condemnation to the endless torments of hell] **has no power over them, but they will be priests of God and of Christ and will reign with him for a thousand years"** (Revelation 20:6).

You may or may not be aware of it, but you have a priestly ministry in service to God and to your Savior Jesus. You are authorized and equipped to represent him during your life on earth and invited to intercede for others through your priestly prayers. In fact, the entire New Testament era (here "1,000 years" in Revelation symbolism) will see the living church carrying out its life-giving ministry. Satan with all his power will not be able to snuff it out.

Yes, you are that valuable to God. Yes, your work is that important. Yes, you will live forever.

Revelation benediction #6: The Bible is a big deal

Pastor Mark Jeske

Procrastinators have a way of pretending that the day of accountability will never come. Students know that there will be final exams but can't resist going out for some beers when they should be studying. Company accountants know that the audit is coming, but they don't budget enough prep time. Branch managers know that inspectors from the central office are coming someday, but that day seems far off.

Here's a big question for your life—do you really believe that Jesus Christ, the Son of God, is going to come back to earth, end human history as we know it, and command his angels to sort out the believers and unbelievers? Do you actually believe that unbelievers will be condemned to a miserable eternity with the devil? Do you accept the information presented to you in the Bible about the end times? Here is your warning: **"Look, I am coming soon! Blessed is the one who keeps the words of the prophecy written in this scroll"** (Revelation 22:7).

"Keeping the words" means believing them to be true and living out the implications of what you believe. "Keeping the words" also means believing that eternal life in heaven is going to be as good as the Bible says it will be. Today as you go about your tasks, connect with people, enjoy some relaxation, keep one eye on the sky. He might just come back today, you know.

Revelation benediction #7: Your clothes are clean

Pastor Mark Jeske

So many different tribes of people on earth; so many different languages; so many different cultures, histories, and achievements; so many different nations. But on judgment day, there will be only two—those whose clothes are clean and those whose are dirty. **"Blessed are those who wash their robes, that they may have the right to the tree of life and may go through the gates into the city. Outside are the dogs, those who practice magic arts, the sexually immoral, the murderers, the idolaters and everyone who loves and practices falsehood"** (Revelation 22:14,15).

Human sinfulness is disgusting to God, and he will not have it in his heaven. On judgment day, those who are found living in rebellion against his holy laws—sexual immorality, murderers, idolaters, and the rest—he will call "dogs" and banish them from his sight. Here's a terrible irony—they wanted to be free from God. On the awe-filled day, they will get what they wanted.

But the believers in Christ have clean clothes. Their sins are the equal of any of the "dogs," *but their clothes were cleaned!* Faith in Christ brings the forgiveness of sins, the washing of our robes in the blood of the Lamb. People with clean clothes may enter the gates of the golden city, the new Jerusalem, and they will be permitted to eat the fruit of the tree of everlasting life. Forgiven, pure, restored, and holy, we are now permanently part of this splendid new life.

All your needs

Sarah Habben

Would you believe it if someone told you, "I can meet your every need"? What if that someone was your future spouse? your doctor? your boss?

Most of us have been around long enough to realize that such a claim has more holes than a slice of Swiss cheese. Nevertheless, someone has made that promise to us. That Someone doesn't say he *can* meet all our needs. He says he *will*.

"And my God *will* meet all your needs according to the riches of his glory in Christ Jesus" (Philippians 4:19).

The apostle Paul wrote these words in prison. He lacked privacy. He lacked privileges. His death sentence loomed. How could he claim that God had met all his needs? Three simple words show the root of his conviction: In. Christ. Jesus.

Perhaps Paul's situation resonates with you. Perhaps you feel imprisoned by your own body, or barred by circumstances you can't control. To you, too, God makes his daring promise. He will meet all your needs. Not by rooting around in his pocket lint, but according to the "riches of his glory in Christ Jesus." That's no back pocket—that's a bottomless barrel. Out of that barrel God draws a brimming ladle of forgiveness. Of salvation. Of resurrection comfort. Of ascension power. Out of that barrel, who is Christ, God scoops a rich helping of patience, trust, hope, and contentment . . . and then says, "Dear one, there's more where that came from!"

Enough for *all* your needs.

The best treat of all!

Linda Buxa

"Let the little children come to me, and do not hinder them, for the kingdom of God belongs to such as these" (Mark 10:14).

In just a few days, little Cinderellas, Darth Vaders, ninjas, and ballerinas—children whom Jesus loves very much—will ring your doorbell. They seem to love all the pretend scary elements that come with trick-or-treating. In reality, though, each one of these children may have life circumstances that are truly dark and scary. What they may not know is they have a Father who loves them deeply and watches over them—and he will always be there when they are afraid.

That's why you are in the neighborhood! Don't miss this once-a-year opportunity. When you open the door, smile and show God's love to every one of his little children who come to your door. Add a Bible passage to your candy or include a card inviting them to church with you.

Then come up with a plan for the rest of the year. Walk around your neighborhood and pray for the homes and people in it. Then get to know the neighbors God has put around you. Be the one in the community who always has a smile. Talk to them about Jesus, the one who changes darkness into light. Let them know about the one whose perfect love casts out fear.

Really, Jesus? Love my enemies?

Pastor Mark Jeske

Nobody could accuse Jesus of pandering to an audience.

The prophetic task of proclaiming the Word of God was once described (apologies to journalist Finley Peter Dunne) as "comforting the afflicted and afflicting the comfortable." Nobody could afflict the comfortable like Jesus. He could dish it out to the smug Pharisees, but he also turned up the heat on his own disciples. His famous Sermon on the Mount took some comfy "church people" assumptions and turned them upside down. Such as: **"Love your enemies, do good to those who hate you, bless those who curse you, pray for those who mistreat you"** (Luke 6:27,28).

Really, Jesus? Yes, really. Jesus not only taught that kind of love; he lived it. The first of his few statements from the cross of Calvary itself asked for mercy for his tormentors. You and I were born enemies of God, but he chose to love us in advance and arrange for a Savior even before we were born. You and I depend for our very souls' salvation on God's gift of forgiveness to the unworthy. God absolutely expects that we will show that same mercy *to people who don't deserve it.* **"If your enemy is hungry, give him food to eat; if he is thirsty, give him water to drink. In doing this, you will heap burning coals on his head, and the Lord will reward you"** (Proverbs 25:21,22).

Nobody is a better rewarder than the Lord.

Really, Jesus?
Hate my father and mother?

Pastor Mark Jeske

The Fourth Commandment expresses God's timeless will for all families, directing all children everywhere to honor their parents. Jesus himself loved his mom and stepdad. Scripture tells us that he was a dutiful and obedient son as he was growing up. His tender words of care for Mary, spoken in his agony on the cross, demonstrated his compassion and determination to put others' needs before his own.

How then could he seem to encourage family hatred? **"Large crowds were traveling with Jesus, and turning to them he said: 'If anyone comes to me and does not hate father and mother, wife and children, brothers and sisters—yes, even their own life—such a person cannot be my disciple'"** (Luke 14:25,26). Really, Jesus? Hate?

Understand a few things. Jesus was employing an ancient Hebrew figure of speech called a *mashal*, in which you make a point by exaggeration to an extreme. In English class we would say it is a type of hyperbole. Jesus wasn't promoting hatred. Rather, he was insisting that the triune God needed to come first in people's lives, more beloved and more important even than one's parents or children. Yes, even they can crowd God out of a human heart. Even they can become deadly idols. *And if a choice has to be made* between following one's parents and following Jesus, choose Jesus.

Any path that leads away from him is spiritual suicide.

God and politics

Pastor Mark Jeske

'Tis election season (actually, it seems like it's been election season for two years. Just sayin' . . .) Is there anything in the Bible that can help us sort our way through the chaos of the choices we will have to make?

Well, not much. Election of government officials by popular vote was pretty much unknown in Bible times. Leadership and authority in those days came either from your family and clan or from the king. Kings aren't elected. They attain their power and rank either by birth or by massive display of armed violence.

But that doesn't mean God is silent on what he expects of public officials. After all, they exercise their authority with his permission and direction (see Romans 13:1-7). The mother of a mysterious king named Lemuel gave him some wonderful advice on how people in high office should behave: **"Do not spend your strength on women, your vigor on those who ruin kings"** (Proverbs 31:3). Nothing good ever came from King David having a harem.

"It is not for kings, Lemuel—it is not for kings to drink wine, not for rulers to crave beer, lest they drink and forget what has been decreed, and deprive all the oppressed of their rights. . . . Speak up for those who cannot speak for themselves, for the rights of all who are destitute. Speak up and judge fairly; defend the rights of the poor and needy" (Proverbs 31:4-9).

As you ponder your voting choices, it seems to me that Lemuel's priorities still matter.

Turn on the light

Linda Buxa

We had friends over one night, and six kids were playing in the bedroom. The slightly bigger kids were turning the bedroom into a haunted house, complete with spooky noises and no lights.

Justin, the one toddler in the room, ran to turn on the lights, saying, "Scary!"

The other five wanted the lights off, enjoying the elementary-school level of fear they were trying to create. Back and forth the disagreement went. The toddler wouldn't give up. Finally, the other kids gave in.

But it wasn't the same. You just can't have fear when the lights are on.

Grown-ups live in an actual haunted house because this world is full of actual scary situations. Children contract life-threatening diseases, marriages crumble, parents suffer from dementia, paychecks barely seem to cover the bills.

With faith like a child, you run to the Light. Shine the light of truth on your fears. Because Jesus suffered the ultimate darkness on the cross—separation from the Father while paying the consequences for our sins—he is more than qualified to handle the darkness of our daily lives. He gives you his light and his strength to face each challenge. Now you get to say, **"You, Lord, are my lamp; the Lord turns my darkness into light. With your help I can advance against a troop; with my God I can scale a wall"** (2 Samuel 22:29,30).

november

"Give thanks in all circumstances; for this is God's will for you in Christ Jesus."

1 Thessalonians 5:18

The grand reunion

Pastor Mark Jeske

I'm kind of glad that I didn't live in Bible times.

I sure do look up to the heroes of our faith—Abraham, Moses, Samuel, David, Esther, and all the rest. But the biblical narrative does not hesitate to tell the stories of their terrible weaknesses as well as their triumphs.

Maybe that's why I still hold these people in such high regard. God achieved great things through them, but they were just frail, sinful mortals like you and me. They lived and worked and suffered and overcame and then died, all the while waiting to see the magnificent revelation of the full might and presence of God. They lived and died in hope and in faith, sustained by the power of God's Word. Only together with us will they experience the grand reunion.

The writer to Jewish Christians in the first century urged them to remember and imitate the saints of old: **"These were all commended for their faith, yet none of them received what had been promised, since God had planned something better for us so that only together with us would they be made perfect"** (Hebrews 11:39,40).

This All Saints' Day take a moment to give thanks to God for the men and women of centuries past on whose shoulders we stand, people whose courage and steadfastness serve as examples and inspiration for us. Soon, soon, comes the grand reunion when we can thank them in person.

Really, Jesus? Carry my cross?

Pastor Mark Jeske

Wouldn't you like to think that becoming a Christian and living the Christian life will make your life better? Doesn't Scripture promise that God will bless faith and obedience . . . that it will go *well* with us and actually extend our lives on this earth? How then can Jesus tell us to carry our *crosses*? Wasn't that supposed to be his nasty job?

He actually said it various times: **"Whoever does not carry their cross and follow me cannot be my disciple"** (Luke 14:27). **"Whoever wants to be my disciple must deny themselves and take up their cross daily and follow me. For whoever wants to save their life will lose it, but whoever loses their life for me will save it. What good is it for someone to gain the whole world, and yet lose or forfeit their very self?"** (Luke 9:23–25). Really, Jesus?

Yes. The one who bore the cross for us invites us to be ready and willing to pick up our own if and when we need to. Our own comfort and our wealth and pleasant environment can become idols, idols so compelling and seductive that to keep our position we just might sacrifice our faith and our worship of God as our number one.

I personally have to work on this more. I would much rather pick up my golf clubs or my vacation luggage or some NFL tickets than a cross. But there will be times when accepting a hardship *for Jesus' sake* is the highest form of worship.

Really, Jesus? Be perfect?

Pastor Mark Jeske

One of people's favorite ways of shucking off responsibility for their weaknesses and misdeeds goes like this: "Hey, I'm not perfect, y'know." That excuse is intended to allow just about anybody to skate away from actually having to *repent*. Only an uptight and unrealistic perfectionist would actually expect other people to be perfect.

Well, Jesus does. Part one of the Sermon on the Mount concludes, **"Be perfect, therefore, as your heavenly Father is perfect"** (Matthew 5:48). That was always one of God's main messages to the human race: **"Keep my decrees and laws, for the person who obeys them will live by them. I am the Lord"** (Leviticus 18:5). God's commandments are made of iron, not pasta. They are laws, not suggestions or helpful tips.

The very unattainable perfection they demand is the main reason we need a Savior. Our clouded minds and broken willpower guarantee that we fall short of the glory of God. Jesus achieved perfection in our place, and our faith in him credits his perfection to our account. What a miracle of grace!

God's commandments, however, still remain. God's believing children are forgiven of the burden of old guilt, indwelt by the powerful Spirit of the Lord, and illuminated by the Word of God. With joy we now study God's Word and will and seek to bend our will and minds toward pleasing God all the way all the time.

We want to be the complete package. Nothing less will do for the King of kings.

Lord, cast your vote through us

Jason Nelson

We are excited, Lord! This week we can participate in democracy. We can choose our leaders. We enter a voting booth like it was a confessional and with only you watching make choices that reveal our politics and reflect our faith. Out of our isolated votes comes a consensus. The will of the people is done. And your will is done. Let us cherish this privilege and never neglect our duty to cast our vote. It is a righteous act of citizenship. Brave people died to secure it for us. Move us to cast our votes and honor their sacrifice.

There are many competing things to consider. Help us sort through the positions among candidates. Help us sift through the positions of each candidate. None of them is a perfect choice. In the course of human events, no candidate has ever been perfect. This is not the City of God. It is the city of men and women. And you have always made exceptional use of flawed people.

We are not electing a national pastor, poet laureate, king of the hill, or ceremonial prima donna. Help us remember what we are doing: electing leaders and legislators who must work together to solve problems in our collective best interest. Remind us that you sent your holy Son to serve and not be served and give himself as a ransom for many. Fill us with hope that comes from him. Lord, please cast your vote through us. Amen.

November 5

God isn't broke

Pastor Mark Jeske

The most obvious beneficiaries of the financial gifts of Christians are their churches, schools, and charitable ministries. That's where the gifts become visible.

But those are just the secondary recipients of our gifts. The more important intended beneficiary is God himself. Our gifts are given first to him. But it's not that he *needs* our money. He isn't broke: **"I have no need of a bull from your stall or of goats from your pens, for every animal of the forest is mine, and the cattle on a thousand hills. I know every bird in the mountains, and the insects in the fields are mine. If I were hungry, I would not tell you, for the world is mine, and all that is in it"** (Psalm 50:9-12).

This is a great paradox. The great Lord of all, Creator of the world's gold and silver, opens his hands to receive our dimes. The serene Master of human history, self-sufficient and eternal, actually cares about our offerings and eagerly scrutinizes what we bring him. Why?

What do you give a God who has everything? Give him what only you possess—your heart. The amount of the gift, the actual money or goods that you let go of, is not for his heavenly balance sheet. It is a marker for you, so that you may put an emphasis on your words of worship and adoration.

The God who isn't broke is so thrilled with your heart-gifts that he will soon give you back more than you first gave him.

God's secret agents

Pastor Mark Jeske

How does God get his agenda for earth accomplished? Let me count the ways: He can act unilaterally, with his unlimited almighty power, as when he commanded the great flood to begin. He loves to use his holy angels, a heavenly host of powerful spirit-creatures who hasten to do his bidding. He uses pastors and teachers, prophets and apostles, evangelists and deacons, and the vast army of believers who grasps his mission and heeds his call.

And he can use people you'd think would be his enemies. The Persians were not known as believers in the God of Abraham, Isaac, and Jacob, but their king, Cyrus (whom we call "The Great"), had a special relationship with God: **"This is what Cyrus king of Persia says: 'The Lord, the God of heaven, has given me all the kingdoms of the earth and he has appointed me to build a temple for him at Jerusalem in Judah'"** (Ezra 1:2).

Is that amazing or what? Here is a ruthless warlord, fresh off his conquest of the Babylonians, master of the entire Middle East, who humbly acknowledges that it was Israel's God who had given him his victories and who now felt a personal obligation to assist the Jews both in returning to the land of Israel and in rebuilding the sacred temple in Jerusalem.

Do you suppose that God has secret agents working for him in our day as well?

Making friends

Jason Nelson

I still think friending people best occurs in the wide open spaces of the here and now. I know people can start relationships online. I know people can share content about themselves and virtually keep in touch. But let's remember these are cyber alternatives to the real deal. I am also willing to say that establishing friendships without firewalls in place is way more satisfying.

"Whoever loves a pure heart and whoever speaks graciously has a king as his friend" (Proverbs 22:11 GW). Kindheartedness, respectful talking, and a willingness to listen don't just ingratiate a person to the high and mighty. They gather a circle of friends among ordinary people in our everyday lives. Many lonely people are looking for a nice person with whom they can just talk and talk. If they see you as that person, they will open up.

My wife works in a local bank. I am very proud of her service to our community. She meets interesting people and expresses amazement at the things they are willing to tell her. She's concerned that Internet banking could make her position obsolete. But I've noticed that the most significant contribution she and her colleagues make isn't keeping track of people's money. It is befriending them the old-fashioned way. And that is why folks keep walking through the door.

This is how we do it in a small town: a) look people in the eye; b) smile; c) say, "Hi!"; d) start a conversation; e) and be ready. If people trust you they will tell you anything.

Fast company

Pastor Mark Jeske

People fast for various reasons. Sometimes they need to clean out their digestive systems completely to prepare for an upcoming surgery, or perhaps they do it to lose weight. In Old Testament times, refusing to eat was a public way of demonstrating that you were really upset or distraught. And then there's religious fasting. Have you ever temporarily denied yourself food for religious reasons?

There are no New Testament rules about religious fasting. God neither commands it nor discourages the practice. It belongs to the vast set of religious behaviors where God invites you to use your own judgment. God's priest Ezra once asked Israel's leaders to join him in a time of intense prayer, and he invited them furthermore to take no food for a set period of time to intensify the experience: **"I was ashamed to ask the king for soldiers and horsemen to protect us from enemies on the road, because we had told the king, 'The gracious hand of our God is on everyone who looks to him, but his great anger is against all who forsake him.' So we fasted and petitioned our God about this, and he answered our prayer"** (Ezra 8:22,23).

If you are easily distracted, fasting probably won't work too well for you—your constantly growling stomach will keep you focused on your stomach, not on God. But as a discipline of self-denial, just as when the church in Antioch commissioned Paul and Barnabas (Acts 13:2,3), it can help you give 100 percent of your attention to your prayers.

There's an app for that

Linda Buxa

Need the most minor problem solved? There's an app for that! Apps help you manage your finances, diet, fitness, sleep, and shopping. (Time of Grace even has an app to give you spiritual support and encouragement.)

Sometimes, though, some of them make me shake my head, such as Drunk Text Savior. Its webpage shares, "Tired of getting yourself into trouble from your drunk texts after a crazy night out? Let the Drunk Text Savior help." It was designed to stop you from waking up one morning to discover you texted someone you dated four years ago or your boss or someone who isn't as attractive in the light of day.

Don't you simply want to ask, "How about you not make poor choices that lead to bad texting decisions in the first place?"

Deep down we know the answer, don't we? Making wise choices is rarely "fun." I don't want to change my behavior; I simply don't want to suffer the consequences. I'd rather cover up my transgressions than not transgress in the first place. Maybe I don't need Drunk Text Savior, but I sure could use Quick Tongue Savior. Or Nagging Savior. Or Wasting Too Much Time on the Internet Savior.

There's an app for that too. My Perfect Loving Savior came, not to cover up or downplay my idiotic choices but to wipe them away completely. No matter what my personal sins are, I have a Savior who won my forgiveness. He did it for you too. Through his Word, his Spirit is downloaded in your heart and mind.

Clear authority

Pastor Mark Jeske

All believers are royal priests of God with a personal ministry to share the gospel with people in their lives. But not all believers are cut out to be teachers and pastors. Why not? **"Not many of you should become teachers, my fellow believers, because you know that we who teach will be judged more strictly"** (James 3:1).

Judged in which ways? The first and most important is that public ministers of the gospel must know the Word backward and forward. They must be masters of its content. Second, they need to have the gift of communication. You not only have to know it; you need to be able to break it down for people in terms that they can understand.

Ezra the priest was one of God's agents to get the worship life of the returned exiles functioning in a better way. He organized a huge Feast of Tabernacles, as Moses had commanded. Just as important as the ritual was the teaching that went with it: **"The Levites—Jeshua, Bani, Sherebiah, Jamin, Akkub, Shabbethai, Hodiah, Maaseiah, Kelita, Azariah, Jozabad, Hanan and Pelaiah—instructed the people in the Law while the people were standing there. They read from the Book of the Law of God,** *making it clear* **and giving the meaning** *so that the people understood* **what was being read"** (Nehemiah 8:7,8).

Congregation members, insist that your pastors and teachers do this for you. Pray for them, encourage them, and hold them accountable so that their proclamation is clear and understandable.

No greater love

Pastor Mark Jeske

Everybody remembers 9/11. But only a few remember the significance of 11/11. Originally it commemorated Armistice Day, the blessed point in time when World War I was finally over. Eleven million military personnel and seven million civilians perished in that dreadful conflict. Now 11/11 is known as Veterans Day, America's opportunity to show some appreciation and support for its men and women in uniform.

We remember especially those who are assigned to service outside the country. Some are able to take their families with them to base housing. Many have to manage long-distance marriages, burdened with the realization that their children are growing up without them. Many have served in live-fire zones and for the rest of their lives will have to live with the fear of IEDs and snipers.

In his last few hours of freedom before his own death, Jesus spoke of the honor, sacrifice, and worth of saving the lives of others at the risk of your own: **"Greater love has no one than this: to lay down one's life for one's friends"** (John 15:13). He laid down his so that you and I could receive the forgiveness of our sins, the favor and blessings of God, and a resurrection like his. He calls us friends. It is our most priceless asset.

The people whom we remember today are showing that kind of love. They are risking their lives to help preserve yours and mine. We are grateful for them all.

God's antidepressant

Pastor Mark Jeske

At the time when George Washington was president, over 90 percent of Americans were engaged in agriculture or agriculture-related work. In today's work life, we tap at computers, stare into screens, and talk on the phone. When so little of our work lives is physical, how can our stress level not go up? And how can stressed people not experience more depression? I am surprised neither by the number of people I know who struggle with depression nor the number who depend on antidepressant medications to get through their days.

Doctors, nurses, and medical scientists can explain to you about chemical imbalances in the brain and how antidepressant drugs are not merely addictive crutches. To the medical advice you can get, I would like to add some from God: look away from yourself.

In a depressed person's mind, everything revolves around him or her. "I wonder what they're saying about me—probably all bad." "I am such a failure." "Nothing goes right for me." "Nobody really cares about me." The way out of that dark hole is to let God speak to you of his unconditional love, that you have immense value to him, so great that the Son of God himself thought you were worth dying for.

Second, let God invite you to turn your face outward and look for people to serve. Service to others heals the soul: **"Be devoted to one another in love. Honor one another above yourselves"** (Romans 12:10). Making someone else's life a little better will make yours better.

Fill your tank

Sarah Habben

Have you ever bypassed a gas station only to find yourself driving down a highway on fumes? It sure sucks the fun out of a car trip.

Jesus' friend Martha once had a similar moment. She had her pedal to the metal in the kitchen. Her sister, Mary, was lounging at Jesus' feet. It wasn't fair. Martha was trying to make a yummy supper for Jesus. But she was driving down the highway with her gas gauge pointing to E. Her mistake, as someone once said, was "thinking she was the host and Jesus the guest." Martha needed to be filled up by Jesus before she could serve.

We've all had Martha moments. We want to sit at Jesus' feet and listen, but there's all this *stuff* to do! We take on a task only to sputter and stall. We're overwhelmed. Tense. Angry. We scold Jesus: Don't you care about my many duties? How can I possibly find time to listen to you?

Jesus gently rebuked Martha (and us). Not for serving him, but for foolishly trying to serve him on an empty tank. Jesus told Martha, **"You are worried and upset about many things, but few things are needed—or indeed** *only one.* **Mary has chosen what is better, and it will not be taken away from her"** (Luke 10:41,42).

We are Jesus' guests, and he's giving away fuel: Forgiveness. Peace. Patience. Joy. Take time to fill your tank. Then, strengthened, go and serve.

November 14

A picture of God

Linda Buxa

A picture is worth a thousand words. Except when it isn't. A photo might capture a glorious moment accurately, but it can also be misinterpreted because it only captures a fraction of a second in your whole entire life.

If you took a snapshot of a moment in your life, you could misinterpret God, couldn't you? Sure, in the good times it's easy to spot his blessings. But in a rough patch? Well, you might think that at best he is distant from you. (After all, why would any God take the time to notice little, unimportant you?) You might think he is angry and giving you the silent treatment. (After all, you've done some pretty horrible things, so I bet there's no way he wants to be around you.)

That couldn't be further from the truth. In reality, the God of the universe is your dearest friend. He is kind and gracious, slow to anger, and abounding in love. He is your confidant, inviting you to leave your weariness and burdens with him so he can give you rest. He is an encourager, sending the Holy Spirit to live inside of you and giving you the strength for each day.

If today is one of *those* days—or this year is one of *those* years—please don't believe the snapshot. There's a bigger picture, one that reminds you, **"Do not fear, for I am with you; do not be dismayed, for I am your God. I will strengthen you and help you; I will uphold you with my righteous right hand"** (Isaiah 41:10).

Love stinks

Sarah Habben

Love stinks. No kidding; it really does.

Victorian sweethearts worked this to their advantage. A love-struck lad would peel an apple and cup it under his arm until the fruit had soaked up the bracing scent of— armpit. Then he would send his "Love Apple" to his beloved for her to sniff at leisure.

But love started stinking long before the Victorians. The world's first sweethearts, Adam and Eve, trashed God's love when they bit into a forbidden piece of fruit. Sin oozed into the world. Love began to smell fishy. Not of BO, but of something worse: *ego*.

Ever since, selfishness has scribbled *me-firsts* over God's script. Love is patient . . . *when I'm first in line for the bathroom*. Love is kind . . . *to my coworker's face*. Love is not easily angered . . . *as long as my kids stop whining, like—NOW*.

The love I offer up is more odor than ardor. It stinks. But instead of sluicing his world clean of me and other reeking sinners, God turned the fire hose of his anger on his Son. In so doing, God redefined love. **"This is love: not that we loved God, but that he loved us and sent his Son as an atoning sacrifice for our sins"** (1 John 4:10).

Though I reeked of sin, Jesus lived for me. Though I served my ego, Jesus died for me. Though I stumble in love, Jesus forgives me. And so he enables me to serve and forgive others.

That's Christ's love.

How sweet it smells.

God, could you pitch in?

Linda Buxa

When we lived in California, ducks were hanging around our creek. Our three kiddos were building nests, hoping the ducks would lay their eggs in them. On the way home from church one Sunday, my daughter asked, "Mom, can you pitch in around the house today? We'll be so busy with our nests."

I laughed, because she was only seven at the time and had no idea what she was saying to the woman who made her meals, washed her clothes, drove her to school.

I often do the same thing to God. I don't really pay attention to all the ways he is working in my life; then when I get busy or stressed, I ask him to pitch in.

We call out, "God, where are you?!" when things are going wrong. When in reality he is the God who chooses to live inside of us and promises to never leave us or forsake us.

To the God who created and owns everything in the whole entire world, providing so we can pay the rent is not a problem. Still, we fret and stew and worry.

We wonder why God doesn't seem to care about our problems but forget that **"Christ Jesus who died—more than that, who was raised to life—is at the right hand of God and is also interceding for us"** (Romans 8:34).

Jesus performed the ultimate act of "pitching in" when he came as *God with us.* He's not about to act uninterested now.

RSVP your wedding invitation

Pastor Mark Jeske

The English language apparently is inadequate for all of life's situations. You have to learn some Italian to play the piano (*Allegro! Andante!*), German when somebody sneezes (*Gesundheit!*), and French to answer a wedding invitation (RSVP-*Respondez s'il vous plait*). It is considered very rude to fail to respond to this important piece of paper. If you are chosen to join the select groups of family and friends at a wedding, you are shown great value. If you blow them off, you show that they are of low value to you.

The Bible compares Jesus Christ to a heavenly bridegroom and the church (i.e., all believers together) as his bride. He is making preparations for the bridal procession and coming soon to gather us together for the grand feast. In the meantime, the Bible brings the invitation to believe in Christ and to prepare for his return. It comes with an RSVP: **"The Spirit and the bride say, 'Come!' And let the one who hears say, 'Come!' Let the one who is thirsty come; and let the one who wishes take the free gift of the water of life"** (Revelation 22:16,17).

Don't put off answering. Do it now. You are guaranteed no tomorrows—today might be the last day of your life. Pray with me: Lord Jesus, thank you for loving me enough to want me in your heavenly mansions. Thank you for the beautiful clothes of righteousness that you bought for me. I accept your invitation with great pleasure and eagerly await the feast. Amen.

Come soon, Lord Jesus.

November 18

Expressing love

Jason Nelson

Our lasting impression of love is formed by our earliest experiences at home. Home is where we discover a thing called love and how to express it. G.K. Chesterton said that the meanest fear is the fear of sentimentality. That fear can make a home or a life austere. It can create doubts about love. I hope this isn't a pain-filled question for you, but what were your first impressions of love?

Here are five things about love from the Bible:

- Love is the evidence of God among us and dwells in flesh and blood (1 John 4:16).
- Love is reciprocal, teachable, and repeatable (1 John 4:19; John 13:34,35).
- Love is not a stable condition in our hearts (Matthew 24:12, 1 Peter 1:22).
- Love is self-sacrificing (John 3:16).
- Love never fails (1 Corinthians 13).

It's not too late to make our homes more loving if we invite Jesus to be a member of the family. His place is set at our table when we

- insist that loving interaction is our family's priority.
- are transparent about our love for him and each other.
- verbalize affection and gratitude for each other often.
- establish routines and celebrate with traditions that include everyone.
- grow together in faith as churchgoers.
- leave a generous amount of wiggle room for people to grow on their own.

You will be able to see if your family learned to express love when everyone gets together and reminisces.

Leaders accept responsibility

Pastor Mark Jeske

Anyone can blame somebody else for what's wrong. It takes a leader to accept responsibility for the misdeeds of the group.

Nehemiah was a Jew, still living in exile during the reign of the Persian king Artaxerxes around 444 B.C., even though the Jews had been freely permitted to return to the land of Israel 92 years earlier. Nehemiah had demonstrated enough ability to have been promoted to a position of high trust in the royal court, that of cupbearer to the king. His heart was stirred by a sad report from Jerusalem about the sluggish progress in rebuilding the city and especially its walls. Without those walls, the city was vulnerable to every band of raiders that came through.

Nehemiah had the soul of a true leader. As he formed his plans to jump-start the rebuilding of Jerusalem, he came to the Lord in prayer and showed that he had learned the lesson of the reason for Israel's painful exile: **"We have acted very wickedly toward you. We have not obeyed the commands, decrees and laws you gave your servant Moses"** (Nehemiah 1:7). Nehemiah did not blame his grandparents' generation. He used the pronoun *we* and meant it. He knew he was a sinner too. He approached the Lord in a posture of humility, asking for mercy, not demanding what he thought Israel had a right to.

When a group of people looks to you as its leader, accept the authority that comes with it, but take the responsibility too.

Leaders call on God's promises

Pastor Mark Jeske

When you want to get somebody to do something for you, there are various tried-and-true strategies. You can recite all the things you've done lately for the person to justify your request. You can try flattery. You can nag and pester, hoping he or she will cave just to get rid of you. You can try to buy people's goodwill, offering to trade something you've got that they might want. You can make promises of what you will do for them in the future.

But don't try any of those things when you pray to the Lord, especially when you are acting as a leader of a Christian group. When your prayers are in alignment with God's mission, you don't need flattery, nagging, or self-justification. You can simply call on the promises that God has already made. Listen to Nehemiah: **"They are your servants and your people, whom you redeemed by your great strength and your mighty hand"** (Nehemiah 1:10).

Through your faith in Christ, God has declared himself to be your Father, and he accepts the obligations that come with Fatherhood. Call on them without fear or hesitation! He is waiting to be asked. He promises a listening ear, daily bread, angelic protection, the Spirit's gifts, steady guidance, restoration when you are knocked down, and the free and full forgiveness of all your sins.

When he does what you ask, don't forget to say thank you.

Leaders dream big

Pastor Mark Jeske

Have you ever seen (or used) the Twitter acronym GBGH? It's used when someone wants to challenge another to up the game. It stands for "Go Big or Go Home."

Good leaders dream big. When you are tackling a spiritual mission or project, the size and level of difficulty show what you think of your God. Nehemiah could not be accused of a small-time vision. In fact, his project drew the withering abuse of the governor of the neighboring province of Samaria: **"When Sanballat heard that we were rebuilding the wall, he became angry and was greatly incensed. He ridiculed the Jews, and in the presence of his associates and the army of Samaria, he said, 'What are those feeble Jews doing? Will they restore their wall? Will they offer sacrifices? Will they finish in a day? Can they bring the stones back to life from those heaps of rubble—burned as they are?'"** (Nehemiah 4:1,2).

Sanballat preferred the status quo—Jerusalem weak and vulnerable. Nehemiah believed that the little band of Jews in Jerusalem could indeed rebuild its walls if they all worked together, if they all brought maximum effort, and if they all devoted their hearts to the Lord.

What are you and your congregation daring for the Great Commission? Jesus was apparently quite serious with his instructions to proclaim the gospel to all the world. Are you pushing yourself with goals worthy of that mighty mission? We're running out of time.

GBGH.

Leaders exhibit courage

Pastor Mark Jeske

Good leaders assess risks. And not just the risks to their organizations' reputation and financial health, but the personal risks that come with being out in front.

Nehemiah was informed by a man named Shemaiah that the wall-building project had aroused such hostility that there were death threats against him. Shemaiah counseled him to run to the temple and hide there, begging for mercy from the very altar steps. Nehemiah refused to wilt. **"I said, 'Should a man like me run away? Or should someone like me go into the temple to save his life? I will not go!'"** (Nehemiah 6:11). It wasn't that he was being reckless, carelessly throwing his life away. It's that he refused to be intimidated. He kept praying and kept working.

Nehemiah had his workers keep their swords with them as they troweled mortar. He also organized armed patrols to watch for saboteurs and raiders. Because of his courage, the little band of Jews got their project done in an astonishing 52 days. What a boost for the morale of the city! What an ongoing source of pride as each family gazed on its stretch of completed wall. Even more—what a faith recharger! God had come through for them and rewarded their courage: **"When all our enemies heard about this, all the surrounding nations were afraid and lost their self-confidence, because they realized that this work had been done with the help of our God"** (Nehemiah 6:16).

Leaders take care of God's house

Pastor Mark Jeske

You can tell a lot about a congregation by the appearance of its property. Mown grass, trimmed shrubbery, immaculate rest rooms, and an adequate sound system send a message that the people who claim the place take pride in it and are serious about their mission of sharing the gospel. It also means that they love the God they worship and want his house to be fit for a King.

Leaders take care of God's house. They build a culture in their congregation where all the members feel a sense of ownership and responsibility for their place of worship because it is dedicated to the name and glory of the Lord.

Nehemiah chapter 10 is an extraordinary document. The provincial governor (Nehemiah), regional tribal leaders, priests, and Levites all prepared and signed a covenant document in which they committed as a nation to reform their national life. All the people bound themselves to its provisions with a solemn oath. One key feature was their promise to honor their God by the way in which they cared for his house: **"The people of Israel, including the Levites, are to bring their contributions of grain, new wine and olive oil to the storerooms, where the articles for the sanctuary and for the ministering priests, the gatekeepers and the musicians are also kept. We will not neglect the house of our God"** (Nehemiah 10:39).

If your church building and property look great, whom can you thank? If they don't, who needs to lead the charge?

Peace is a gift of God

Pastor Mark Jeske

It is a pleasant fantasy of well-meaning people to want to believe that human nature deep down inside is good and kind, that conflict and violence are aberrations, and that we are evolving into a kinder and gentler human race. In fact we are corrupt from birth, selfish, me-oriented, and prone to conflict. Already in Genesis chapter 6, God sadly observed that the mind of man was only evil continually.

This side of heaven, warfare is the natural state. It's the law of the jungle, but it's also the law of the desert, prairie, and forest. Humanity isn't growing more peaceful—the last century, the 20th, was the bloodiest in history. Thus when people experience a stretch of peacetime, it is time to lift up their eyes to heaven to show some gratitude.

King David knew nothing but conflict for most of his reign. He had to battle not only the warlike nations that surrounded Israel but also had to run for his life from his friend and mentor Saul and even from his own son Absalom. Finally at the end of his life, there was a stretch of peace, and he wanted the crown prince, Solomon, to appreciate where it came from: **"He said to them, 'Is not the Lord your God with you? And has he not granted you rest on every side?'"** (1 Chronicles 22:18).

I hope you never get tired of praying for peace. I hope you never get tired of saying thank you for peace.

THINK

Linda Buxa

As we were leaving a picnic, my daughter spoke up, "I want to go with Grandma." I piped up, "Ah, but does Grandma want you to go with her?"

That's when my firstborn asked, "Mom, did you THINK about what you said?"

She was referring to the sign we had posted in our home that read, "Did you THINK? Is what you say . . ."

True: Do we exaggerate the grievances we have against each other? Do we look clearly at the issue, or are we tainted by previous grievances?

Helpful: Do your words support the people around you? Do they offer solutions to problems? Do you bring comfort in sadness? Teasing can be fine; sarcasm, not so much.

Inspiring: Do our words encourage others? Or do we squelch their dreams by putting down their ideas?

Necessary: Does it have to be said? Do we speak when silence would be best? If someone is feeling guilty, do we add to their burden?

Kind: Nice doesn't mean kind. Sometimes kindness means saying hard things because someone needs to be called to account. It's looking out for their best interests. But do you speak the truth in love or do you intentionally cut someone down?

Each day is another chance to live this truth: **"Finally, brothers and sisters, whatever is true, whatever is noble, whatever is right, whatever is pure, whatever is lovely, whatever is admirable—if anything is excellent or praiseworthy—THINK about such things"** (Philippians 4:8).

Saving money God's way

Pastor Mark Jeske

As recently as the mid-1980s, Americans were saving money at a 10 percent rate. That is, for every $100 they grossed, they would save $10. Do you know what the savings rate is these days? It's around 0 percent. Yep, you heard me—0 percent. That sounds to me like the behavior of people who either think they have no future, think only about NOW, or who are simply assuming that someone else will take care of them when they are old.

The Bible does indeed warn us of the dangers of materialism. Money can easily become a god that people adore and trust. Loving money is indeed a root of all kinds of evil. That doesn't mean, however, that poverty should be a *life goal* for Christians. God vigorously approves of the concept of building wealth for you and your family.

A few fortunate people build their retirement funds through a large inheritance or gift. The rest of us need to grow it bit by bit. It is a wonderful discipline to spend less than you make and save the difference. Here is Solomon's advice: **"He who gathers money little by little makes it grow"** (Proverbs 13:11). Financial security means not only being able to pay your obligations and not be a burden on others. It also means that you can be generous to ministries and projects that you care about.

Start young. Time and compounding are your friends.

Light a candle for hope

Pastor Mark Jeske

Back in the day, candles or oil lamps were the only way you could illuminate the inside of your house after dark. Candles were a big deal.

Today, not so much. In the age of electricity, only a few uses remain for candles. One of them is for emergency preparations. Disaster relief organizations want all homes and businesses to stash bottled water, blankets, some canned food, and candles and matches in the event that all utilities are disabled or cut off. Candles are part of survival gear.

A sweet, ancient Advent custom is to light a candle each week for the four weeks in the run-up to Christmas. It strikes me that lighting an Advent candle is a reminder that our coming Messiah, Jesus Christ, will help us not only survive the coming judgment but triumph with him.

As you light the first candle, ponder the powerful Christmas reality that our Advent waiting anticipates: Jesus Christ is God himself, come in human flesh to relive your life for you and die your death for you. While you are waiting for Christmas, and waiting for the second coming, rejoice that God is with you. **"The virgin will be with child and will give birth to a son, and will call him Immanuel"** (Isaiah 7:14).

Let that first candle remind you of the hope that Jesus brings.

Remember the martyrs

Pastor Mark Jeske

I have never attended the funeral of a martyr, i.e., someone who was killed because of his or her faith in Jesus Christ. It is a gift to live in an age and in a country where I can practice my faith in relative peace.

But there have been many, many thousands of martyrs in past ages, and there are parts of the world today where being a Christian is costing people their lives. Right now would be a good moment to reflect on those brave souls and celebrate the powerful impact made by their testimony. Their relationship to their Savior was more important to them than their comfort, money, or life itself. They believed that whatever they lost on earth would be more than compensated for in eternity.

Meanwhile, their souls wait in heaven, wait for God's public vindication on the great day of judgment: **"When he opened the fifth seal, I saw under the altar the souls of those who had been slain because of the word of God and the testimony they had maintained. They called out in a loud voice, 'How long, Sovereign Lord, holy and true, until you judge the inhabitants of the earth and avenge our blood?' Then each of them was given a white robe, and they were told to wait a little longer, until the full number of their fellow servants, their brothers and sisters, were killed just as they had been"** (Revelation 6:9-11).

Dear Lord, thank you for the faith, example, and testimony of the martyrs.

Becoming intimate

Jason Nelson

If you read on hoping for some sex talk, you're in for a letdown. Sex and intimacy were decoupled a long time ago. Intimacy has little to do with taking your clothes off in front of someone. It has everything to do with letting your guard down and baring your soul. That is the kind of naked that really makes us afraid.

Jesus had disciples and intimate disciples. He invited Peter, James, and John to see him suffer from the inside out (Matthew 26:36-46). Too bad they slept through it. Intimate friends are hard to come by. It is a wondrous love to know someone and be known by them through and through.

There are over 500,000 sensory fibers on our skin connected through our spinal cord to our brain. God wired us for lots of touching. We can distinguish affectionate touch from sensual touch. A bear hug, two-handed shake, or little poke in the ribs is the language of people who really like each other.

Intimacy doesn't happen by appointment. It develops when we have the leisure to talk over a nice meal or on a long quiet trip in the Prius. We break our silence. We tell a little more, and some honest feelings spill out. Someone tries to understand us.

Mark Twain said, "I can live for two months on one good compliment." We might not get one that often. Any affirmation and encouragement from a confidant has lots of staying power in our lives. Therefore, **"encourage one another daily"** (Hebrews 3:13).

Pass the salt

Sarah Habben

Salt has a humble spot on our grocery lists. It's not fancy or expensive. But imagine life without it! Salt preserves crunchy pickles, melts stubborn ice, adds zing to a bland steak, and helps heal a sore throat.

God also wants salt to season our speech. **"Let your conversation be always full of grace, seasoned with salt, so that you may know how to answer everyone"** (Colossians 4:6).

So how well-seasoned is your speech?

Salty speech preserves relationships. It stops the rot of resentment with words like "I'm sorry" and "I forgive you."

Salty speech melts stubborn hearts by being quick to encourage and compromise.

It sparkles with thanksgiving, putting zing into a bland day.

Or it helps heal the rawness of death by pointing to the Savior and his promise of heaven.

Salty speech is full of grace, ready to answer watercooler questions about our faith.

Sadly, the meals I make are usually better seasoned than my speech. I can talk all day without ever once giving away a clue to my listeners that I am a child of God. Instead I grumble, hold grudges, gossip, go dumb when I should share grace.

Forgive me, Jesus, for being stingy with the salt of your grace. You rescued me from the rot of sin. You melted the grip of death and the devil. Before I speak, let me pray, "Please pass the salt!" And teach me to season generously.

december

"For to us a child is born, to us a son is given, and the government will be on his shoulders. And he will be called Wonderful Counselor, Mighty God, Everlasting Father, Prince of Peace."

Isaiah 9:6

Where else would we go?

Jason Nelson

It was a roller coaster week for Jesus. **"A large crowd was following him, because they saw the signs."** These were hungry people who tagged along. Jesus tested Philip: **"Where are we to buy bread, so that these people may eat?"** Philip had no idea. Andrew found a kid with a lunch. **"Jesus then took the loaves, and when he had given thanks, he distributed them to those who were seated. So also the fish, as much as they wanted."** The people liked what they saw. **"This is indeed the Prophet who is to come into the world!"**

Jesus said something obscure: **"I am the bread of life; whoever comes to me shall not hunger, and whoever believes in me shall never thirst."** He became explicit: **"For my flesh is true food, and my blood is true drink."** Now it was getting weird for people who liked what they saw but didn't understand what they heard. **"After this many of his disciples turned back and no longer walked with him."**

He turned to the ones he picked: **"Do you want to go away as well?"** Peter could have been a little more diplomatic. He said, **"Lord, to whom shall we go?"** It was like he was saying, "We thought about it, but you seem to be the best messiah available." Peter clarified: **"You have the words of eternal life, and we have believed"** (John 6). An awkward confession is still a confession of faith.

I also follow Jesus because I don't know where else I would go.

December 2

Get plugged in

Linda Buxa

The deadline for my devotions came up right in the middle of a busy time. Between school things and kid activities and work responsibilities, I had overcommitted myself. To add to that, as far as First World problems go, my phone battery died. I was a little panicked because I had people to call and e-mails to check and texts to send. But instead of a useful tool, about the only thing my phone could do at that point was to serve as a paperweight.

The Holy Spirit then tapped me on the shoulder (figuratively, of course) to remind me that I'm an awful lot like that phone. I was using up all my energy and forgetting to plug back in. Without recharging, I wouldn't be useful to anyone.

It's not that busy is bad. But busy all the time is. Jesus knew what it was like to be busy. After all, he showed up in lonely places and crowds of thousands would follow him, wanting to listen to him, to be healed by him, to be forgiven by him. He could easily have gotten tapped out, but he made it a habit to recharge: **"Very early in the morning, while it was still dark, Jesus got up, left the house and went off to a solitary place, where he prayed"** (Mark 1:35).

Today, make it a point to find just a few moments of solitary time. Pray. Plug in. Recharge.

Show and tell

Sarah Habben

Did you ever show up at kindergarten without an object for show-and-tell and decide to just do the "tell" part? Your classmates got fidgety fast over your lengthy description of an absent item.

God isn't fooled when his people are all tell and no show. Nor is he pleased. He warns us in James 2:17, **"Faith by itself, if it is not accompanied by action, is dead."** God takes no more pleasure in a deedless faith than we would take in a dead body slumped on our couch.

Such a faith is no witness either. If our works don't match our words, we won't have any more impact on our neighbor than a dead battery has on a cell phone. What good is our Sunday confession that God so loves the world if on Monday we refuse to show love to the "slacker" in our office? What good is our mealtime confession that God provides all our needs if by bedtime we are losing sleep over our investments? Such a faith is not only no good; it is dead.

Thanks be to God! He loves us despite our flaccid faith and timid deeds. The proof of his love is found in his Son. Jesus—whose words and actions were in perfect sync from his cradle to his cross. Jesus—who not only spoke forgiveness but gave his life to win it. Jesus—who enlivens our faith with his love.

Now that's something to tell—and show—the world.

Light a candle for love

Pastor Mark Jeske

Candles are not essential to our lives anymore, but they have some profoundly important symbolic uses. One is to provide an aura of romance. Any young Romeo (or older one, for that matter) who wishes to score points with his girlfriend over dinner will want to have candles burning on the table. The soft golden light, low and flickering, conveys a powerful emotional message: I love you.

As you light a candle in your wreath for the second Advent week, light it for love. Light it to celebrate the amazing romance going on between God and you. Celebrate the commitment of the Father who has become your Father, who did not hesitate to send his Son to buy your redemption at the cost of his life. **"'Though the mountains be shaken and the hills be removed, yet my unfailing love for you will not be shaken nor my covenant of peace be removed,' says the** Lord, **who has compassion on you"** (Isaiah 54:10).

Light the candle also to send an "I love you" message back to God. Let that second candle be your reminder this week that the only appropriate response to the majestic and tender and expensive love of Jesus Christ is to love him back with all your heart and soul. When Satan's attacks make you feel small and insignificant, a failure and a fool, let that candle glow remind you of the unconditional commitment Jesus Christ has made to you.

Let that second candle remind you of the love that Jesus brings.

Make a difference

Linda Buxa

On September 25, 2000, Kevin Hines paced the Golden Gate Bridge, ready to kill himself but hoping for something else. "I said to myself, 'If one person comes up to me and says, "Are you okay? Is something wrong? Can I help you?" I was going to tell them my whole life story and they were going to make me safe.'"

The bridge is an incredibly busy place with cars and bicyclists and pedestrians. It is incredibly easy to overlook just one. No one asked. He jumped—and survived. And now he tells his story of healing and hope to others who are struggling.

It's easy for our churches to have a similar problem. Between meetings and multiple worship services and so much to be accomplished by so few people, it's easy to overlook just one. But each of us can make a difference. This week, look at the people in your church and community with fresh eyes. Try to pick someone who is pacing, wishing someone would ask, "Are you okay?" Look at the visitor and smile. Ask a worn-out, busy mom, "Can I help you?" Be willing to tell your story of healing and hope. Talk about the God who loves you, who gives you a certain hope when situations seem bleak, who comforts you when you are lonely.

In this life you are surrounded by others for a reason. **"In fact God has placed the parts in the body, every one of them, just as he wanted them to be"** (1 Corinthians 12:18).

Let's look out for one another.

Follow his example

Linda Buxa

"Follow my example, as I follow the example of Christ" (1 Corinthians 11:1).

Have you been socked? With this Christmas equivalent of Halloween's "You've been boo'ed," you'll find gifts on your doorstep with an accompanying note: "You've been socked." Then you pass along the season's joy to another neighbor.

It's the modern-day take on St. Nicholas, an Eastern Orthodox Christian whose wealthy parents died while he was young. Obeying Jesus' words to "sell your possessions and give to the poor," Nicholas used his inheritance to help those who were needy and suffering. When a poor man couldn't provide a dowry for his girls, three bags of gold were tossed at night through an open window, providing a future for the man's daughters.

This story would be neatly tied up with a bow if following his example meant we should be generous. However, following Nicholas' example—who followed Jesus' example—also means being willing to suffer. Bishop Nicholas was exiled and jailed for his faith by Diocletian, the Roman Emperor who jailed so many Christians that there was no room for true criminals. After his release, he attended the Council of Nicaea in A.D. 325. From this council, the church was given the Nicene Creed, and two thousand years later the church still declares these truths.

On St. Nick's Day, as we follow his example of generosity, we also follow his example of proclaiming Jesus—even when it costs us more than money.

Satisfaction guaranteed

Sarah Habben

Customer churn. That's the term for when clients defect from a company that hasn't delivered on its promises. Companies know that today's customers expect immediate results in order to stick around. Guarantee our satisfaction, and we'll wake up whistling.

When it came to God's promises, Moses was a loyal customer. At first glance, it would appear that he didn't have much reason for his loyalty. His job was unenviable: 40 years of desert wandering with millions of mulish Israelites. His diet was monotonous. His home was a tent. What was the source of Moses' loyalty? It's apparent in his prayer to God: **"Satisfy us in the morning with your *unfailing love*, that we may sing for joy and be glad all our days"** (Psalm 90:14). Moses' loyalty was the product of *God's* loyalty.

When Moses looked in the mirror, he saw his sin and mortality. He saw a person who deserved the terror of God, a person desperate for a merciful God.

Look in the mirror—you'll see the same.

When Moses looked at God, he saw unfailing, loyal love. A God who sent bread from heaven to meet each day's physical needs. A God who promised to send the Bread of Life, the Savior, to meet Moses' needs for eternity.

Look at God—you'll see the same.

Our God makes big promises. One of them is unfailing love. It's delivered in his Son, satisfaction guaranteed.

No matter what our wilderness, we can wake up whistling.

Repairing the breach

Jason Nelson

"You shall be called the repairer of the breach, the restorer of streets to dwell in" (Isaiah 58:12 ESV).

The mission of God was carried out when Jesus healed the broken relationship between God and his dearly loved people. We have been reconciled to God in Christ. We are on a mission to bring others to him. We are on a mission to live in harmony with one another along the way.

How can we repair our relationships with others when we fail in our mission?

Really pinpoint the problem. What people argue about is not always what they are mad about. Face this disturbing possibility. *Is it me?* We are nose blind to our own obnoxiousness. *Is there something about me that stinks?*

Give it some time but don't act like everything is fine. Ignoring problems is the recipe for a simmering breach waiting to boil over. And it will boil over.

We need to apologize when we are wrong or maybe just a little wrong. Apologies are unqualified like God's love is unconditional. *I'm sorry*—period. Adding *but . . .* isn't an apology. It's an excuse.

Rush to forgive as humbly as Christ has forgiven us. Vaporize grudges so lessons learned don't become axes to grind later. And don't trash each other to family and friends. You will get over it before they do.

"Lord, when we are wrong, make us willing to change. When we are right, make us easy to live with."—Dr. Peter Marshall, former chaplain to the U.S. Senate.

Finding strength

Sarah Habben

Are you feeling strong today?

You can . . . even if your fingers are bent by arthritis. Even if cancer has come or come back. Even if your heart is shrouded in mourning colors. Even if debt just slipped through your mail slot. Even if your mind is letting go. Even if you don't belong. Especially then.

No matter what your circumstance, the psalmist says you are "blessed"—spiritually happy—when you find your strength in God. **"Blessed are those whose strength is in you, whose hearts are set on pilgrimage. They go from strength to strength, till each appears before God in Zion"** (Psalm 84:5,7).

The writer of this psalm longed to worship God in Zion. He couldn't wait to get there to praise his King. How about you, fellow pilgrim? Do you long for a heavenly Zion? Are your eyes fixed on that final home? Have you set your heart on pilgrimage, or have you hammered in your stakes on Planet Earth?

God doesn't want us to think of the world as our permanent residence. Sometimes he allows us to pass through painful places. But he has an astonishing name for those waysides. He calls them "strengths." God takes our roadblocks and makes them rest stops. He does it through his Son. Harried and helpless, when we arrive at our crosses, we think of his cross. And what do we find there? A payment for our sin. A promise of Paradise.

Are you feeling strong today?

Because in Christ, that's what you are.

Bless the next generation

Linda Buxa

"He decreed statutes for Jacob and established the law in Israel, which he commanded our ancestors to teach their children, so the next generation would know them, even the children yet to be born, and they in turn would tell their children. Then they would put their trust in God and would not forget his deeds but would keep his commands" (Psalm 78:5-7).

For thousands of years, millions of believers have been teaching children to put their trust in God and remember everything he has done for them. Now it is your turn to keep up this vital work of teaching the next generation.

Yet it can be a long slog, a thankless job. On the hard days of being a parent, grandparent, uncle, aunt, or family friend, you wonder if your work is making a difference. On the days you watch your teens question if God is really who he says he is, you pray like crazy. There are days you want to yell instead of modeling God's faithful, patient discipline. Through it all, the Holy Spirit is ridiculously busy, taking the Word you speak and planting, nurturing, and growing it in young hearts. God is using you, and the gifts he has given you, to bless the next generation.

The people you tell today are the ones who get to tell the next group of people yet to be born. Someday our children will be telling their children about their Savior, knowing God's Word and his story of grace, because you model it and share it every day. Because you put your trust in God.

Light a candle for joy

Pastor Mark Jeske

We don't need candles for illumination in our home; so when one is burning, it means "something's up." If my wife comes home and spots one, her first question is, "Is somebody coming over?"

She asks that because if she had invited someone, lighting a candle is the first thing she would do, even before vacuuming and cleaning up dirty dishes. She loves the scent. Candles make our home smell nice. They not only mask the tired aroma of old socks and dust bunnies, but they add enticing whiffs of cinnamon, balsam, and vanilla. They take us away from our ordinary street and suggest that we are somewhere else, somewhere exotic or romantic or exciting.

When you light the candle for the third Advent week, let the scent of the match and the wax and the wick take you away. Think of the burning of sacrifices on the Old Testament temple altar that are no longer needed because the Lamb of God has been slain once and for all. Think of the lake of burning sulfur, the ultimate and horrible place of banishment in hell, that you will never see.

Think also of the sweet aroma of incense burned in the Holy Place that brought the prayers of the believers to the throne of a Father who eagerly listens to his children, children who smell good to him now. **"The Lord is my strength and my shield; my heart trusts in him, and I helped. My heart leaps for joy and I will give thanks in song"** (Psalm 28:7).

t third candle remind you of the joy that

December 12

Magnificat:
They will call me blessed

Pastor Mark Jeske

A magnifying glass makes things look really big, and a magnificent event is huge fun. The title of the virgin Mary's poetic outburst of praise is "Magnificat"(from its Latin version), and its keynote idea is that Mary was responding to God's amazing grace and in gratitude chose to make the Lord a really big part of her life. That's what true worship really is—we lift God up high in our hearts and organize our lives around him.

Mary was shocked and awed and delighted that she had been chosen to bear the child who would save the world. She was aware that believers in the future would look back on her day and bless her name for her service on their behalf: **"My soul glorifies the Lord and my spirit rejoices in God my Savior, for he has been mindful of the humble state of his servant. From now on all generations will call me blessed, for the Mighty One has done great things for me—holy is his name"** (Luke 1:46-49).

Mary's simple and humble faith is an inspiration to countless generations of believers. She believed an unbelievable message, endured a hard journey to Bethlehem while nine months pregnant, gave birth in a barn in the dark, and the royal Son she bore put her life so at risk she and her husband and baby had to flee for their lives.

Mary, you are blessed indeed.

Magnificat:
The humble will be lifted up

Pastor Mark Jeske

Billie Holiday's most famous song was a bitter lament that people were stuck in their life destiny—"Them that's got shall get; them that's not shall lose." It sure does seem that the rich get richer and the poor get poorer, doesn't it?

Except when God reverses everything. Mary must have laughed out loud to herself at the outrageousness and absurdity that the King of kings should be born to a poor commoner like her. **"He . . . has lifted up the humble. He has filled the hungry with good things"** (Luke 1:52,53). She didn't know the half of the humble part—she was probably expecting to give birth in Nazareth with her mother and aunts around as midwives to help her with the delivery. Her baby, though, would come during an unplanned overnight "camping" stop in a stable in Bethlehem, attended by only her scared husband and the animals.

But God guided all of these humbling circumstances, and the baby was fine. As she predicted, humble Mary was indeed lifted up. Though she probably never became wealthy, this little "Nazareth nobody" has become the most famous woman in the history of the world.

God enjoys making great things out of small things and using ordinary people for extraordinary missions. If you feel small and insignificant, Mary would counsel you to not be surprised when God taps you for something big.

Magnificat: Not too big to fail

Pastor Mark Jeske

During the 2008 economic meltdown, Americans were treated to the spectacle of the government's decision that certain financial firms were "too big to fail," i.e., too big *to be allowed to fail.* They needed to be propped up at all costs and protected from normal market forces. That's how little folks at the bottom see the upper crust—that the system is rigged to protect the big guys at the little guys' expense. They fear that nothing ever changes.

Except when God does one of his celebrated interventions in human history and changes the unchangeable. Mary had the Spirit-given perceptiveness to see that she was living in just such a moment: **"He has performed mighty deeds with his arm; he has scattered those who are proud in their inmost thoughts. He has brought down rulers from their thrones . . . sent the rich away empty"** (Luke 1:51-53). It's not that God hates wealth and the wealthy or that he hates power and the powerful. Some of his most productive believers in history were wealthy and powerful.

But the people who put their trust in their wealth and power are leaning on a broken stick. In God's eyes, nobody is too big to fail. He can take people and their institutions and organizations down as fast as he built them up. What matters is faith in Christ.

Money makes a lousy god.

Magnificat: He kept his word to Abraham

Pastor Mark Jeske

Mary's Advent joy was communal. She was excited not only for herself but for her nation as well. And not just because of a chauvinistic pride of race. At the core of the identity of the Israelite nation were the triple promises that God had given to Abraham two millennia earlier, that Abraham's little family would grow to nation size, that this nation would inhabit the land in which Abraham now roamed as a landless Bedouin sheep tender, and that his descendants would bring the Savior into the world.

Mary was given the insight to see that Israel's national purpose was about to be fulfilled. Through her, God was about to keep a 2,000-year-old promise: **"He has helped his servant Israel, remembering to be merciful to Abraham and his descendants forever, just as he promised our ancestors"** (Luke 1:54,55). A faithful core of Jewish believers kept the Word and promises alive even in centuries of spiritual decay, military and economic reversals and collapse, occupations and exiles, and everything else Satan could throw at them. How we Gentiles appreciate and respect them!

And how thrilled we are to see God taking his historic promises so seriously. We depend on his Word, often having to believe what we cannot see: God's forgiveness of our sins, God's favor on our daily lives, God's angels bringing their protection, and God's resurrection power to reassemble our dead bodies.

With Mary, our souls glorify the Lord.

December 16

Inarticulate Spirit-groans

Pastor Mark Jeske

Perhaps you know the story of Cyrano de Bergerac (modernized as the movie *Roxanne* with Steve Martin). Cyrano's friend Christian was clumsy and full of self-doubt as he tried to court the noble and beautiful Roxane, and so the glib-tongued Cyrano whispered elegantly romantic things for him to say.

Normally when we need communication assistance, we get someone who is a better writer than we are (an editor), who knows the law better (an attorney), or whose poetic speech is better than ours (Cyrano). Most of us would agree pretty quickly that it would be great if we had a little help in our prayer life. Amazingly enough, the Holy Spirit himself volunteers to do that for us, but in the strangest way—through *inarticulate groans*: **"The Spirit helps us in our weakness. We do not know what we ought to pray for, but the Spirit himself intercedes for us through wordless groans. And he who searches our hearts knows the mind of the Spirit, because the Spirit intercedes for God's people in accordance with the will of God"** (Romans 8:26,27).

Not to worry—the Spirit can communicate more in one groan than you or I can in an entire stammered paragraph. What a promise! Imagine—the Spirit himself so strongly wants our needs to be communicated to the Father's throne that he will carry them himself, edit them, and even write copy for us when we hit writer's block.

Diversify

Pastor Mark Jeske

These are great days for the concept of diversity. Universities offer diversity studies. Consulting firms provide facilitators who provide diversity training for executives and boards. Corporate headhunters help companies develop a candidate pool that doesn't consist exclusively of older white males.

Every financial advisor will counsel you that the first rule of savings and investment is to diversify your assets—that way if one sector of the market sags, another may pick you up. That's what a mutual fund does—it spreads the risk around by investing your money in a wide range of companies, large and small, domestic and international, providers of goods and providers of services, and a variety of commodities producers.

Solomon advises you to diversify your education and life experiences too so that you have a number of ways to earn your bread: **"Sow your seed in the morning, and at evening let your hands not be idle, for you do not know which will succeed, whether this or that, or whether both will do equally well"** (Ecclesiastes 11:6).

Never before have these words been truer. Our country's economy is changing constantly, and skills that were valued yesterday may be automated tomorrow. The more things you can do, the more people you know, the more life experiences you've had, the better equipped you will be to take care of your family in the constant uncertainties of tomorrow's job world.

Light a candle for peace

Pastor Mark Jeske

We don't need candles for illumination in our church, but any church with an altar looks barren without its candles. Some are mounted on a three-branched candelabrum, suggesting the Trinity, our God who is one God in three persons. Some altars feature a pair of candlesticks, suggesting the two natures of Christ, the divine and human Savior who invites you to that altar to receive the Supper. Sometimes that candle is a giant single column, representing the constant presence of Christ among his people.

Inside the temple's Holy Place, an oil lamp burned each night as a visual reminder of the rock-steady presence of a God whose unconditional love never wavers. As you light the fourth candle in the fourth Advent week, let it remind you of the constant and faithful presence of God in your life. Let it be a symbol of the living relationship that you enjoy now and will enjoy forever in heaven.

Let it fill your heart with serenity and calm, for it is lit in honor of the One who came just as he said he would and did just what he said he would. All is good between you and God. You are loved, forgiven, and immortal. **"To us a child is born, to us a son is given, and the government will be on his shoulders. And he will be called Wonderful Counselor, Mighty God, Everlasting Father, Prince of Peace"** (Isaiah 9:6).

Let that fourth candle remind you of the peace that Jesus brings.

Seek him; see him

Sarah Habben

Imagine you're a shepherd in first-century Israel, smelling of campfire and sweat, rough around the edges. Imagine the hem of the night sky being snapped like a sheet, making light and noise and angels spill out. Imagine those alien beings announcing a birth—the Messiah's birth. "You will find him in Bethlehem," they cry.

When the lightning-bright creatures vanish and your eyes readjust to the midnight black, you turn to your companions. What now? You have just received a royal invitation. You're wrapped in layers for a night in the field, but you feel stripped bare by your glimpse of heaven, as if your sin is on view for all to see.

When you speak, your own words surprise you: **"Let's go to Bethlehem and see this thing that has happened, which the Lord has told us about"** (Luke 2:15). You are lowly and sinful, but God's message of grace compels you to *seek* your holy Savior.

In Bethlehem, beneath a strange star, is an animal's stall filled with straw and with warm, belching beasts. In the stall is a manger. In the manger is a baby. There is no king here; not if one goes by appearances. But despite the child's lowliness, you *see* your royal Savior. The angel's announcement has ensured that you regard this tiny bundle of life with eyes of faith.

Listen again to that heavenly invitation. Though you are sinful, *seek* your Savior. Though he is humble, *see* your Savior.

God of the others

Jason Nelson

"When a foreigner resides among you in your land, do not mistreat them. The foreigner residing among you must be treated as your native-born. Love them as yourself, for you were foreigners in Egypt. I am the Lord your God" (Leviticus 19:33,34).

Much of what God reveals to us early in the Bible is the making of a chosen people. He preserved the line of Adam-Abraham-Isaac-Jacob-Judah-David-Joseph and Mary to bring us Jesus. He favored their race and set them apart from all the others. He told them to avoid the others and made their culture and religion so odd the others would want to avoid them. There are tough stories in the Bible of segregation, exile, and regulating ethnic groups.

But God was also God of the others. He never sanctioned or promoted xenophobia (fear or hatred of strangers) among his people. He expected tolerance within their community so they would have an inkling where the story was headed and humbly realize they weren't so exceptional after all. They had experienced the hardships of being socially and politically out of favor. They had a history of being the underclass. The only thing that distinguished them from the others was God's favor, not their favorability. This was grace they received because God was in the process of reconciling the world to himself through Jesus Christ.

Ours is a world where all have fallen short. And the most gospel-leaning way to live is to love all of your neighbors as you love yourself and those like you.

What do you mean "repentance"?

Pastor Mark Jeske

Contrary to what a lot of people think, it is not their sins that threaten to put them in hell forever. It is their lack of repentance.

God has a lot of patience with sinners. He knows that we are weak. It is for that reason that the Father sent the Son to live and die for us so that when we die we might live again. The great work of Christ brings God's favor and forgiveness to all, and those who believe it have it. Repentance involves three changes in a sinner's mind and heart: 1) honest acknowledgement of one's sins and acceptance of personal responsibility; 2) faith in Christ the Savior, trusting in his words of forgiveness; 3) sincere desire to amend one's life. **"Whoever conceals their sins does not prosper, but the one who confesses and renounces them finds mercy"** (Proverbs 28:13).

That sounds simple, but it isn't in practice. Not because we can't understand the process. It's that we're so reluctant to do it. Just as alcoholism counselors know they have to hammer on a problem drinker's willingness even to admit he or she has a problem, in the same way the words "It's my fault" don't want to come out of our mouths.

Stop struggling. Stop pretending. Stop evading and avoiding. Just tell God the truth (he knows it anyway). Dump the bag, all of it, and let the Savior's love wash over you.

You will find mercy.

Flame on!

Sarah Habben

He was in his 80s, and he'd been through a lot. Exile. Conscription. Promotion. Betrayal. A failed execution-by-lion. And now a revelation from God.

Old prophet Daniel described his vision of a divine man in Daniel 10:6: **"His body was like topaz, his face like lightning, his eyes like flaming torches, his arms and legs like the gleam of burnished bronze, and his voice like the sound of a multitude."**

Picture Marvel Comics' Human Torch, and you'll get the idea. Daniel could hardly breathe. And the divine man brought troubling news. A spiritual war was raging. A time was coming of unprecedented distress. Judgment day would divide humanity into two camps: those who would gain everlasting life and those who would face everlasting contempt.

If we awoke on Sunday and saw God's "Human Torch" blazing above our beds, we'd probably be less likely to skip Bible study in favor of brunch. Less likely on Monday to bite our tongues instead of sharing our faith. Less likely on Friday to unleash our pet sin.

But God doesn't leave us with terror as motivation. In this vision God promised Daniel—and us—that **"everyone whose name is found written in the book—will be delivered"** (Daniel 12:1).

The Divine Man, Jesus, let his love blaze from the cross and empty tomb. In Baptism he enters our names in the book of life. Rescued, we delight to shine Christ's light in a dark world.

Redeemed, we will shine like the stars forever.

If church were a gym

Linda Buxa

"Physical training is of some value, but godliness has value for all things, holding promise for both the present life and the life to come" (1 Timothy 4:8).

The more I'm at my CrossFit gym, the more I apply their unwritten rules to my church life too.

- **Check your ego at the door.** I'm working out to get stronger, not to show off how awesome I am. But do I walk into church hoping everyone will admire my faithfulness? Arrogance has no place in the body of Christ.

- **Cheer for others.** The people who finish the workout last and struggle the most don't get judged because they aren't in great shape. They get the loudest cheers. Yet sometimes I judge those who are struggling in life. Shouldn't my congregation be the place where the weak get the most compassion and support?

- **Tell your trainers about any injuries.** How can they help you if they have no idea what hurts? Still, I walk into church and hide my struggles and pain. The people God put in your life are there to help you. Let them serve you.

- **You get out what you put into it.** Going through the motions doesn't change anything. Want your faith to grow? Get involved. Open up your Bible. Think about the words you are singing. Put the Word into practice.

My gym is fabulous, but it's for this world only. Our churches have an infinitely more important message about eternal life.

What kind of God is this?

Jason Nelson

On this holy night, we wonder, *what kind of God are you?* This is the question for the ages. You lack origins, but there is no denying your existence. We see your imprint everywhere but can't make out your face. You won a primordial battle over the evil one, but the struggle continues for us. You control everything but manage not to be controlling it seems. What kind of God are you to hide behind mystery?

Not too soon, not too late you laid your infant self in a mangy crib resting on sawbucks. Your special mother took good care of you. She knew you were special and wondered about you herself. So did the shepherds who found you and the kings who were on their way to find you by calculating your location from a star. Everyone who seeks you out has questions about you and questions for you. You answer, and we wonder deeply at the kind of God you are. You laid down your life, lifted up on crossbeams before your prime. You visited your own grave only briefly. You lived. You died. You live. We live for you. We die trusting you. We will live forever with you. You make and keep promises. You are the promise itself, the eternal Word come in flesh like ours. On this holy night, we worship you and wonder, *"What child is this? What kind of God is this?"* Gloria in excelsis Deo. You are God with us.

The gift of being God's child

Pastor Mark Jeske

You don't hear the word *orphan* much anymore, but there are plenty of children in the world who don't have homes. The Bible teaches us that by nature we are spiritual orphans. We are cut off from God, hostile to God's Word and ways, and doomed to die physically and eternally, unable to save others and unable even to save ourselves. Only a bleak, lonely, painful eternity lay ahead.

What if Christmas had never happened? We would have stayed in that miserable twilight zone. But the fullness of time did come; God sent his Son; the One who was eternally begotten of a Father without a Mother became the son of a mother without a father.

What you do with the Christmas story will determine your eternity. Your attitude toward Jesus means life or death: **"To all who received him, to those who believed in his name, he *gave* the right to become children of God"** (John 1:12). Think of it—as you believe what the Bible says about Jesus, you receive the ultimate Christmas gift—you become a member of God's family. You become a child of God. The Christmas baby becomes your Brother; his Father is now your Father.

God now obligates himself to do for you what all good fathers do for their children: provide security, daily provisions, and life guidance. When you pray to him, you don't have to beg like a panhandler or argue like a lawyer. You can ask like a member of the family.

Which, of course, you are. Because of Christmas.

Whose ethics?

Pastor Mark Jeske

It's interesting to see how often business conferences will have serious workshops and keynote addresses on the topic of business ethics. Left unsaid is where those seemingly universally adopted ethical principles were derived from.

Companies pretty much know that they have to obey the laws—there are legal and illegal behaviors, with penalties attached to the latter. The concept of "ethics," however, implies that there are certain practices that are intrinsically right and wrong. There is an assumption that everybody knows what those things are and is in agreement. Ha! Not so. Is it unethical to leave out certain unpleasant information in negotiations so that you can close a deal? Is it evil to shade information you submit to the government in order to evade taxes, or is that just a fun game you play and you hope you don't get caught? Does anybody in your company have a problem if you sabotage your competitors' bids? Does the end justify the means?

There are no ethics without God. Without his word in Bible and conscience, there is only the law of the jungle, and all successful businesses would be red in tooth and claw. God's wonderful words reveal to us how to treat one another, personally and in our commercial transactions: **"I meditate on your precepts and consider your ways. I delight in your decrees; I will not neglect your word"** (Psalm 119:15,16).

He's watching us, you know. What's in your ethics?

Joy for the journey

Sarah Habben

Consider what you've endured for the sake of a future joy. The drudgery of pregnancy and the pain of delivery take a backseat to the joy of holding a newborn. Twenty hours crammed into an economy car are bearable when you're en route to your dream vacation. But to endure life's journey, we need a bigger, better joy in sight than Disney World. We need a heavenly joy—won for us by *Jesus'* endurance.

Jesus bore countless crosses before he felt the nails of Golgotha: the limitations of human flesh, the temptations of Satan, the hostility of those he came to save. And yet, **"For the joy set before him he endured the cross, scorning its shame, and sat down at the right hand of the throne of God. Consider him who endured such opposition from sinners, so that you will not grow weary and lose heart** (Hebrews 12:1-3).

When the whip fell on Jesus' back, he remembered the peace he was making between his Father and us. When the crowd screamed Jesus' guilt, he focused on the *not guilty* verdict he was winning for sinners like you and me. When the cross loomed, Jesus willingly endured its shame—because being pinned to its planks would gain our salvation.

Consider what Jesus endured for the sake of our future joy. Consider the price he paid to make us his children. Consider his extraordinary love. It will fill your weary soul with strength. It will give you joy for the journey.

Sitting in the cell

Linda Buxa

"For even the Son of Man did not come to be served, but to serve, and to give his life as a ransom for many" (Mark 10:45).

Sgt. Joseph Serna, a Special Forces soldier, served four combat tours in Afghanistan in his almost 20 years of military service. He was almost killed three times. He has three Purple Hearts and post-traumatic stress disorder, which led to struggles with alcohol. After he was charged with driving under the influence, he entered a veteran's treatment court program where he had to report to Judge Lou Olivera. At one visit, he admitted he lied about a urine test. Judge Olivera sentenced Serna to one day in jail.

Then the judge drove Serna to the jail in a neighboring county, and Joe was put in a cell. He barely had time to sit down when the cell opened again and the judge walked in. The judge, who had served in the Gulf War, was concerned that leaving Serna in isolation for a night would trigger his PTSD. So the judge sat with the criminal the whole time.

You have a judge who sentences you for your crimes too. God knew that sin had locked us in a cell with no chance for escape. But then he crawled into our cell with us. He sent Jesus to be *God with us*, to suffer the ultimate punishment for our sins, death on a cross.

On Easter morning he rose again.

And we are set free.

Philosophy of dating

Pastor Mark Jeske

Single? Think of the top five criteria that you look for in someone you'd want to date. Where does the person's Christian faith rank in your top five? Is it even in your top five?

I know, I know. You will say to me that marriage evangelism has been happening for centuries, that dating and marrying an unbeliever is no big deal because the believer can bring the other person to faith. Two of the women in Jesus Christ's own ancestry, Rahab and Ruth, were non-Israelites brought up to worship false gods. Both were led to the true God by their husbands. Indeed that happens.

But so does the reverse. Sometimes the unbelieving spouse drags the believer down. Even the wisest man in the world lost his spiritual bearings: **"As Solomon grew old, his wives turned his heart after other gods, and his heart was not fully devoted to the Lord his God, as the heart of David his father had been"** (1 Kings 11:4). How do you know which is going to happen? You don't.

If your boyfriend or girlfriend won't go to church with you while you are dating, he or she probably won't when you're married either. How long can you keep your faith life going if your spouse thinks praying, Bible reading, and churchgoing are stupid wastes of time? Abraham went to great lengths to find a believing wife for Isaac.

How can I be sure I'm saved?

Pastor Mark Jeske

The handwriting is shaky from age but the fear is real. A man named Bob writes, "I wish I could have a rock-hard, undoubting faith. I wish I knew I was saved. But I have doubts and I am a big sinner."

Bob's dilemma (shared by many millions of people) is that in spite of knowing about Jesus, he can't quite shake the idea that his eternal salvation depends, at least in part, on his own life performance. Our good works are indeed important, but only as our gifts of gratitude to God for his forgiving love for us. *They are not the cause of our salvation!* **"It does not, therefore, depend on human desire or effort, but on God's mercy"** (Romans 9:16). Salvation is God's gift, not our wages.

Our lives of service and obedience to God will always be flawed; we are works in progress, and we sin every day in some way, either by what we do or fail to do. Don't somewhat believe in Jesus. Don't sorta believe in Jesus. Listen to the Bible's message and believe it all: Jesus Christ is 100 percent human (without the sin), and so he qualifies as a substitute for you in God's court. Jesus Christ is 100 percent God, so the blood he shed is far bigger than your pile of sins.

How can Bob be sure that he is saved? He can stop looking at himself for reasons for hope and simply lift up his eyes to the One who loved him enough to go to the cross for him.

The straightest shooters

Jason Nelson

My little grandson, Noah, doesn't mince many words. One time I picked him up from preschool and gave him a convenient snack when we got home. It was a package of yogurt and nuts in separate compartments that you tip together upon opening. I didn't get it mixed to his satisfaction. I said, "I'm sorry, Noah, I am not familiar with how this product works." He said, "Well, Papa, maybe you should take a class." *Booyah!*

My heroes have always been kids because they are the straightest shooters. I have been taken to school by the unfiltered comments of elementary, high school, and college students in a lifetime of teaching them. Sometimes they are the only ones God can count on to say what needs to be said. **"From the lips of children and infants you, Lord, have called forth your praise"** (Matthew 21:16). *Hosanna! Hosanna!*

The joy of Christmas for many adults comes from watching the children. They are mini beacons of the joy of salvation. They love the little Lord Jesus, and it shows. We think back to the time when our faith was like theirs. We wonder what happened to us. At what age did we start holding back? What disappointments piled up to dampen our praise?

Jesus likes kids too. And he warned us, **"Truly I tell you, anyone who will not receive the kingdom of God like a little child will never enter it"** (Luke 18:17). My New Year's resolution is to hang on to my boyish tendencies as long as possible.

devotions for special days

What if?

Pastor Mark Jeske

The saints in Old Testament times had only *promises* that the Messiah, the Servant of the Lord, would live again after his suffering and death. You and I have the fabulous advantage to hear the story of the bodily resurrection of Jesus Christ as an accomplished *fact*. And yet—there is a downside here. Since Easter is old news, some of the suspense and anticipation can leak out of our celebrations and our hearts. When there's no tension, there's no relief. When there's no fear, there is no comfort.

What if Easter *hadn't* happened? What if Jesus had failed in his mission? What if he had sinned somewhere? What if he had caved in to even one of Satan's littler temptations? Started hating instead of loving? How would our world and our lives be different if his body had stayed on earth and decomposed like everyone else's?

Here's what: **"If Christ has not been raised, our preaching is useless and so is your faith. . . . If Christ has not been raised, your faith is futile; you are still in your sins"** (1 Corinthians 15:14,17). The physical resurrection of Jesus Christ guarantees the Father's approval of the Son's work, all of it. The physical resurrection of Christ guarantees the integrity of the church's gospel message for 20 centuries. The physical resurrection of Christ guarantees your forgiveness and your own personal resurrection.

That's why Easter is such a big deal.

Behold your mother

Jason Nelson

Of all the writing assignments I have ever done, this one intimidates me the most. What's left to say about mothers? Love for mothers is deep, and expressions of appreciation for her are exhaustive. Champions and thugs have this in common: they love their mothers. I can't say enough about my own mother's sacrifices and the faith she passed on to me because it lived in her first. I know anything I write will not do justice to your mother either. So let me borrow a few of Jesus' last words: **"Behold, your mother!"** (John 19:27 ESV).

This is the end to an untold story. The perfect Son honored his special mother with his last breaths. What does that say to us? In the spirit of Christ, behold your mother. Take a good long look at her. She is easy to overlook because she is probably the lowest-maintenance person in the house. Her dependability is epic, so we take her for granted. Her scolding is quotable, and she bites her lip often to spare our feelings. Behold your mother. She never stops working or thinking about what needs to be done. Every time she is summoned, she answers the call. She looks very tired sometimes because she is. Behold your mother. Reward her love for you by taking good care of her. Never let your mother down.

Fathers, be good

Diana Kerr

The song "Daughters" by famous musical artist John Mayer has a chorus that begins, *"Fathers, be good to your daughters; daughters will love like you do."* He goes on to say that those daughters, influenced by their parents, become mothers and, therefore, continue the chain of influence on the next generation.

Without a doubt, fathers make an impact on their sons and daughters, especially in their early years. My mom always said that fathers are so influential that most girls end up marrying someone like their dad, for better or worse. I was blessed with a godly, supportive, amazing dad, but I know that isn't the case for everyone.

What legacy did your father leave you? Was he "good to you," as the song "Daughters" says and as God's Word instructs? Or did he leave you with some scars? God provides biblical guidelines for fathers, but sin taints parenthood. Ephesians 6:4 is a classic verse for dads: **"Fathers, do not exasperate your children; instead, bring them up in the training and instruction of the Lord."** Unfortunately, some of us can probably relate more to the first half of that passage than the second half.

So how do we handle Father's Day? First, thank God for your father and for any lessons he taught you, either through positive *or* negative actions. (If Dad is still around, thank him too.) Second, thank your Father God that he fills in all the gaps where earthly fathers don't always measure up.

Great things

Sarah Habben

"What have you done for me lately?" Maybe that question has crossed your mind (or lips) recently. It's in our DNA to object when someone wants something for nothing. Why should we expend effort, time, or money on someone who has nothing to offer us?

Maybe you feel like that about God. Maybe you are out of a job, out of love, out of money, out of options. *"What has God done for me lately,"* you wonder. *"Why should I pray/ worship/offer my time or talents when I get so little out of the bargain?"*

It's true—you may be having a tough week, or year, or life. You might feel forgotten by God. Nevertheless, such a view of your relationship with God is shortsighted. It's not too different from a kid denied in a Dollar Store who hollers, "You never buy me *anything!*"

This Thanksgiving, let's remember exactly what God has bought for us with the blood of his Son—not just anything, but everything that matters: Pardon from sin and release from guilt. Peace with God and a home in heaven. We come empty-handed to this banquet of blessings. No marshmallow-topped side dish of good works can earn us a place at this buffet. We have nothing to offer God in exchange, yet **"the Lord has done great things for us, and we are filled with joy"** (Psalm 126:3).

So go ahead. Bring your hungry heart to God and ask, "What have you done for me lately?" Then prepare to be filled . . . with joy.

About the writers

Pastor Mark Jeske brings the good news of Jesus Christ to viewers of *Time of Grace* in weekly 30-minute programs broadcast across America and around the world on local television, cable, and satellite, as well as on-demand streaming via the Internet. He is the senior pastor at St. Marcus Church, a thriving multicultural congregation in Milwaukee, Wisconsin. Mark is the author of several books and dozens of devotional booklets on various topics. He and his wife, Carol, have four adult children.

Linda Buxa is a freelance writer and Bible study leader. She is a regular speaker at women's retreats and conferences across the country. A regular blogger for Time of Grace Ministry, her first book, *Dig In! Family Devotions to Feed Your Faith*, was released in August 2014. Linda and her husband, Greg, have lived in Alaska, Washington D.C., and California. They now live in Wisconsin, where they are raising their three children.

Pastor Matt Ewart and his wife, Amy, have been blessed with three young children who keep life interesting. Matt is currently a pastor in Lakeville, Minnesota, and has previously served as a pastor in Colorado and Arizona.

Sarah Habben is a pastor's wife, part-time educational assistant and piano teacher, church musician, and mom to four daughters. She and her family have lived in St. Albert, Alberta, Canada, since 1999. Sarah is the coauthor of *The Bloodstained Path to God* (2012, Northwestern Publishing House) and the author of *The Mom God Chose: Mothering Like Mary* (2015, Northwestern Publishing House).

Diana Kerr is a certified professional coach, writer, and blogger on a never-ending chase for a life focused on what matters most. Her business and life's passion are all about equipping goal-oriented Christian women with the tools and truths they need to get unstuck and make the most of their time and life. You can find out more about Diana or read her motivational and transparent content on her blog at dianakerr.com.

Pastor Daron Lindemann is pastor at a new mission start in Pflugerville, Texas. Previously he served in downtown Milwaukee and in Irmo, South Carolina. Daron has authored articles or series for *Forward in Christ* magazine, *Preach the Word*, and his own weekly Grace MEMO devotions. He lives in Texas with his wife, Cara, and has two adult sons.

Jason Nelson had a career in church work as a teacher, counselor, and leader. He has a bachelor's degree in education, did graduate work in theology, and has a master's degree in counseling psychology. After his career ended in disabling back pain, he wrote the book *Miserable Joy: Chronic Pain in the Christian Life* (2007, Northwestern Publishing House). He has written and spoken extensively on a variety of topics related to the Christian life. Jason lives with his wife, Nancy, in Necedah, Wisconsin.

About Time of Grace

Time of Grace is for people who want more growth and less struggle in their spiritual walk. Through the timeless truth of God's Word, we connect people to God's grace so they know they are loved and forgiven and so they can start living in the freedom they've always wanted.

To discover more, please visit timeofgrace.org or call 800.661.3311.

Help share God's message of grace!

Every gift you give helps Time of Grace reach people around the world with the good news of Jesus. Your generosity and prayer support take the gospel of grace to others through our ministry outreach and help them find the restart with Jesus they need.

Give today at timeofgrace.org/give or by calling 800.661.3311.

Thank you!